Breaking Free

A Way Out

For

Adult Children of Narcissists

Lisette SQ

ACON PRESS

Copyright Notice

This Book is Dedicated to
Adult Children of Narcissists

WE NEVER HAD A CHOICE

With a heartfelt thanks and a debt of gratitude to **ROH Press** and Nico Lorenzutti for his encouragement, guidance and support in the making of this book.

Disclaimer

This book is designed to provide information, motivation, validation and entertainment to its readers. The book contains speculation, assumptions, opinion as well as factual information. The content of each article is the sole expression and opinion of its author. I have tried to recreate events, locales and conversations from my memories of them. In order to maintain anonymity I may have changed the names of individuals and places. I may have changed some identifying characteristics and details such as physical properties, occupations and places of residence. The author takes no responsibility for any similarity to any person living or dead.

Contents

GuiDe to Commonly UseD ABBreviations anD Acronyms

ACONs write in code. Why? Because Ns cyberstalk the SG and this way our FOO that we've gone NC including MNM, EF, NS and GC plus their FMs won't be able to decipher our language and find us! Well, that and it's easier. It's just easier. I present to you the ACON glossary.

ACON Glossary

ACON = Adult Child of Narcissist(s) – biological parents, adoptive parents, step and foster parent(s)

NPD = Narcissistic Personality Disorder

N = Narcissist

Narc = Narcissist

MN = Malignant Narcissist (not just a turbo Narcissist – a cruel and ruthless sadist)

MNM = Malignant Narcissist Mother

NM = Narcissist Mother

MNF – Malignant Narcissist Father

NF = Narcissist Father

NP = Narcissist Parent

N Brother/Sister = Narcissist Sibling

MN Sister/Brother = Malignant Narcissist Sibling

GC = Golden Child (the spoiled rotten narcissist sibling who can do no wrong in the eyes of the N parents. Also referred to as the "chosen one.")

NGC = Narcissist Golden Child (it's usually implied that the GC is a narc, or at least narcissistic)

SG = Scapegoat (most ACONs are the family SG, but in many NFOOs the scapegoat role is fluid. In my family it shifted from my dad to my brother to me. Of course, the two MN hags – my mother and sister – were never scapegoated because they were in control)

* **N** before anyone – husband, wife, friend, co-worker, neighbor, relative etc. denotes Narcissist.

Nship = A friendship with a narcissist

EM = Enabler Mother (enabled the narcissist father's abuse of his children)

EF = Enabler Father (enabled the narcissist mother's abuse of her children)

EP = Enabler Parent (the enabling parents is morally lazy and looks the other way to make their life easier. Often they are enthralled or afraid of their spouse)

E = also denotes "estranged" so context is important when deciphering the language.

FOO = Family of Origin

NFOO = Narcissist Family of Origin. (Not garden variety "Narcissistic" people, we are referring to full-blown Narcissistic Personality Disorder = Narcissist or Malignant Narcissist)

FOC = Family of Choice, or of Choosing

FM = Flying Monkey (FMs are the Narc's minions that they send in when they cannot obtain access to us. A FM can be just about anyone who does the Narcissist's bidding. They are the Narcissist's proxy abusers)

NC = No Contact (the ACON exit strategy of going no contact is the ultimate goal – leaving the abusive Narcissist(s) in the dust, cutting ties for good and never looking back!)

LC = Low Contact (some adult children of a lesser Narcissist opt for low contact)

VLC = Very Low Contact

FOG = Fear, Obligation, Guilt (the haze, the maze, the fog we were lost in before learning about NPD)

D = Dear or Darling (DH = Dear Husband, DD= Dear Daughter etc.)

MIL = Mother in Law*

FIL = Father in Law*

SIL = Sister in Law*

BIL = Brother in Law*

* (Add an **N** or **MN** in front of any of these and you have a **Narc or Malignant Narc in Law**)

BPD = Borderline Personality Disorder (commonly a Narcissist)

Cluster B = Individual(s) with a whole host of personality disorders (most Narcissists have more than one personality disorder)

FB = Facebook

CBT = Cognitive Behavioural Therapy

T = Therapist

LOL = Laugh out loud

WTF = What the fuck?! (ACONs have been wondering our entire lives)

Introduction

About Me

I am an ACON (Adult Child of Narcissists). I come from a "family" of narcissists. Both parents are full-blown NPD. Mother is a malignant narcissist and older sister is a malignant narc / sociopath. I fought like hell to survive that dangerous system but was unwittingly raised to be 'narcissistic supply' and have been a magnet to pathologicals and predators all my life. Like Jane Goodall - who lived among the apes - I've lived among the narcissists. I have a very personal understanding of their contemptuous and predatory nature, and destructive family and social interactions. I accept the hard cold fact that narcissists are disordered and dangerous and will NEVER change. I'm a firm believer of NO CONTACT, and have always exercised my right to do so.

As an ACON I have an uncommonly high threshold for bad experiences. Especially with bad people who incite shock, horror and outrage – Narcissists.

In 2007-2008 I was under unrelenting attack from all sides by a pack of Malignant Narcissists. No surprise the terrorism occurred during a time in my life when I was extremely vulnerable. The resulting trauma from the malignant narcissist feeding frenzy led to psychological injury.

I spent Christmas 2008 in a psyche ward. The so-called mental health professionals and gloating malignant narcissists would label what happened to me a break-down. I call it a "breakthrough" disguised as a descent into hell. What soon followed was the most terrifying, bizarre, dark and devastating period of my life – a life where my faith in humanity was strongly challenged and my sense of justice outrage. Every door I tried to open in in search of validation was slammed shut on me. The injustice of it all was outrageous. In effect, the whole damn world was gaslighting me. It was me against the world. And like most ACONs, or any person that has had their life shredded by narcissists, I longed to be heard. In fact, my need to be heard was so intense it hurt.

In April 2011 with fight or flight mode in full swing, I launched House of Mirrors blog. The "About Me" blurb is the same one that has appeared on my blog for over 5 years. My avatar is Lady Justice. It is a symbol of my very reason for speaking out on this dark subject – to expose the truth and find some measure of justice.

I started blogging because I needed to tell my story (or at least parts of it). I needed to shout-it from the roof tops that narcissists are dangerous and disturbed and LIARS! I didn't care if anyone read what I had to say or believed me. What I needed was a voice. MY voice that was attached to ME – the person I am inside. NOT the person the narcissists painted me to be.

In an effort to cover-up their crimes the malignant narcissists engineered a false image of me through a smear campaign of projection, lies and third party manipulations. I experienced the very real horror of strangulation by triangulation. The sick and guilty fucks took my strengths and spun them as their very opposites – weakness/illness. Knowing there was a false image of me out there and that I was framed for the very crimes the narcissists committed was a fate worse than death. Even more debilitating was the fact that I was choked into silence and denied a defence. The malignant narcissists had their unanswered say. I was tormented. I needed an outlet for my pain and anger.

To be honest, anger didn't even begin to describe what I was going through. I was enraged (still am) that my life had been bulldozed by a bunch of ruthless moral imbeciles, and my abusers not only escaped responsibility for their egregious acts, most of them masqueraded as the victim. So, not only did these malicious frauds abuse the living crap out of me and intentionally inflict emotional distress, they turned me into the bad guy/the "problem". It was a real life carnival of the absurd. The world became warped beyond all comprehension. I needed to set things straight, right the wrongs and create a venue to shout the truth – a place to let it rip!

Of course this powerful need to be heard, release my anger and right the wrongs of narcissists took hold decades before I even knew what a narcissist was. By the time I was hospitalized for psychological injury, I had already endured a lifetime of emotional and psychological abuse. It just took being hospitalized to do something about it. Like I said, I have an uncommonly high threshold for bad experiences. I come from a "family" of narcissists and I was groomed to be prey and trained to put-up and shut-up my entire life. The blog and book were a long time coming; it just took a lifelong build-up of horrible experiences and one hell of a dramatic crescendo to propel me into action.

This book is not a self-help book. But that's a good thing. According to a study, self-help books make you feel worse. That comes as no surprise considering they are written to sell, not to help. I wrote my blog as a form of therapy for myself and it ended up being a source of information and validation for other ACONs and those victimized by narcissists. The content on the blog has been tested for over 5 years and it works. It gives voice to those troubled and maimed by serious loss and abuse. It provides release, validation, and information and awareness to untangle yourself from the narcissist's web of destruction as well as skills to protect and defend yourself against personality disordered predators. According to many of the letters I have received over the years, it also offers strength, alleviates self-destructive thinking and behavioural patterns and inspires light bulb moments and breakthroughs that lead to positive change in life and relationships. I never, in a million years, would have thought something as primal as expressing my anger (with a lot of swears) would have such a positive effect on others. Here's what one reader had to say:

Lisette, I wonder if you fully realize what a difference you are making in the world?

The analogy that occurs to me is this: you are to the victims of narcissists what Gandhi was to the victims of colonization. Quite late in Gandhi's life, he was asked where he found his courage to fight against oppression. He replied, "After you've been reduced to a zero, there's nothing to fear" (not his exact words) and he was reduced - so were you - so was I - so were all the people you are validating. And that's one of your great gifts to the people you are reaching: validation. Without, few can start the deeper journey to freedom.

One of our great tasks, I think, is to reconcile our Self with our Soul; to survive, we had to split them; they existed on different planets. You are supporting people in that reunion, consciously or not.

One of your other great gifts is the validation of the rage the horrendously abused (including me) feel. We have all been mind-fucked in the past to believe that only sick or evil people feel and express that much rage and not to be one of THEM. We are also scared by the thought that we could resemble the evil narcs in ANY way - so we disown/suppress the rage and instead get ill/go mad/collapse/sabotage our lives, minds and selves. Which is exactly what they WANT US TO DO.

So what you are achieving, Lisette, in my view, is expressing and validating and externalizing and vocalizing that healing rage for the people who cannot yet do that themselves. You are making it possible for them. For us. For me. And also for you. You are saving lives and healing the harmed, and I hope you really know this.

You are one of the most inspirational people I have ever come across. And as well as liberating the chained (the chains are on consciousness for many of the harmed) you also have to fight the rear-guard battle against the evil, they hate people like you, they will never stop trying to discredit and undermine you, their evil feeds on itself in their rotting souls. Yet YOU DO! You prevail! I pray that you will always prevail. Please look after you with great kindness to yourself. Thank you for all the gifts I have received from you. Anna

Thank you, Anna. There's a lot of wisdom there. I don't know about the Gandhi comparison, but I'll take it! And Anna sure is right about the rear-guard battle. Since I wised-up to these predators and began speaking-out about narcissistic abuse the malignant narcissists have done everything in their "power" to silence me, destroy me, kill me or at least neutralize me (living but not a threat). Their end goal appears to be: drive me to suicide, financial ruin, a mental or emotional break-down, physical illness or cause serious injury or death.

The malignant narcissist/sociopath sister is still chasing the power high she got when I ended up hospitalized after her 2 year cyberstalking / gaslighting / strangulation by triangulation psychological murder spree. My downfall would be a triumph to her and the other vipers. These are people who do not wish me well and would have no problem leaving me dying by the side of the road (after they run me down). They are my "family" of origin. And my awareness of malignant narcissism gives me a death-grip on reality. I'm not clinging to a shred of denial.

I fully understand that generational narcissistic abuse is a crime in progress and going no contact does not necessarily put a stop to the abuse. No contact is mainly a safe guard like the witness protection program. The narcs will continue to slime and malign you in your absence and plot and scheme your demise but the distance of no contact will keep you mentally, emotionally and hopefully physically safe. I know where I stand with these ice-people known as "family." I know what I'm up against and I know the problem isn't me, it's them! And they will never change. Blogging about these evil soul-sucking death eaters and receiving validation from other ACONs saved my life.

House of Mirrors blog is now a book. Your natural scepticism and fluff detector will not go off when you read it. It's hard hitting and brutally honest. It's blunt and to the point. It outlines what is going to work and what isn't. It's meant to inform and educate. Instead of being hugged and told to think happy and healing thoughts you will be slapped and told how it is. Denial doesn't work. My hope for you is that you release some of your anger, find validation in knowing you are not alone and gain the understanding and awareness you need to effectively deal with narcissists or avoid them all together.

There are no cures for narcissistic abuse. Invisible wounds are the hardest to heal because they depend on the love and support of others, patience and understanding, and the tender gift of time. This book is about being better equipped to manage what you're going through and what's ahead of you. It's a grieving process and it's messy. It's about accepting loss and removing the narcissist's destructive influence on your thinking, your emotions, your behaviour, your relationships, and your entire life. It's about self-preservation. It's about taking back what the narcissists stole from you.

My greatest wish for ACONs and other readers is that the book gives you the feeling of "breaking through and breaking free" in real-time and leaves you different forever. Certain skills and adages are going to stick and once in a while one will appear in your mind at exactly the right time, and you will feel yourself thinking differently and find yourself doing things differently. It's then you will discover a window is broken open where you didn't know there was one and your world has become a bit bigger, a bit brighter and your load a little lighter.

Enjoy the journey. May the force be with you!

Lisette

You should be angry. You must not be bitter.

Bitterness is like a cancer. It eats upon the host. It doesn't do anything to the object of its displeasure.

Anger is like fire it burns it all clean.

So use that anger.

You write it. You paint it. You dance it. You march it. You vote it. You do everything about it. You talk it.

Never stop talking it.

--- Maya Angelou

MALIGNANT NARCISSISTS

Malignant Narcissists. On the outside they look like you and me, but on the inside they are very different. They are the real life Vampires, Zombies, Witches and Werewolves. They don't hide from daylight and suck blood; they hide in plain sight and suck your soul. They aren't dead and flesh eating; they are emotionally vacant and parasitic. They don't cast harmful spells and concoct toxic potions; they plot and scheme to poison your life and systematically destroy you. They don't morph into Werewolves; they are the real life Wolf in sheep's clothing; charming and innocent on the outside and predatory and vicious on the sly.

13

They'll steal your soul if you let them, but don't you let them.

You can spend your time in fantasy reading about fake Vampires, Zombies, Witches and Werewolves OR wise up and learn about the real life predators in our midst. Because by the time you've read one page of fiction, one of these vipers will have lied, cheated, stolen, slandered or generally harmed you in some way. I suggest you read on... right here... about these human prowlers that subsist on the life-blood of others, but keep one eye on the page and the other one looking over your shoulder because narcissistic/psychopathic abuse is a crime in progress, it's a worldwide epidemic of evil, there is no cure and it's happening right now... to all of us.

WHY WE SHOULD EXPOSE NARCISSISTS

Malignant narcissism is a dark subject. And blogging about it is intense.

It takes going to an uncomfortable place to find my rage. It requires mental and emotional face time with bad memories. And in the case of this blogger, it's requires embracing my own darkness: my unadulterated hatred of what passes as human. If this seems extreme to you then you've probably never stared into the dead eyes of a smirking malignant narcissist.

Blogging about narcissism and the more malignant variety isn't just about the writing. It's also about the reading. The interacting. It's about the environment where we are "free" to express our truth. And it's about maintaining that freedom by keeping watch over our environment and fighting for our convictions. It's a battle in the real world and online.

Hey Narcs, you stop lying about me and I'll stop telling the TRUTH about you.

The bull-shit never ends.

I'm not done exposing them... doubt I ever will be. I can't just switch my bull-shit detector to "off." It doesn't work that way. It's not about "healing" or "recovering" from N abuse and then becoming complaisant. Now wouldn't the narcissists love that? For all of us to miraculously "heal" from their atrocities - Hallelujah! - and fade away into the background. That must mean you're "well" right? When you are no longer outraged by injustice.

As long as there is a personality disordered abuser or some other unspecified fuckhead getting all up in my grill in real life or online, I will challenge them. It's the narcissist's nature to harm others and it's my nature to go after bullies. My desire to speak the truth, my truth, will remain long after I stop blogging. It's my passion.

I tell you this because I am damn sick and tired of people labeling truthful blogs, vulnerability, authenticity and righteous anger as a sign of weakness or being "stuck", or not "healed" or not "recovering" or "playing the victim" ... blah de blah blah. Does it ever occur to these pinheads that maybe some people are natural fighters, truth tellers and supporters and that are why they are writing about this stuff? Does it ever occur to these scaredy cats that the bloggers and commenters are brave? Airing so-called "dirty laundry" is about exposing the nuances of abuse. It's about participating in a dialogue and keeping the information on narcissists alive and out there? Does it ever occur to these "silencers" that the movement to expose the pathologicals among us is bigger than the sum of its parts? When people march in a rally are they doing it just for themselves? No. They're doing it for the cause, the greater good. I know all of this sounds idealistic. But frankly, I don't know where the hell I would be if it weren't for the brave souls who first took to the internet to carve the way.

A difference is being made. For me, blogging on this subject is about activism.

You're either part of the problem or part of the solution. So what's the solution? So much exposure that being able to spot a narcissist and run like hell before they bite becomes second nature to all. And if you can't run before they harm you, you expose their sorry ass because it's the societal "norm" to do so. I look forward to the day when emotional and psychological abuse is considered a crime punishable by law.

COMMENTS:

And with any malignancy, early detection is paramount to contain the damage they do.

You can sterilize Narcs now or euthanize ACONs later. Same difference. Except the Ns miss out on torturing us for a life time.

Lisette, I love your fire, your ability to express yourself and I love that you are always, always, always willing to tell the truth, even when it's ugly or disturbing. Especially when it's ugly and disturbing, hell, maybe because it's ugly and disturbing. Thanks for keeping your bullshit detector on. And loaded.

No one can inspire more hatred in another human being, even the most gentle, peace loving person, than a narcissist. In fact, that's a sign they are a narcissist - that they are absolutely HATED by those near and dear for *mysterious* reasons. Well, the reasons are not at all mysterious to their victims. The narcissists abuse the living shit out of us on the sly behind closed doors and then play sweet and innocent and meek and mild to the rest of the world. That is why it is so important to expose them and their covert abuse. They have been getting away with it for far too long.

The word "healed" is a load of crap. Yes, who really heals from abuse and things that have happened in this life? I'm convinced that those who say that they are "healing" are in denial.

Questioning the bullshit paradigm of the did-the-best-they-could aka the Family Romance (dare I say it), is a healing thing to do in itself.

I'm an ACON and I tend to attract narcissistic people into my life. It's true that they smell out vulnerability in a person and slowly move in to control and abuse the intended victim. Unfortunately narcs are everywhere in strange almost demonic abundance. Please. How do you stop them for good and keep them away from a person? Thank you for you great articles. You are helping to free many many people from abuse.

May we all be beacons of light for those following after us and liberate all worthy folk from their narcissist tormenters!

The Malignant Narcissist Death Personified

Malignant Narcissists lack empathy, compassion, insight and the ability to love and be loved. Moreover, they lack a conscience and are largely under the control of their base instincts: anger, fear and envy. Despite their contempt of people for being *'feeling saps'* they are secretly intensely jealous of others precisely because others have what they lack. So, anyone who is authentic, or capable of feeling or who loves and is loved – in other words, anyone who is a normal human being – is a threat to their delusions of superiority and an object of their irrational malice. All of this, along with the Narcissist's pathological sense of entitlement, greed, control freakism, and need to win at all cost makes them extremely predatory and very dangerous. Because they lack normal human feelings, they don't relate to people on an emotional level and instead operate entirely through mind control and manipulation.

The Narcissist's expert ability to read others' reactions and respond accordingly make them very skilled at projecting convincing images and synthesized emotional states. Outwardly, they *appear* to be like everyone else, but inside they are very different. They lack normal human emotions, they have nothing inside to draw on – they don't have interior lives – so everything they do is an act. They are the ultimate phonies, total impostors and they are empty inside.

Malignant Narcissists are predators driven by the fear that others are, and will always be, superior to them (for being human) and this hard reality is such a threat to their existence that they must destroy anyone who has what they lack. Their battle ground of choice is in the realm of the mind and their weapon of mass destruction is manipulation/mind control.

Malignant Narcissists do not become depressed, anxious, emotionally conflicted, incapacitated or self-destructive. They depress others, make others feel anxious and conflicted, incapacitate others and drive others to self-destructive acts. It is always others who suffer, not the malignant narcissist. Without a moral compass to guide them, or a conscience to restrain them, MNs cause a hell of a lot of human suffering in this world. They do whatever works to fuel their lifelong obsession with ruining others so they can be triumphant. This includes causing suicide, stress diseases, a host of anxiety disorders and mental illness, addictions, divorce, the total destruction of families and the annihilation of gene pools: they wipe out the next generation.

The Malignant Narcissist is synonymous with death. They are parasitical creatures, always on the hunt for a potential host they can sink their evil tentacles into. They are predators and their intent is murderous – they ruin lives. Since homicide is usually out of reach - and not as satisfying as a long reign of terror - the MN operates in the realm of the mind by administering a drip-drop of poison through gossip, lies and slander. They plant evil seeds of doubt and confusion that kill relationships, destroys mental, emotional and physical health, ruin reputations and sabotage everything that others have worked for. The destruction Narcissists wreak on the victim's life is so gratuitously evil it would appear that the ultimate victory for the MN would be to drive the victim to suicide or a complete mental breakdown or physical collapse.

Suicide, insanity, debilitating anxiety, drug dependencies, agonizing death by a stress cancer or psychological enslavement is the perfect outcome for the bloodthirsty Malignant Narcissist. The victim, once thoroughly injured by the MN's systematic destruction, ceases to exist as a separate identity. Instead, they are merely a tool used to carry-out the Malignant Narcissist's will – their own execution. Yet the MN won't suffer any consequences for what they manipulate the victim to do – *they literally get away with murder.*

The Narcissist views others as property and will stop at nothing to assume ownership. They get inside the victim's head, take-up permanent residency and take-over the victim's thoughts and ultimately their life. What better power rush for a Malignant Narcissist than gaining *absolute control* over another's body and mind? Talk about pathological control freakism and an avaricious greed to have it all. The Narcissist's manipulations and mind control has at last reached the grotesque proportion of total possession of another's being – they are in charge… and they do not wish you well. What's the term we use when a demon has entered someone? We call them *possessed.*

The Malignant Narcissist is a hungry beast of prey that stalks minds and souls and violates every conceivable human boundary. Once they have slithered in and taken over a person's being, they literally need to be exorcised out. Their MO is to weaken their prey's defences, throw them off balance and make them doubt their own reality so they can control and manipulate the target into executing their own self-destruction. And, if they don't succeed in total annihilation of their prey, the Narcissist takes pride in the fact that their mental and emotional terrorism will long haunt the victim.

Picking-up a gun and blowing the victim's brains out would be more humane. But we're not talking about humanity here; we're talking about the Malignant Narcissist. And, a swift kill would fail to provide the drug they so hungrily crave – *the continual power rush they get from eroding your identity and feeding off your pain and confusion.* Besides, the sinister game of gaslighting is wicked good fun and they need minds to play with. In fact, seeing people squirm seems to be the only time the Narcissist experiences true pleasure.

Ever notice 'the look' a Malignant Narcissist gets when you are in mental, emotional or physical pain? It's as if they're a junkie who has just received a hit of smack and as the drug courses through their veins, they are being soothed by Satan. The look that crosses the Narcissist's façade is so vile it's as if a demon has just peeked out from behind their mask and winked at you. Here's what happens time and time again to men and women of the Malignant Narcissist variety: they smirk, their pupils dilate, their eyes squint and glaze over, and their mouth goes slack as if they are experiencing what can only be described as something akin to an orgasm. Sometimes, if it's a super intense hit of the dark drug, they convulse in ecstasy and their eyes roll back in to their skull and they gurgle and foam at the mouth.

So, it is with unbridled determination that these predators stalk their prey and methodically destroy the victim's life – they have to, the power high they get from another's demise is their drug of choice and they are addicts.

Comments:

Finally, someone who has lived what I have lived through!

This is the best and most real thing I have ever read about narcissism. I always felt like my ex was like Satan walking the earth and I appreciate your validation.

Thank you so much for your articles. It is the exact and precise descriptions I would give of these people too, having come from a family of them.

This is a really good description of the living ghosts that they are, like vampires, only able to survive by sucking the life-blood from others.

I can relate to EVERYTHING that has been written here. My mother is a MN, and I have had no contact with her for five years now. I found this blog after googling, "stalked by narcissist mother", and I feel so validated. She doesn't know where we live, and I cut myself off from the whole family because they became her minions in bullying me, (although they are well aware that the woman is batshit).

What's really alarming is how many people are like this. They are EVERYWHERE, it seems, and they have just about everyone else under their spell, believing them and not you, even if they've known you longer.

How did we do it? How did we survive? They had all the power and they were demonic; we had no power and they were relentless in their evil; we were soul captives and experienced this abuse day in day out for years and years. Yet we did survive, without help, without support, without any of the basic nurture that infants and children need. What does that say about us? What does it mean?

Truth is, those of us who have endured the MN family insanity are strong people because we had no choice but to be strong. We've just never received support and validation for knowing what we know. That may be the cruelest part of being the MN family scapegoat... having nowhere to turn. People don't want to hear about it, they don't get it, and they don't want to even try.

WHAT CAUSES MALIGNANT NARCISSISM?

What causes malignant narcissism? Who knows? Who cares?

….. The End

Seriously. Does it really matter what causes malignant narcissism? Not to me it doesn't. I look at MNs the same way I look at grizzly bears: as dangerous predators. I don't need to analyze the hell out of why a grizzly bear will claw me to death and eat me for dinner. I know that's their nature. So I stay far away from grizzlies. Same thing with narcs. They like to harm others. That's their nature. Stay away from them.

This blog post is inspired, in part, by a comment that "depthpsych" left on a post. Instead of publishing the comment, I decided to vault it and bring it out for a full dissection. It's attitudes like this narcissist sympathizer that warrant discussion.

Your description is accurate but what is missing is that you have no curiosity for the etiology of NPD or empathy for the plight of those beset with the disorder. We don't have the chance to see it in

Ordinary People but there is usually some kind of wounding that occurs that causes flight to false self.

· Your description is accurate

Okay. Thanks for telling me my description is "accurate." I am the daughter of a narcissist father, malignant narcissist mother and sibling to a malignant narcissist/sociopath golden child sister. I write through the lens of my experience and my descriptions of narcissists are neither accurate nor inaccurate. They just are. My eyes, my life, my experiences, my perceptions, observations and insights. They may be familiar and relatable to some, but they cannot be judged for accuracy.

· What is missing is that you have no curiosity for the "etiology" of NPD

How do you know I have no curiosity? You seem to think you know me and you are really quick to judge. Depthpsych? Why is it that you arrogant know-it-alls are always associated with, or like to be associated with psychology or psychiatry or some other nonsense? And yes you are a know-it-all, but I will get to that later.

So you've decided from reading one post on my blog that I have no curiosity for the "etiology" of NPD? Umm... do you know the books I've read? The research I've done? The documentaries I've watched? The people I have spoken to on the subject? The questions I've asked myself? The late night pondering of why? why? why? Why are they like that? So yes, I do have curiosity for the "etiology" of NPD, and what I've learned is that no one knows what causes it. And anyone who claims to know the cause (like a flight to false self) knows way less than the people who admit they don't know.

Is it nature or nurture? Is it nature and nurture? Is it nature, nurture and a scientific component? Is there something wrong with their brains? Are they missing the empathy chip? Or, do the narcissists create their own disorder by all the evil choices they make? Are some people just born bad?

Why do we expend so much energy on the etiology of malignant narcissism/psychopathy? Is there a worldwide phobia of the existence of evil? Is there worldwide denial of the banality of evil? We accept that people are good without explanation or analysis. So why can't we accept that people are also bad?

Trying to figure out why narcissists are the way they are gives them power. Once again we give the narcissists what they crave - attention - and spoon feed the big babies excuse after excuse for their wretched behaviour. Accepting what they are, without a sound explanation, is liberating. I don't need to know how they got that way. I don't care how they got that way. But I sure have thought about it.

· What is missing is that you have no "empathy" for the "plight" of those "beset" with the disorder

Bahaha! You sure got that right! I have no empathy for narcissists. ZERO. I reserve my empathy for a species I can relate to - NORMAL human beings. You know; the ones who also have empathy. The ones that narcissists target for mental, emotional and physical beat-downs. It is just ludicrous to suggest that narcissists deserve even a drop of my empathy. Besides, empathizing with another requires being able to put yourself in the other person's shoes and I just can't wrap my head around being a narcissist.

Wait a second… I'm not being entirely truthful. I suppose I could understand what it's like to be a narcissist if I took my contempt of MNs and I applied it to the population of normal, feeling people and then flipped it. In other words, if the population was say 90% MNs then I would have contempt for most "people" out there and I would want to hurt them, and see them suffer. Yes, this is probably the closest to embodying a MN as I will get. And admittedly, I really love getting under the skin of MNs. Thinking about them with bright red faces, and veins bulging out of their foreheads, and smoke coming out of their ears as I mess with them, gives me a bit of a rush. Better yet, is the fact that they have absolutely no control over what I say or do. They can't stop me. So yeah. I guess I can sort of understand what it would be like to be a MN. But wait… I have a motive. I hate MNs because they harm others, they have harmed me and I want to see them pay. MNs, on the other hand, harm for no reason, they have no tangible motives for hurting others. So I guess that cancels that. There is no way in hell I would be able to hurt another person who has never hurt me and never would hurt me.

· The "plight" of the narcissist

Plight, eh? Ok. Let me whip out my trusty thesaurus. Plight: dilemma, predicament, quandary.

Yes, being a narcissist is a difficult predicament to be in. Poor them. Those narcissists have quite the dilemma: they must choose between right and wrong, good and bad. That's quite a quandary to be in, isn't it? It's not unlike what we normal folks have to go through on a day-to-day. But here's the difference: narcissists choose to do wrong. Why? Because it makes them feel good. Their malicious way in the world is a choice. Narcissists know damn well that what they do is wrong but they do it anyway, and they ALWAYS do it when they know they won't get caught. Waiting to inflict harm until there are no witnesses present proves consciousness of guilt. Of course, that doesn't point to a guilty conscience. It only means malignant narcissists want to fly under the radar and never been seen for who they really are.

· "beset" with a disorder

Okay. Got my trusty thesaurus out. Beset... beset...ah... beset: plagued, tormented, and harassed.

Narcissists are "plagued" with a disorder. Huh? Do you think they are tortured souls who just can't help themselves? To suggest that they are "tormented" is to suggest that they experience shame and remorse and have a normal functioning conscience. Or *gasp* secretly hate themselves.

News flash: Narcissist enjoy their twisted way of being in this world. They like being narcissists. And they sure as hell don't want or need our empathy. Let's get real. What would make a normal person feel any sympathy for a narcissist? Maybe because the narcissist will never be able to love and be loved? They will never experience the joy of a deep and profound human connection. The narcissist is thinking; love, connections? Who gives a shit about love and feelings and all that crap?! What the narcissist "loves" is feeling superior to us mere mortals. Narcissists don't need others to love them, they need others to enable and support their narcissism. And in the case of malignant narcissists (sadists), they "love" supreme power and control. They get a perverse thrill dominating others to the point of usurping that person's will. Abusing others to such a degree that the only way for the victim to survive is to check-out of their own body and mind is one of the malignant narcissist's destructive goals. Absolute Possession of another is what turns the narcissist's crank. That's what the narcissists love. Malignant narcissists are the original soul snatchers flying below everyone's radar. They don't want us to have empathy for them; they just want us to be capable of empathizing so they can continue to exploit us. And never forget, they will always have contempt for us for having the very qualities they proudly lack but love to exploit.

The best example of a malignant narcissist smugly staking claim to their fucked-up-ness, is when MN sister said to me; "Why do you expect ME to act a certain way?! Why can't YOU just be complaisant?!" Crossed-arms, a big Hmpf! and a stomp of her feet. Classic narc. Translation: Why should I have to behave like the rest of humanity?! I'm special! I'm superior! The rules of common decency don't apply to me! You should just obey me!

Narcissists don't want to be like us. So don't waste your empathy on them. They are "beset" with free-will just like the rest of us. The difference is; they are plagued with ill will. But again, it's starts out as free-will. It all boils down to choice.

·   There is usually some kind of wounding that occurs (with the narcissist) that causes "flight to false self"

Flight to false-self, eh? So are we supposed to "empathize" with the vile narcissist because their real-self flew away? Yeah right. And the dish ran away with the spoon. Spin me another tale. Now where did the "real-self" fly off to? Did it go to that place where socks go? Is that what happened to their soul, their conscience and their hearts too? They flew away? ·

What proof do you have that the narcissist's "self" takes flight? And isn't the narcissist's "false-self" just another word for what they really are – assholes.

I get that some people believe that the narcissist's alienated self somehow springs completely out of control, to a pathological degree, and they will protect that alien self at any cost. Of course, the cost is always to others, NEVER the narcissist. That's why narcissists are so... well... despicable. These cretins can never admit a wrong, or any fault because THEY don't want to experience the misery of having a personal flaw. We are the ones who suffer the consequences of the narcissist so-called false self. The narcissist bears no burden. EVER. And let's face it; the narcissist's so-called false self is their real self because it's the one that actually exists.

Oh and then there's the whole shame thing. Apparently, to the narcissist, shame is so intolerable that they have developed the means not to experience it at all. As far as I'm concerned, the narcissists have repressed their shame so completely that it no longer exists. So who cares if it's deep-rooted and repressed? It's non-existent! And of course, we pay the price for the narcissist's pathological need to "appear" perfect, shameless and blameless. We are on the ones who pay for these self-serving freaks to avoid the inconvenient and ugly truth of who and what they really are. We pay by being at the receiving end of their denial, delusions, pathological lies, indifference, rage, projection, scapegoating and superiority to name a few. We pay for these high maintenance fucks by being at the receiving end of their abuse. No, I have no empathy for narcissists.

"Flight to false self"?? Gimme a break. Oh and some kind of wounding occurs? Let me fill you in on a little something, "Depthpsych." Some kind of wounding occurs to all of us, and we all don't turn into depraved narcissists. It's self-serving illogic like this that allows these hateful, selfish, vicious predators to justify their abuse of others. Thanks for giving the narcissists the excuse they have been searching for, and it's a lame one at that. Based on your reasoning that logic could be applied in the following way; "Hey, I didn't diddle that little boy, my false-self did." Awe, gee. I feel bad for the creepy old child toucher, he's got such a burden to bear, juggling those false-selves and all. Or better yet, the devil made me do it. Now that's more likely to be true. The devil inside, the devil inside...

So what causes malignant narcissism?

Who knows?

As for all this talk of causes originating in wounding, flight to false-self, nature, nurture, genetics, science, society, brain damage, early attachment disorders, too much attention, too little attention, abandonment, abuse, blah blah blah. So what! Who cares?! Any scientific break-through or reasonable explanation of the "etiology" of malignant narcissism is not going to make a lick of difference to me. It's not going to change anything, including the narcissist.

As far as I'm concerned, the cause of malignant narcissism can remain as mysterious as the existence of Big Foot. And frankly, I wish there was a folk tale surrounding a rare malignant narcissist spotted on occasion, captured in blurry photographs and living a solitary existence deep in the woods.

COMMENTS:

"And the dish ran away with the spoon..." BWHAHAHAAA! That's exactly how much I need to know about the "Etiology of Two-Legged Predators" aka, MNs.

I always love the "well he had a horrible childhood/she was abused" etc. excuse for horrifying behavior. Because if that was Cause & Effect, then every single person who lived to walk out of Auschwitz or the like would have turned out to be a narc, an abuser. I have sympathy for someone's pain and 'crazy' and suffering. But when it impacts anyone else but THEM, I want them to grow the fuck up, or die. I have NO sympathy for anyone who refuses to stop abusing. None. I wish them death, nothing less.

You wrote - they want us to be capable of empathy so they can exploit us. So very true. In turn they hate us even more because we are human and have empathy.

"Is there a worldwide phobia on the existence of evil?" To the smartarse psychology student who has the arrogance to think we are not aware of the psychological theories she parrots, and instructs us as if she was gifted with unique knowledge and we are ignorant bystanders who need her enlightenment to see the real picture. I am extremely well versed in the pathetic one eyed, one dimensional religion of academic psychology, and not the only one here I am sure. How dare you offer us your "expert" observations (for our own good!)Your apologist stance enables MNs to flourish by trying to exploit the sympathies of potential victims. I wonder what motivates you to protect their evil? Self-interest? Your comments are outrageous and enormously offensive. Fuck off.

So, what about the VICTIM'S "wounding?" of their REAL "selves?" Repeated intentional infliction of damage to others particularly their own family members.

I reserve my pity for the victims of the MNs, especially for the children who grew up with vile pieces of shit like this for parents. The world would be a better place if all Ns just sterilized themselves...And just in case there are any people reading this thinking, "But if Ns were sterilized, you wouldn't have been born." Yup, I'm aware, and my position remains the same.

Warning: Do Not Feed The Narcissists

I came across an article about how to talk to a narcissist. I was intrigued, hoping it would be a juicy step-by-step guide on how to mess with the narcissist's mind; how to confuse and destabilize the narcissist; how to control the narcissist. No such luck. Not only was I disappointed, I was pissed-off. No wonder narcissists are multiplying like cockroaches; they've got a good thing going. In the land of entitlement they get to act like Baby Huey, lofty Kings and hungry predators and *we* adjust to their temperament by pacifying the wailing baby so it won't have a tantrum; obeying his or her majesty so we won't be banished from court; and backing down to the vicious predator so we won't be attacked. It seems there are three ways to deal with a narcissist: tolerate (indifference), obey (fear), and/or run like hell (despise). I hope they're feeling the love.

Behold. My spin on the *rules* of how to talk to a Narcissist:

1. **Demand little. Expect Little** – You are merely a foot servant in the narcissist's court. Your role is one of support, acknowledgement, praise and recognition. You must cater to his Majesty's every need without being asked. For his Majesty should never suffer the indignity of acknowledging you.

2. **Be willing to listen a lot and listen carefully** – You must be admiring of his Majesty at all times. You are beneath his notice so you must not look at or speak to him. Simply listen and nod in approval.

3. **Find ways to provide positive recognition frequently** – You must feed his Majesty's ego at all times. Constantly check his reactions to make sure you have understood precisely the type of recognition his Majesty desires at any given moment.

4. **If it is at all possible to do so, be honest and sincere in your acknowledgement, praise, and recognition** – This is not possible. Besides, his Majesty does not require sincerity; he simply requires that you obey the laws of his court.

5. **Don't worry about making the narcissist become more self-centered** – (this part is real, read it and weep) "Narcissists need help of course, though they usually are very reluctant to seek it. If you think the narcissist in your life might want to alter his or her outlook, considering making an intervention." Hahaha! Though the N would thoroughly enjoy the attention an intervention brings - is there a reality show in the works?

6. **Avoid challenging the narcissist's wishes or desires** – his Majesty has the mentality of a three year old and thus does not tolerate frustration or interference of any kind. He is never to be judged. To fault him in anyway is unthinkable. He is righteous by virtue of *who* he is, not what he does.

7. **Failing these, smile a lot and keep quiet** – behave exactly how his Majesty expects you to: as his humble servant. Challenging his magnificence will result in a vicious attack: you will be swiftly banished from court or be-headed. Shut-up and know your place.

How to talk a narcissist? How to appease a narcissist more like. But why would you want to? Those rules might be helpful in getting what you want from a narcissist, if you must work or do business with one. But other than that, why would anyone in their right mind put up with that kind of abuse?

I have one narcissist in my life who I speak to a few times a year long distance: that's all the abuse I can handle. Even knowing full well what a narcissist is all about, having absolutely no expectations, and psyching myself up, I still feel lousy after speaking to the narcissist precisely because of their degrading rules. Here's an example, you call up a narcissist – who never calls you because they are too self-absorbed to even think about anyone but themselves, and aside from the obligatory "how are you?" they drone on and on about their dull as dishwater life without one iota of interest in you; even though you have just returned from an African Safari where you wrestled a tiger. The narcissist might say; "Hmm, Africa eh? I remember when I went to the bathroom…." You get the idea: Rule #2. Narcissists literally shit on you every chance they get.

We exist to fulfill the narcissist's every desire; we exist for the narcissist's sake. Narcissists are the original "what have you done for me lately?" "What can I get out of this?" Before I learned what a narcissist *really* is, I used to call them "Takers." No wonder everyone refers to them as Vampires: they drain us and leave us for dead. I suffer from stomach aches, headaches and exhaustion around narcissists. I tense up even if they are only on the telephone line. And, in the past, when I've managed to extricate a narcissist from my life, I lay down for a long winter's nap and sleep and sleep and sleep. Only when they have finally flown off into the night to set their evil tentacles on another target can you exhale. Not only are narcissists "Takers" they are "Haters of Mankind." Can you imagine the narcissist living up to the standards that he or she sets for us? The narcissist can't even abide by the standards of common decency. And we treat these freaks like Royalty.

A relationship with a narcissist is a non-relationship: a never ending stream of psychologically abusive messages that let you know - in no uncertain terms - that you have no value. They are constantly manipulating our feelings to make us feel bad. It more closely resembles a master/slave arrangement than anything. The narcissist feels entitled to all of the attention and views you as unworthy of any of it. Not only that, you have no right to resent the narcissist's arrogance and flagrant disregard. So, you swallow your pride and your anger and you end up with a psychosomatic illness.

I worked for an extreme narcissist whose wife worked part-time in the office, ran the household and cared for the three kids while he got to focus on his fun and sexy career which often took him away from home for months at a time. The narcissist treated his wife like his slave and he totally messed with her mind. She was completely under his control and would often come to work with bizarre inflammations that I sensed were physical reactions to having to continually swallow her pride and anger. I ended up quitting the job not only because of this creep's narcissism but because I couldn't bear witness to the abuse of this woman any longer. Less than two years after I left the job, she died of leukaemia. I contend to this day that the narcissist killed his wife through a stress cancer.

Here's another example of narcissism at its finest: I once had an N friend whom I'll call 'Neil.' He possessed all of the wonderful qualities of narcissism including being a control freak, a big baby and an insufferable 'know it all.' One summer evening we took a stroll through the city and began a discussion about a certain film. Neil was convinced that the actor who played the lead was a man by the name of XYZ. I informed Neil that it wasn't that actor; it was another fellow but people often get the two men confused. Neil refused to believe me and the discussion went back and forth with me presenting facts to support my position and Neil denying these facts.

Eventually, Neil and I stumbled upon a Blockbuster Video and we agreed to go inside and settle the debate once and for all. There on the shelf was the movie in question, with the actor in question. I picked-up the piece of hard evidence and presented it to Neil. I also pointed to a gigantic poster of the film on a wall that exposed the glaring truth in black and white.

Neil surveyed the evidence, let out an arrogant 'humph' and snipped, "I still don't believe it." He was then overcome with fatigue and informed me he was going home. In a huff, Neil stormed out of Blockbuster Video. I was left standing there holding the video case – aka, the undeniable proof he was wrong.

Despite all the evidence - in his deluded mind – Neil was still right because his ego would not allow him to admit defeat. He was right not because of any facts supporting his claim, but by virtue of who he believes himself to be – a superior being who is always right. And, through his behaviour, Neil sent me a very clear message about what he thought of me in relation to all knowing and powerful him – I was beneath him. You might think that this kind of thing is harmless, but it's not. Yes, you can say to yourself, "Okay, this guy's an arrogant fuckwit" but it goes deeper than that. For example, Neil would not have behaved like a petulant child if there was someone else around. In other words, he would not have let his mask slip and disrespected me if there was a witness present.

Whereas Neil was downright obnoxious, this type of aggressive control and pathological sense of entitlement can be manipulated very subtly. It's always going on, even when it's beneath the surface. Break one of the narcissist's rules and see what happens. Go on, try it. I dare you.

Full-blown narcissists, malignant narcissists, sociopaths - whatever you want to call them - supposedly make up only 4% of the population give or take. I believe it's much more. Let's say they make up 10% of the population. It would appear then that we are adapting to *them,* instead of them adapting to us – the majority. What gives? I thought majority rules.

We comply with their demands because it's just easier. They're just *that way* and we don't want to have to deal with some kind of a temper tantrum, exile, assassination or attack. We don't want to upset the poor little narcissist because then they'll make *our* lives hell and being around them is already bad enough. Narcissists don't change; they don't have to. They've got us exactly where they want us – under their control. Hello Big Brother. No wonder so many of them have climbed the ranks of politics straight on up to running governments.

We have identified evil: malignant narcissists, sociopaths, psychopaths. Now we must isolate evil and force it to adapt to *our* rules. If this 'entity' refuses to adapt it will not be able to survive and it will just die off or go somewhere else.

It's high time we organize a world-wide "starve the narcissists rally." This could be followed by a "starve the narcs festival." Perhaps Bono and Sting would jump on board and George Clooney could organize a call centre to provide telephone support to all of the narcissist's minions as they take a stand to "starve the narc."

We need to act on principles NOT in reference to the narcissist. Perhaps only then – when we have the courage of our convictions – will the narcissist submit to our values of common human decency.

I have a dream: that starvation might someday lead to the narcissist's extinction, or, better yet, their evolution.

Comments:

WELL FUCKING SAID!! I totally agree, why the fuck should we walk around on eggshells and feel like the only way to survive is to help boost their fucking ego when really they need to lose it in order to realize that they can't receive the satisfaction they demand from us unless they glorify us in the same way they do themselves!

It only just now occurred to me why I really am a magnet for Ns - Not only was I trained to put up with more shit than most, but compared to my MN mother, a run-of-the-mill N wouldn't initially seem that bad. I really do have a problem recognizing the lesser Ns because they don't seem as evil as my mother. Back when I first escaped the family home, I had ridiculously low standards. I was susceptible to the charming ways of Ns and unable recognize the abuse; actually thought they were nice... All because the abuse was less than what I suffered at the hands of my mother, and all because these people actually seemed to be nice in between - something that my mother rarely bothered to do unless she had a reason (her thing was mostly get the hell away from me/don't bother me, then abuse when I didn't comply).

I can relate. The "nice in between" used to trip me up all the time. Now I look for people who are nice all of the time and show compassion for others. These types of people are hard to come by.

I never knew my NM was a Narc until a couple years ago, but I always (as in from childhood) knew that I would not share with her how I feel or stuff that goes on with me, unlike what I observed with my friends and their moms.

It's only been 11 months since I initiated NC, and I'm still struggling with the de-programming. Since the MN in my life was my mother, she conditioned me since birth to put up with her shit, and because of this, I was the poster child for the illusion of powerlessness. As a married woman in my 30s, I still couldn't wrap my brain around the fact that I had the right to stand up for myself, and didn't have to tolerate any of her b.s. Now that I'm away from this crazy bitch, I can really see how insane and toxic she was. Had I not cut her out of my life, I'm sure that I would still be just as brainwashed as I always was.

38

Never Show Vulnerability to a Narcissist

Never show signs of weakness around a narcissist because when you are down that is precisely when they are going to kick. This is true for all narcissists, from your garden variety straight on up to the malignant. All narcissists salivate at the sign of a vulnerable target - be it mental, emotional or physical vulnerability.

Narcissists are spineless bullies. They are insecure, jealous, inadequate, attention seeking little brats trapped in the body of an adult. Have you ever referred to a narcissist as a strong person? I doubt it. Narcissists are immature weaklings and cowards. Their personality disorder makes them so. When they see an easy opportunity to strike they can't help themselves. They are nasty little children and they don't fight fair.

Malignant narcissists are predators by nature and predators devour the bleeding and the injured. They can't help themselves; it's their animal instinct. They respond to your vulnerability like a rabid junkyard dog to a meaty bone: they've gotta chomp on it.

So I ask you, are you going to show insecurity around a sadistic little brat who is always looking for ways to vaunt themselves at your expense? Are you going to show signs of weakness around a vicious predator whose very nature is to attack vulnerable prey? Narcissists are unsafe, period. But they are especially dangerous when you are in a weakened state. Sharks sniff out blood.

All narcissists identify with other abusers, so if you have been harmed by another person – most likely another narcissist - do not tell them. The narcissist will not only pathologize you but defend their fellow narcissist. Feel better now? The narcissist does. Narcissists are always scrounging around for validation of their abusiveness. If you offer up proof of another harmful person – in the narcissist's eyes – you have justified their own cruel behaviour. Birds of a feather and all that.

In the most sinister way; the vile narcissist will attribute virtues to your abuser while giving you a good kick. For example, you are in utter distress because a co-worker has been bullying, undermining, and sabotaging you for over a year. He's trying to get you fired; he wants your job. You are at wits end, losing sleep, nervous, stressed-out and ready to quit your job because of the situation. The narcissist - let's call her "Sheila" - will simply be delighted to hear of your dilemma, and react to your predicament by saying, "Oh, come on. He's not a bad person. He's just a hard worker and his job is important to him. Maybe he's been taking notes on you. You're just not taking very good care of yourself."

See what the narcissist did? Sheila just defended her fellow narcissist saying that he's a good guy, a hard worker, cares about his job and obviously has dirt on you. The narcissist just told you that you are bad, lazy, you don't care about your job, and that you're obviously doing something that warrants note taking and the narcissist's abuse. Furthermore, the narcissist assigned the cause of your distress to *you* for not taking care of yourself. It's your fault. Get it? You were asking for it. That's why the co-worker narcissist abused you, and that's why Sheila is justified in abusing you. The vile narcissist feels better now.

Here is another example of the narcissist's callousness. You have been in a traumatic accident in which you sustained serious injury to your face. The injury is so bad that it required plastic surgery. You are still in a state of shock from the accident; you are beaten-up, stitched-up, battered and bruised. You are distressed at the state of your face; you are weakened and run down from surgery. Laid up in bed, you make the mistake of sending a *fact based* email notifying a narcissist of your accident. Let's call the vile narcissist "Myra." Myra responds with a one line email that says, "Keep it in perspective." To drive home her point, she adds a link to a YouTube video of a some dude with no arms and no legs. Feel better now? The vile narcissist Myra does.

Let's take a look at what both of the narcissists did. They placed themselves above you as your judge: "Keep it in perspective." "You're not taking care of yourself." This condescending superiority aggrandizes the narcissist. They denied you any attention and let you know that you don't matter. They blamed you, the victim, and attributed virtues to your abuser. They dismissed and minimized your experience. They let you know that you have no right to even bring up your accident, let alone *feel anything* because someone out in YouTube land has no arms and legs (as if they care). They justified their outrageous callousness and derived pleasure from you pain.

And get this: Sheila calls you up bawling her eyes out because her date stood her up, and she expects you to comfort her. Myra calls you up bawling her eyes out because her sister doesn't have time to frame her paintings for her upcoming art show, and she expects your sympathy.

Ugh! You get it: they are narcissists. They are big babies and parasitic bottom feeders who are always scrounging the surface of every interaction looking for ways to feed. Their entire existence is based on deep-rooted selfishness.

Here's one final example of a narcissist taking advantage of your vulnerability. You've had a bad fall in which you suffered a massive cut to your face. You are still recovering and you are coming to terms with the fact that your face is going to be permanently scarred. The narcissist knows that you are self-conscious about the scar on your face and how it is healing.

You visit the narcissist and notice that he needs a few things around the house. Although you are the one in need of care, you go out and purchase a bunch of helpful and thoughtful items for the narcissist. You package everything up really nice and with a smile present the big bag of goodies to the narcissist. The narcissist takes the gift bag, and with a big smirk on his face and an evil glint in his eye, snarks, "That thing on your face is really red." You can't hide the fact that he hurt your feelings. In a trance-like state, the narcissist drinks-in your pain and looks high on drugs.

When you are in a weakened state or even doing something thoughtful and kind, the narcissist's fangs and claws spring out. Dropping your guard and being vulnerable will make you the perfect target to abuse, control, manipulate, toy with and jerk around. Never let a narcissist know that someone has done you wrong. Never let them sniff-out insecurity. Never let them see you sweat. What elicits warmth and compassion in normal people provokes an act of shocking inhumanity in a narcissist. They will respond to your kindness with contempt, attack when you cannot defend yourself, and deny you whatever you are in need of, be it serious medical attention, a roof over your head or an ounce of sympathy.

Do not ignore the twisted aggression inherent in all narcissists. Do not engage in fantasy and magical thinking. Do not try to penetrate their callousness. When we refuse the truth of what the narcissist really is, we leave the door wide open to abuse.

Whatever is ruling your emotions at the time will be used against you by the narcissist. Do not involve them in the sensitive areas of your life, don't let them into your head space, keep them away from your wounds. Protect yourself. If you must be in contact with a narcissist, play your cards very close to your vest. Do not display any signs of neediness. They are the enemy of goodwill and the *last* people you want around during a time of crisis.

Narcissists are terrorists who invade mental and emotional borders. They are constantly engaged in an invisible war of control. It's ALWAYS about *their* boundaries, *their* terms, *their* agenda, and *their* conveniences while you lay dying by the side of the road.

Comments:

They'll accuse you of being "all about yourself" for setting limits and terms of your own.

I found about NPD last year, it basically blew the veil off describing how my mother worked and several other relatives.

Seriously! You can NEVER do anything nice enough or selfless enough for them. They will ALWAYS deny you, confuse you, and leave you feeling invalidated.

They will totally attack you at your lowest state. It is so exhausting having to constantly protect yourself in any and every way you can possibly imagine.

I completely agree with this article and I've noticed that other people seem afraid of the mean N and redefine his or her behaviour, calling cruelty strength.

Every sentence or so that I read here conjures up people from life and I think, 'that's what Karen did to me!' or (my sister, mother, cousin, aunt, "friend" etc...) I'm seeing my whole life in a brand new way and I'm finally feeling validated and not stupid, weak or flawed beyond all repair. I finally see that I'm okay after all and that it's the Ns in my life who are character disordered.

No wonder the Ns in my life, which is pretty much everyone I know; including my doctors, have ramped up their N behaviour since I've become disabled and unable to work. No freaking wonder! OMG. I feel like I should have known this, but even college courses on psychology don't teach us to prepare for this. A comment on here said that learning about Ns is so intense because of the constant revelations we have. It is so true!

I recently went no contact with the evil that is my parents and brother. The worst part is that everyone wants me to just move on. If they were that bad it should be easy right? I have suspected a couple of these people to be narcissists before this and now I am certain. They are already trying to use me and prey on me at this vulnerable time. Isolating myself with just a few for support may be just what I need to feel better, slowly, when I am ready. Thank you for putting this information out there.

I've read many articles about being genuine and having the 'courage' to be vulnerable and I say, don't buy that bullshit. It is insane to be vulnerable around unsafe people. Be vulnerable around people you can trust. This means you don't talk to everyone about your problems. If you did it in the past, stop doing it now. You don't tell everyone that you were abused as a kid. Not everyone has to hear your life story or how people took advantage of you. N's will see you as potential prey; if those other abusers got away with it, I can too. Don't feel ashamed of yourself for being human; we all get burned sometimes.

44

Narcissists Are Always in Attack Mode

The last post got me thinking... Okay, it's a given that we should never show vulnerability to a narcissist because that's like dangling bait before their eyes. Narcissists are predators and they can't resist the temptation to attack when a juicy opportunity presents itself. Also, narcissists are cowards and being vulnerable means that you cannot properly defend yourself. So, being in a weakened state around a narcissist means you are dead meat, or deader meat.

But I ask you, when are narcissists NOT on the offensive? My experience is that narcissists are ALWAYS engaged in an invisible war of control and that means narcissists are ALWAYS on the lookout for an opportunity to mess with you.

Why do narcissists abuse? Because it makes them feel good. They undermine and attack because of their incapacity to love. Narcissists need to triumph over others in order to feel superior and accept themselves. They must destroy to find affirmation. They are junkies always chasing the next high. And narcissists know many ways to get their next fix.

First and foremost, narcissists are attention whores. They've got to have every last drop of it and that means you are not allowed any of it. They flagrantly deny, dismiss, minimize and invalidate your needs, rights and feelings. Narcissists are emotional tight wads who withhold positive regard of *any* kind including: sympathy, praise, support and approval. It's as if giving you *any* positive attention might actually kill the narcissist.

I remember once having some fantastic news that I shared with two narcissists. The narcissists didn't know one another other, they never even met. They lived at opposites ends of the country, but their gruff response to my news was identical. Both of the narcissist, with clenched jaw, gritted teeth, and vexed tone could barely spit out, "I'm (pause) happy (pause) for (pause) you." Afterwards, they both took a deep breath because they seemed to have given their last breath of life (attention) to little old me. This act of begrudging cordiality almost suffocated them. Then they immediately changed the subject away from me and my news. That's as good as it gets with a narcissist. They are all from the same factory assembly line and they are all interchangeable.

But the narcissist will give you *negative* attention. Their critical sense is highly developed. They spend a lot of time disparaging, humiliating and insulting everyone and everything, this makes them feel all powerful.

Here's an example; you get dressed-up, you're looking good, feeling great and excited about the event you're heading to. The narcissist will give you a demeaning side-eye and a noticeable smirk when you walk by. The narcissist wants to bring you down with a glance. Or, they will look you up and down and bark, "You're not wearing *that* are you?"

Or, let's say you call up a narcissist and tell them that you just won a very competitive arts competition and you are receiving a hefty financial grant for your project. The narcissist will snipe, "Hmpf. Well, then you better get cracking." No congratulations, no nothing. And, this nasty bite after all the encouragement and support you have given the needy, greedy narcissist over the years.

Even if they are incredibly privileged, narcissists feel spiteful irritation at the sight of the happiness and the accomplishments of other people. Their driving force is envy. It's an abusive mentality based on the perception of what you possesses and they lack. Narcissists gotta have it all and that means pillaging you while giving NOTHING in return.

In addition to being greedy, entitled, dismissive, withholding attention whores; narcissists – in their dead eyes – think they are better than you. And, they will demonstrate their pathological sense of superiority in every interaction. Showing you that you are beneath their notice is how they prove that they are better than you.

If you are excited about something the narcissist will change the subject and direct the attention back to *anything, anything* but you. A narcissist I know put the focus of his attention on a radish while I excitedly told him about something I was interested in. He rudely interrupted me to point out the radish's skin. If there isn't a fascinating radish lying around, the narcissist will walk out of the room while you are talking; they will talk over you; or suddenly yelp, "Ouch!" Seriously, one narcissist I know would yelp, "Ouch!" and suddenly look at his finger or down at his foot whenever I spoke enthusiastically about a subject. Talk about diverting the attention back to him. I think my happiness caused him actual pain.

This makes sense, considering what makes narcissists happy – *your* pain. The narcissist's deficiencies are continually shown up by your healthy desire to attain goals. So, the feeble narcissist is like a human voodoo doll that receives painful stabs at the sight of your joy and zest for life. I think we should all kill them with our vitality – best revenge ever!

But a note of caution regarding the more conniving malignant variety: Malignant narcissists are very good at feigning enthusiasm and interest in your life: it's a combat manoeuver. What they are doing is gathering intelligence – ammo – that they will use to attack you with at a later date. Too much personal information in the dirty paws of a narcissist is a dangerous thing. Also, by feigning interest and enthusiasm in you, the narcissist is getting you to drop your guard and that's when you become a vulnerable target of opportunity for them. Narcissists are like dogs that lick your face while they figure out where to pee on you. Beware the narcissist playing nice – it's a strategic move - they are constantly engaged in an invisible war.

So, if your life is in dire straits the narcissist will attack. If you are on top of the world, the narcissist will attack. They want to kick you when you're down; they want to rain on your parade; they want to dampen your spirits; they want to dim your bright light. And, by the time you figure all this out and you can give the narcissist a taste of their own medicine, you've already said to hell with them.

However, should a new narcissist enter your sphere, treat them like the predators they are: whack them on the snout, get in their face and yell back, humiliate them, call them on their bull-shit. Do anything to deter the predator from viewing you as prey - protect your borders.

Here's what I know about narcissists, it's simple: the norms of human interactions do not apply. Narcissists don't have "human" relationships because they lack everything that makes us human. And for that reason, narcissists are not cognizant of any common humanity between you and them. They can't relate to you, or your feelings at all. Your inner person is as far from regard to the narcissist as the inner soul of a bug is from you when you squash it. Get it? They are empty, the well is dry... actually the well is a fire pit of hell. Do not try and draw water, you will get burned.

So, here's how I am when I am visiting planet narcissism – without witnesses - in the presence of the only narcissist I have a relationship: I am a robot. Yup, that's right. No noticeable joy and happiness, no sadness, no anger, nothing much in between. No feelings, period. I don't want to give the narcissist any ammo. I keep a low profile and don't draw attention to myself. Sadly, this is exactly what the narcissist wants: for others to be mindless automatons, a non-person who will not make them feel bad or usurp their attention. The thing is; I give the narcissist nothing. I've grown completely indifferent to them. No attention, no regard, no reason to attack. Hell, I'm a robot; just like the narcissist and I'm not capable of a normal human interaction and I'm devoid of supply.

But... on planet earth, I am a human being, living a human life, and it's a valuable one – despite what the narcissist may think. So, other than that one narcissist, the way I deal with them is simply to get and stay far, far away. For life is short and too good to waste on them and their dirty war.

Comments:

I'm still learning to live on planet Earth, but I have realized, to my profound relief, that I am in fact an Earthling.

Thank you so much for this post! This is the most concise example of narcissistic behavior and abuse that I have read so far. It ALL resonated with me!

Nfoo could care less if I was dead or alive... They have no interest in my life, never did. They've already proven that I don't exist to them. It's still hard to wrap my head around that.

Your blogs are definitely 'food for thought.' I've been NC with my narcissistic siblings now for about five months and in LC with my NM - and I feel so liberated.

Also an adult survivor, I just want to say THANK YOU for your fantastic blog.

MN's are always in attack mode, if they're not attacking they're just planning the next one. They are sharks who never sleep. Every conversation is a mind game and every sentence is a move on the chessboard.

They know the difference between right and wrong, yet choose to do what feels good at that moment in time regardless of anything else. How do I know? Because I've seen my own mother behave different ways in front of different people. If she didn't know whatever she was doing was wrong, her behavior would be consistent regardless of who was around. She committed crimes, yet knew enough to cover them up. Did that bother her? Nope. That bitch was able to pass a polygraph test without batting an eyelash, only to come back and brag about it later.

Since I started reading your blog a week ago or so -- I've now read every post, some twice -- I'm finally losing the guilt about going LC/NC and I'm not as angry and I even find myself laughing about some of the crap my Ns have pulled. The MNs and Ns in my life had me feeling suicidal for years, but now I feel happy to be alive and more in control of the situations in my life. I feel SO validated! I know that doubt and anger can easily slip back into my life but now I have resources to turn to like this one and I finally have a game plan that I feel confident about.

The Narcissist's Shock Tactics

Narcissists are mental and emotional terrorists, and like terrorists, they strike when you least expect it. At any given moment, the narcissist will launch an attack by reacting to a situation the polar opposite of what would be considered normal and humane. It's is a shock tactic: a deliberate blast of terror designed to leave you stunned and immobilized.

Narcissists will react to your physical injury by laughing at you. Narcissists will react to your psychological injury by mocking you and calling you crazy. Narcissist will react to your kindness with contempt. Narcissists will react to your happiness with misery. Narcissists will react to your joy with hate. Narcissists will react to a smile with a look that could kill. Narcissists will scream and yell at you when you're barely hanging on. Narcissists will react to your pleas for help with anger – you've got a lot of nerve inconveniencing them with your distress. Narcissists will react to your basic human needs with spiteful irritation. Narcissists will view other people's disturbing and disgusting behaviour as funny. Narcissists will boldly defend other abusers who are rotten to the core, just like themselves. What makes normal people shudder in horror gives the narcissist a cheap thrill.

Narcissists are perverts. Their ass backwards reactions to things are all part of their strategy to catch you off guard and run you over. Narcissists are emotional and psychological snipers and drive by shooters. Their behaviour leaves you morally stunned, and mentally scrambled; shaking your head; pinching yourself and wondering in disbelief if that really just happened? When you are off balance, you cannot properly defend yourself. The narcissist's goal is to amass power by derailing you with their inexplicable inhumanity.

The effects of shock are intense feelings of insecurity, psychological distress, and physical and psychological isolation. The narcissist pulls-off their perverted stunts on the sly, where there are no witnesses to their evil. As a victim of a narcissist, you are left startled, astonished, confused and fearful of it happening again. Who are you going to tell? Who would believe you anyway? Only when a witness appears on the scene will the narcissist "fake" some semblance of humanity. Proving once again that the narcissist knows that their impulses are warped, but they choose to act on them anyway - when they can get away with it.

Here's an example: About 12 years ago I went to see a psychotherapist. During one session the shrink spoke to me in a soft and gentle manner, as I began to drop my guard, I told him that I felt very vulnerable and alone. I related the feeling of abandonment to being on the top of a hill in an empty world with no other people. When I paused, while lying on a sofa with my back to him, the shrink ATTACKED. In the most vile and hateful tone he screamed, "ARE YOU COVERED IN SHIT?!"

BAM! A deliberate blast of terror out of nowhere. This scumbag blindsided me while my defences were down by doing the mental and emotional equivalent of smashing me over the head with a baseball bat. I was startled, confused, frightened and humiliated. Before I could recover, the evil shrink quickly changed his tone to very soft again. I named this creep Dr. Full O' Crap, and was aware that his shock tactic and toxic projections blatantly revealed that he sees *himself* as a piece of shit. Needless to say, I got the hell out of that psycho's line of fire.

TERRORISM

Dr. Full O' Crap is a quintessential malignant narcissist: a dangerous and destructive predator working in the so-called mental health field that got his kicks messing with vulnerable people's minds. This sicko and the Soul Murdering practice of psychiatry warrants future in-depth posting. But my point is, narcissists are everywhere, in every profession and every walk of life, and they all draw from the same playbook. So be on the look-out for perverted behaviour. There is a reason why narcissists act the way they do.

The idea behind the narcissist's shock tactics is to prevent the victim from relaxing and therefore recovering. When someone is in a state of shock they are open to suggestion and likely to comply. That is why shock tactics are a popular weapon of narcissists. Narcissists require total obedience and mental awareness is a threat. Attacking you off guard and keeping you disoriented is a way for the narcissist to blur the lines of reality, snuff out the fight in you and keep you under their control. It's a crime against your humanity and it is done entirely for effect by only the lowest of the low.

In warfare, a shock tactic is an offensive manoeuver which attempts to place the enemy under psychological pressure by a rapid and fully committed advance with an aim for the enemy to retreat. This is exactly what the narcissist is doing. They advance with shockingly cruel, bizarre and offensive behaviour designed to trigger confusion and discomfort so you feel insecure and fearful around them. Narcissists continually undermine your perceptions of reality so that you end up without any confidence in your intuition, memory, or powers of reasoning. This makes you easier to manipulate. In the case of psychiatry, it ensures the narcissist a dependent patient and an income.

The vilest of narcissists will use shock tactics to compound your pain and suffering when you are already under extreme duress. Reducing you to a puddle on the floor makes them feel all powerful. Therein lies the malignancy in malignant narcissism - sheer perversion and evil.

The thing to keep in mind is that shock wears off. So, the best defence against these sickos is a strong offense: *know* that you are under siege and stay oriented. When you are in the presence of a narcissist be hyper aware of *what* is happening to you and *why*. If possible, stay focused on the *narcissist's behaviour* not on how they make you feel. When we stayed focused on the narcissist's behaviour we remain in a position of strength.

Shock tactics, like gaslighting are the most sinister forms of "clean" violence and the reddest, of all the red flags of dangerous people. If someone you know has shocking reaction to things, that's a sign that they are deliberately trying to destabilize you and they are extremely dangerous. I liken being around the hostile narcissist to walking alone down a dark alley in a dangerous neighbourhood. Be cautious, heed the warning signs, stay alert and keep your wits about you. Crystal clear awareness of how the narcissist operates is the best way to protect yourself from their twisted aggression.

Comments:

They are predictably unpredictable.

I saw a comment on a thread about truth being stranger than fiction. That bitch on wheels that calls herself my mother really pushes the boundaries on that.

I read something from your blog every single day so I don't become complacent and fall into the guilt trap, which I often do because I actually have too much empathy (the only one in my narcissist family who does).

Something I got from your blog this week that has helped me tremendously. Can people who are supposed to LOVE you really and truly be this evil? YES THEY CAN AND ARE.

Each day I get stronger and stronger and develop more and more resolve to ditch these harmful people from my life. Thank you again. Your blog has literally SAVED my life!

Great post, I have been at the receiving end of MN abuse when I was foolish enough to have empathy or feel sorry for them. That's when the narcs tone of voice turned evil and there was a sick gleam in their eye. Even if they appear to be behaving, just wait a moment because that is when you will get a knife in the back. It is so true the MNs want to control and destroy. It is a tricky twist they play.

Excellent and truthful post. People have been brainwashed into thinking that we need to be sympathetic and nice to the narcs because they have a "disorder and need help." I have no sympathy for them... People look at me as though I have no heart because I won't feel sorry for them. Their thinking is just as distorted as the narcs.

I was just sitting here wondering why I don't recognize the Ns right away. I have had a lifetime of experience dealing with their shit, so I should spot their tactics rather quickly. I think I do, but one additional side effect of being an ACON is that I don't trust my own judgment; I frequently second guess myself, and that brief moment is all that a skilled N needs to infiltrate my life. Next thing I know I'm spinning my wheels trying to figure out how to get rid of them.

Yes! Stay focused on the narcissist's behaviour. I think they use shock tactics to shame us. They want us to look inward (like they trained us to do) and wonder what "WE" did to make them act that way. If they can get us to doubt ourselves, feel the need to explain ourselves, and question our perceptions and judgement, they can get us to back down, or give in. If we don't trust our gut instincts then the narcissist will succeed at manipulating and controlling us.

Malignant Narcissist, Sociopath, Bully, Liar, Slanderer

It doesn't matter what you call them: malignant narcissist, covetous sociopath or bully. They are one and the same. They are all predators who target people that provoke in them a desire for something they have, or something they are. The covert power game and systematic destruction of another who put puts their wretched self to shame *is* sport for the malignant narcissist. They excel at it. They've been practicing since birth. It gives them a thrill and makes them feel alive. That is why malignant narcissists are unsafe for human interaction, period. If you have been targeted by a malignant narcissist and they have access to you, they will try and destroy you. That's their nature. It's not complicated. Run like hell.

Having two narcissists as parents was no picnic (they divorced long ago). Though, I sometimes feel lucky that my mother was the only truly malignant one. Unfortunately, my sister made up the difference. She is a malignant narcissist like my mother and I have had a target on my back since birth. Not one, but two dangerous predators working as a team have been hunting me all my life. When we were kids, the malignant narcissist sister tried to physically kill me. The MN mother twice slipped me a note that suggested I should commit suicide. They have both been unrelenting in their desire to psychologically murder me.

I've stayed out of reach of these two dangerous MN predators for 20 years and yet they still managed to stalk me and wreak havoc on my life over the phone, online and through email. Truth be told; that's the main reason I'm writing on the subject of malignant narcissism - those two crazy bitches, and others who are *exactly* like them. Take it from someone who has been there: If you've been targeted by a malignant narcissist – particularly a family member – you will NEVER be safe in their sphere of influence because they will *never* stop trying to destroy you.

If the malignant narcissist can extract information from anyone, and I mean *anyone*, who is in contact with you, they will. They will create a smear campaign over the most innocuous slice of your life. For example, you tell Bob that a car rear ended you; the malignant narcissist knows that you're in contact with Bob, and even though the malignant narcissist doesn't have a relationship with Bob, she calls him now and again just to see if she can dig up dirt on you – that's how brazen and predatory the malignant narcissist is. The blood thirsty malignant narcissist manages to pry this tiny titbit of information – about a minor car collision - out of Bob. The malignant narcissist then concocts an elaborate pathology of you based on a 5 second mention of a fender bender. She spreads her work of fiction far and wide in order to generate a negative view of you in everyone's eyes. Remember: the malignant narcissist is ravenous; she hasn't had her supply since you went no contact; she is irritable and aggressive and is chomping at the bit to destroy you by *any* means possible.

If the malignant narcissist can't violate *your* mind directly, the next best thing is to dirty up other people's minds with bad thoughts of you. This is achieved through lies, slander, false rumours, undermining, creating doubts and suspicions and by encouraging and manipulating people to withhold information and spread misinformation.

Don't think for a second that sharing an innocent piece of information such as being in a fender bender is harmless – it isn't. *Any* information about you is ammunition for the devious malignant narcissist and it will be used to attack you. That's why it is so important to sever all lines of communication that are open to your abuser. Even if you don't care what her cohorts and copycat abusers think, she's still getting a power rush out of the game. And the worst part: the slimy bitch will malign you all under the pretence of "concern". It's enough to make you sick. She puts on a schmaltzy performance as a "caring" person; meanwhile, behind closed doors, she's plotting your destruction. And, the brain dead 'pod-people' buy her act. What a joke! It's no surprise that narcissists surround themselves with imbeciles.

No wonder people are taking to the internet to expose the truth. Narcissistic abuse is not only an assault of a person's human dignity; it's a never ending cycle of re-victimization by an abuser who literally gets high and mighty through the process of your destruction. In short, narcissistic abuse is an assault on a person's humanity by those who are inhumane – that is an outrage!

Malignant narcissists are disgusting, filthy, reprehensible creatures. They are violent mental and emotional rapists, and as such, they think like rapists. A rapist knows that they are dirty. They are secretly ashamed of themselves for their perversions. So, in order for the mental rapist to feel clean, they must dirty up their victim. That's where spreading rumours, lies and slander comes in. But we all know that slander is just projection. So, whatever LIES the vile narcissist is spreading about you, is actually the TRUTH about the narcissist.

Unfortunately, most people are easily duped into swallowing the narcissist's load of crap. Female narcissists are masters at manipulating people through their emotions, beliefs, attitudes and perceptions. Malignant narcissist sister once said to me with a spooky giggle, "It's *so* easy to use the *power of suggestion* on Dad." Creepy, eh? There is underlying sinister intent to everything she says and does.

Another thing that people don't get is that the narcissist needs NO reason to be hostile to their target. Normal people attack for natural motives like revenge or retaliation. Not so the narcissist. They simply attack people who possess something they want. For the narcissist believes that everything belongs to her, and if someone has a little of it, then she's not getting all of it. Pathological greed, entitlement, and covetousness are what make the malignant narcissist a dangerous predator. They are forever out to take, keep from, destroy and besmirch whatever they can get their grimy paws on: be it your job, you home, your relationships, or your reputation.

It is sheer malevolence to want to damage the most valuable possessions of another. It is sheer malevolence to be hostile to others getting what makes them happy and feel good about themselves. And, it is beyond sick to have ill will toward people who aren't harming you, have never harmed you, and have never threatened to harm you. Malignant narcissists are pure evil. Just look at who they target: vulnerable children, people who love them, family, and the innocent.

Convicted criminals who steal out of necessity, or shoot someone who tries to fight them off in a robbery, or commit murder out of anger or for revenge, are better than the malignant narcissist. The criminal is not a threat to anyone else because he doesn't go around wishing to hurt others or see harm come to them. But the malignant narcissist does - in every waking moment of her sad, sorry existence. The malignant narcissist is a pestilent, disease spreading low-life and the driving force behind her predation is insecurity, greed, entitlement and covetousness. Remember; she's not normal. She's incapable of acquiring positive attributes for herself, so she must *take* from others to even the score.

The malignant narcissist's spiteful envy compels her to steal from you and she wants to make damn sure that you are severely harmed in the process. This clandestine power game is priority number one, and all of the malignant narcissist's energies are devoted to it. The objective is POWER, CONTROL, and DOMINATION and she will stop at nothing to win. Causing the downfall of others gives her pleasure and victory means disempowering the target to a state of suffering and loss while aggrandizing herself. So sad, that the pathetic little narcissist must resort to such tactics but she knows no other way, she's abnormal: socially, morally, emotionally and psychologically retarded.

However, beneath her extreme treachery, the malignant narcissist is still able to project an "image" - albeit campy and over-the-top. So, when people don't incite her jealous rage, she lays on the smarmy charm thick with a spoon and slyly uses those dimwits to spread vicious rumours about her victim. All the while, maintaining a false front as a well-meaning, do-gooder. Blech! That is precisely why these sickos - particularly women - can continue harming people. Why is the average person so dense? Narcissists are lousy actors.

Malignant narcissists love their perverted sport, and they never want the game to end. It's all they have. Let's face it; their lives are sad, so very sad. Take away the narcissist's only reason for living – to hurt others. Don't be their play thing.

Stay far, far away.

Comments:

Why is it when you tell "normal" people that someone you know or someone that they know is a sociopath/narcissist/bully that they look at you like you are the crazy one......??

These narcs are very skilled at what they do. They happily drive wedges between people and pit family members against one another. Unfortunately when it comes to families, the narcs usually win.

This account that you have written about the traits of a malignant narcissist completely struck a chord with me. My younger sister is exactly what was described. It was so scarily accurate that it frightened me.

Wow! I am blown away by what I have read here. I have a malignant narcissistic twin sister and ex-husband. I have read a great deal about them but hearing personal experiences really validates what I have experienced and felt. Not very many believe me...I end up sounding crazy. I could almost cry.

I've always thought this universe works with some kind of supernatural justice and everyone gets what's coming to them towards the end. I believe ultimately they're exposed and humiliated the way they should. It doesn't give me my childhood back, but I can at least revel in this cosmic revenge of some sort.

I've lived long enough now to see "how the story ends" and yes, they are gonna die the way they lived: Parasitic, pissed off and leaving in their wake a life-long, F-5 Path of Destruction. They destroy their families, friendships, employment opportunities and when/if they had any paid minions, once the $$ is gone, so are the minions.

This post pisses me off. Only because it so has my mother described to a T. Would it be considered breaking no contact if all I did was knock on her door and smack her a couple of times and then leave??

Boundaries don't work with MNs despite what the "Pros"/Experts tell you. No, you're *not* doing them "wrong." No, it doesn't matter how hard you try, what you "use." For example: meticulously crafted letters explaining your feelings, requests to be treated with Dignity and Respect etc. as an autonomous human being. MNs don't give a shit about you any more than they know you. In my experience, Boundaries for Adult Children are viewed as Targets of Opportunity by NFOOS. But go ahead and try 'em anyway: The Retribution and Retaliation Campaign will absolutely confirm your beliefs re: how entirely screwed up these NFOOs truly are and remediate any possibility of lingering guilt or doubt. Ultimately, Boundaries will function to set you free on the Road to NO CONTACT. It'll be damn expensive in every way but will pay off exponentially in *every* way for the rest of your life.

I agree 100% that boundaries mean jack shit to a malignant narcissist or any other NFOO member. They see boundaries as just another part of us that needs to be destroyed. I also agree that it's a total waste of time to set boundaries with NFOO. No contact is the only way to stop the abuse, and sometimes that doesn't even work because as you can attest to, some MNs are stalkers. What I do believe is that boundaries deter other narcs. Narcs test people and if they can't bust in, they go away and find other prey. But I think it's useless to start setting boundaries once a narc has already gotten in. If you let a narc in, they think they own you, so boundaries just don't work for former Ns only future Ns.

NARCISSISM IS ALL ABOUT CONTROL

One thing about malignant narcissism that I cannot stress enough is that it's All – About – Control. Perhaps, I'm stating the obvious when I say narcissism is all about control? I don't care. I'll say it again, this time really loud: NARCISSISM IS ABOUT CONTROL. Every single motivation behind the narcissist's abuse stems from a pathological need to control what others think, feel, say and do. Every loathsome narcissistic trait such as covetousness, entitlement, greed and predation is an off-shoot of the narcissist's delusion of control over the entire world, and everyone, and everything in it.

What does it mean to be in CONTROL all-the-time? It means you hold all the POWER. It means you are SUPERIOR. It means you are a GOD.

Narcissists find their "identity" in POWER. The more power they wield, the stronger their identity as an omnipotent God becomes. As a result, every waking moment of the narcissist's wretched existence is devoted to proving to themselves and to those in their pathological space – their mini universe – that they are Masters of the Universe. This isn't hard to do, because like their minds, the narcissist's world is usually very small.

Narcissists discover their "identity" in POWER and CONTROL. They view themselves as supreme beings in charge of everyone and everything. The narcissist also equates "love" with power and control. In other words, you prove your "love" to a narcissist by relinquishing all your power and allowing them absolute control over you. By allowing the narcissist to control and abuse you – have power over you - you are enabling the narcissist's malignant self-love. You are feeding the narcissist's delusion of grandeur. Narcissistic supply is simply allowing the narcissist to control you.

CONTROL of you = POWER over you = "Love"

CONTROL + POWER = The Narcissist's "Image"

= Narcissists LOVE their IMAGE.

Narcissists do not love you. They love the way you preserve their narcissistic image by permitting them to lord over you.

Here's the thing; narcissists only identify with their image and nothing else. Without control, the narcissist is nothing, they are nobody. Without control, the narcissist has no identity. Their image is shattered. That's why they fight like hell to gain control of everyone and everything around them. Their entire identity is riding on it. The narcissist's so-called "identity" is extremely shaky. It isn't a true identity built on human substance. It's a flimsy illusion built on lies. That's why the narcissist devotes all their energy to a lifelong war of control: they are continually fighting a private battle to maintain their narcissistic "image."

NO CONTACT makes the narcissist feel angry, crazy and out-of-control because when you are not available to abuse, the narcissist is rendered powerless, empty, and without an identity. The more they need your supply - to maintain their narcissistic image – the harder they will fight to control you. Going NC puts you in the power position and effectively starves the narcissist and drives them insane. I think that's why every malignant narcissist I know obtains a "Flying Monkey" of some sort. They always need someone to control and manipulate into carrying-out their evil deeds when their intended target inevitably cuts them off. By sending in their "Monkey" they maintain their illusion of power. However, IF the narcissist were to be abandoned completely, and without a "Flying Monkey" or any "narcissistic supply," they would be swallowed alive by their big black hole of inner emptiness, and would surely go insane.

In fact, I've already seen this happen to some extent with both malignant narcissist mother and MN sister. At this point, it would appear that their only source of narcissistic supply is each other and a fed-up Flying Monkey that's flapping its wings into retirement. They are both starving, and they are both feeding off each other, and resenting the hell out of one another in the process. Two malignant narcissists exploiting one another is akin to a starving person eating their own limbs to stay alive. It doesn't end well. I'm convinced that their steady descent into madness is the result of a deficiency of supply. After all, narcissists are parasites and they desperately need a host to feed on.

The fact is, narcissists would have no power over others if people didn't give it to them. Sadly, others unwittingly give the narcissists power over them to the degree that they lack true self-esteem. These fools mistakenly think that the narcissist will somehow endow them with what "appears" to be a limitless stream of self-esteem. This never happens. Narcissists take whatever others have to offer them to gratify their egos and leave them high and dry.

Narcissist's view others as objects/tools to exploit any way they please in order to maintain their image. Since they lack normal human feelings and are not capable of relating on an emotional level, ALL of the narcissist's interactions take place in the "realm of the mind." If you are in a relationship with a narcissist then it is entirely "mental." Though they are able to "simulate" emotional states, there are no real feelings involved at their end. All of the Narcissist's relationships are based entirely on mind control and manipulation. They are cold, calculating reptiles that continually plot and scheme. Every single interaction with a narcissist is a business transaction of sorts; a sneaky power-grab based on what they can manufacture in you and then use to exploit you. A successful hostile take-over means they can control your mind, emotions AND behaviour. Ka-ching! Their image of a superior being remains securely intact.

Narcissists cannot relate to others because narcissists do not recognize their likeness in others. Narcissists only relate to their "image" as a supreme being. They cannot empathize with human beings because they don't see themselves as human beings. They see themselves as above human beings. Narcissists have no idea what humanity is. They mistake their bruised ego/image for hurt "feelings" and call their anger humanity. PATHETIC!

Despite being completely oblivious to your feelings, the narcissist is acutely aware, on a moment-by-moment basis, of your emotions and thoughts. They are essentially technicians: pressing buttons, pulling levers, flipping switches and turning dials all in an effort to produce the desired "human effect." The desired effect could be something as simple as eliciting confusion, shame, guilt, a nervous laugh, a sideways glance, an expression of hurt or embarrassment, or a show of admiration or sympathy, or a reaction of anger, or falling prey to their lies and destructive *powers of suggestion* that leads to you spreading their misinformation, or making a detrimental life choice. Each and every time the narcissist puppet master succeeds in controlling you – no matter how subtly – you have reinforced their delusion as The Almighty Powerful Oz. Oops - I'm sorry narcs. I meant an omnipotent GOD.

But remember this: It's all smoke and mirror folks. Pull back the dark curtain of the narcissist's psyche and you will find a tiny, frightened, impotent little creature at the controls. Their flimsy false-self is hanging by a thread. Narcissists don't have any real self-esteem. NONE. Don't let them steal yours, they can't use it, and they wouldn't know what to do with it anyway.

For true self-esteem doesn't involve a perverse desire to control the entire universe. Healthy self-esteem is about trust in yourself and being true to yourself and wanting others to trust themselves and be true to themselves; it's about being respectful of your own individuality and the individuality of others. True self-esteem is about being sensitive about others feelings, and considerate of their privacy and needs. True self-esteem is about allowing yourself to find your way in life without handing the controls over to someone else; and it's about allowing others to find their way in life without trying to control them. True self-esteem comes from seeing other people as "other," not as functions of yourself or as objects to be used for your own gratification.

COMMENTS:

Thank you for the "business transaction" insight. That helps to explain what often feels wrong in an apparent kindness of a narcissist.

Best, best, best site ever! Others are good but don't focus so much on how to handle narcissists and what is happening to you as a victim and why. Other sites/books focus on what makes the narcissist tick - who cares right? I cannot even tell you how much you have helped me. I feel alive again! Thank you, thank you, thank you!

The people who stand up to the narcissist and tell the truth become enemy number 1. Excellent blog!

The sense of entitlement and control coming from these demons is absolutely beyond belief. Victims unite!

They dangle us to make sure they always have an inroad in case they need us for something, but they want to make it very clear by their ambivalence/dangling and complete lack of total attachment that we never feel comfortable enough to ask anything from THEM. How dare we?

When they are done getting what they want from you, they move further away from the relationship or all together discard you. Not knowing at the time what I was dealing with, I wasted over half of my life with people like this. It sucks being at the age I'm at now and having to start all over. It's not easy.

I continually have to bite back hard on my anger and when I successfully suppress it, then horrible guilt creeps in because I've gone NC with some people and LC with others, and that's something I never thought I'd have to do with anyone in my life, let alone, practically everyone in my life! I'm also an ACON which has been a continual issue throughout my life. I've had many friends, lovers, coworkers and others whom I can now identify as being on the N spectrum. And yes, it is all about CONTROL.

I like how you describe MNs as trying to elicit the desired response from us like pulling a lever, or turning on a switch of some sort. This is what I find the most telling about their flawed character. There is no consistency from one moment to the next. It's like their memory has been wiped each day, and what they did, thought and believed one day magically changes depending on what their current agenda is.

I always thought I was crazy, but that's what my MN MOM wanted me to believe. I have not had in person contact with her for going on five years. I get the occasional phone call from her trying to pull me back into her drama, her sickness, but I see through it now as just her way of trying to make me feel bad and also trying to make others see me as a monster. It has caused me to have to separate from many family members because they are on her side and try to say that I am the one who is cruel but they don't know what I dealt with my whole life. I have a much better life without my mother in it. I can finally be free and be myself without the constant nag of a mother who needs to have control of me and be the center of attention at all times. I am finally at peace in most of my life.

68

The Malignant Narcissist Mother's Mantra....... YOU Have No Right to Live!

I never once entertained fantasies of having a loving, caring mother. How could I? I didn't have time for fantasies. All of my energy was devoted to survival. In fact, I never thought of malignant narcissist mother as a "mother" at all. I saw her as my mortal enemy: someone who was hell-bent on destroying me, and someone whom I feared. That's exactly the way she wanted it: for me to live in fear of her in an "Off with her head!" kind of way.

There are only a few times, that I can remember, that we did something together as "mother" and daughter. Once I asked her if she would take me to the mall so I could buy a tracksuit with some Christmas money that I had received. Surprisingly, she agreed to take me, but there was a catch: the entire outing was just a set-up to get me alone to inflict abuse and relieve her of frustration. She bitched, and moaned, and screamed at me in the car for being so selfish for asking her to take me shopping. She bitched, and moaned, and complained about the parking. She bitched, and moaned, and complained about how busy the stores were. She bitched, and moaned and complained about EVERYTHING as if it was my fault. On the escalator - while minding my own business – she kicked me. Shocked and hurt; I looked over at her and she seethed, "Don't you dare look at me like that!"

Another time - a couple of years after she had abandoned her family – she came to meet me at my job at a department store. She wanted to buy me a coat for Christmas. She seemed in fairly good spirits, and things were going fine until it came time to buy the coat. Impatiently shifting back and forth from leg to leg, she boiled with frustration over the line-up. Then she looked at me and seethed, "You bloody-well better not be as slow as *that* cashier."

Horrors of all horrors, when I was a teen, she took me to a Mary Kay Party. MN mother took me, and not "The Chosen One" for a simple reason: Image. MN sister was awkward and off-putting and she had all the afflictions: braces, glasses, and acne. I was more socially presentable but I had absolutely no self-esteem. I remember those years being incredibly shy and nervous. My hands would tremble and I was too afraid to utter anything out of fear of sounding stupid.

At the Mary Kay Party, I watched as all the mothers and daughters joked around with one another and had fun. I couldn't wait for the party to end. I was so nervous and uncomfortable.

During the car ride home MN mother screamed at me, "You didn't say one word to me at that party! I am so embarrassed. All those other mothers were having fun with their daughters and you just ignored me!"

MN mother expected me to initiate conversation with her. She expected me to give her attention. This is standard pathology for Ns. Both my N parents were like this. If you didn't direct all your attention at *them* by initiating a conversation, and make the conversation all about *them*, then there was no conversation, period. It would be a cold day in hell before they broke the silence by making a general statement, or, heaven forbid, asking me about myself.

At the Mary Kay Party, I was simply too shy and nervous to speak. And, I didn't defend myself while MN mother screamed at me in the car. On the contrary; I winced in fear. I believed that MN mother had a right to be angry: it was my responsibility to make the Mary Kay Party a fun experience and I had failed. No wonder she never wanted to do anything with me... no wonder she wanted to destroy me.

N Parent's marriage completely deteriorated during my teens, and it was around that time that MN mother really stepped-up her abuse. She alternated between refusing to acknowledge my existence, to screaming vicious threats to "annihilate" me.

Normally, when I came home from school I would walk through the kitchen and say, "Hi" to MN mother. She would turn, look, glare at me and say nothing, and I would go straight to my room and hide-out.

This day was different. I came home from school to find her waiting for me. She was sitting at the table holding a newspaper clipping between her sharp pointy finger nails. As I walked into the kitchen she said, "Here" and shoved the clipping at me. I took it, and read it.

It was a question to Ann Landers. A relative of a teen who had committed suicide had written to her expressing grief and disbelief over the tragic event. Landers' callous reply was, "Some people are NOT meant to live."

A cold chill went down my spine. MN mother hadn't spoken to me directly in months and this was the only thing she felt compelled to communicate to me. She didn't show the clipping to my sister, or brother. It was for my eyes alone. I said, "Oh" and handed the article back to her. She went on to say; "I think that's really true what Ann Landers said. Some people just don't have the strength to survive. Some people just aren't meant to live." I was alarmed. I felt like she had just handed me a gun. I said nothing, and went to my bedroom to hide-out.

Many years after no contact with MN mother, I read "People of The Lie" by M. Scott Peck. In the book, Peck describes an evil couple who gave their son Bobby his brother's suicide weapon – a gun – for Christmas. The evil parents described in the horrifying story reminded me of my own sinister parent. I was flooded with memories of the Ann Landers incident.

Fast forward 25 years from the time I first received the menacing Ann Landers article.

I had not spoken to MN mother or MN sister in 17 years, and made the grave mistake of contacting MN sister. My thinking was; maybe after all these years she's become "normal." Maybe I could have a relationship with my sister. I was in complete denial and I had not yet learned about malignant narcissism. It was the biggest mistake I ever made. My brief contact with her wreaked severe havoc on my life.

First, the deluded MN sister took credit for *my* effort to make contact by saying, "Why did it take "us" so long to get in touch?" Keep in mind; when I went NC all that meant was that I stopped initiating all the phone calls, letter writing, gift sending etc. When I stopped bending over backwards to have a relationship with two people who did not wish me well, the relationship ended. Never once, did they reach out to me.

During our "catching-up" I made the grave mistake of mentioning to MN sister that over the years, I had experienced some depression, nothing major, but some times of distress. A few days later, MN sister sent me an email of that exact same Ann Landers article that read, "Some people are NOT meant to live." I shuddered in horror.

Of course, MN sister had relayed everything that I had confided in her back to MN mother. So, 25 years after first handing me that sinister clipping and after 17 years without speaking to me, the MN mother chose to communicate to me - via flying monkey delivery – that exact same ominous message.

Malignant narcissist mother clung to that heartless Ann Landers comment for 25 years. And, probably still is clinging to it. It's the only piece of writing she ever found to justify her own evil. It's also the only way she could communicate to me, without actually saying that she wished I would kill myself.

Thanks to Ann Landers, I had proof positive - in black and white, no less - that malignant narcissist mother and malignant narcissist sister would forever remain my mortal enemies.

Comments:

I'm just glad you are NC with these people. There is a saying "you're dead to me."

How horrific. What a horrible story, Lisette. I am so very, very sorry.

That's really astonishingly evil, recommending suicide.

Coming from a past with an N mother and sister I can relate to your situation. I'm sorry for what you had to go through, but know you were not alone. I too believe in no contact.

Seriously. I want to hug you and strangle your mother and sister. That is all.

I've never had a favorite blog before, but right now I can't think of one more useful or truthful than yours!

To Confront, or Not Confront Your Narcissist Parent?

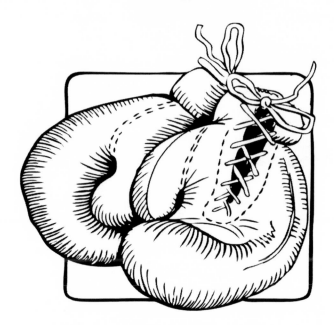

A man in his early fifties *finally* got up the courage to confront his narcissist father. Ed was in therapy at the time, working through some 'issues.' He was beginning to heal and restore some of his self-esteem that had been demolished by his abusive dad. At the urging of his therapist, and as a way to bring about some closure, Ed decided to make a long trip across country to go see his father and speak to him about how his abuse had negatively impacted his life. He decided he wouldn't notify him of the visit, he would just show-up.

Ed booked a flight, arranged a car rental, and reserved a room at a hotel. He was feeling really positive about the plan and figured it was only a matter of time before he would be liberated from his traumatic past. On the plane, he leaned back comfortably in his seat, closed his eyes and envisioned touching moments of him and his dad bonding.

When the plane touched down at the airport, Ed started to feel a little nervous. That's normal, he thought. After all, he hadn't seen his father in years and the only communication he had with the old guy was what *he* instigated. Besides, he was about to embark on a face-to-face mission that he had once deemed impossible.

In the hotel room, Ed started to feel a little edgy so he fixed a drink and busied himself with some work he had brought with him. But he couldn't concentrate. Thoughts of what he would say to his father kept racing through his mind. Eventually, Ed calmed down. He had a relaxing shower and went to bed early. He wanted to be well rested and on the ball for the big day.

The next morning, Ed felt ready to take on the world. He was about to make a very positive step forward in his healing process, and wondered why he had psyched himself out the night before. Eager to get the show on the road, Ed telephoned his dad and arranged a lunch time meeting at his house.

When Ed's father answered the door he seemed *fairly* happy to see him but not overjoyed - then again, he wasn't the 'joyful' type. The two men had a beer, barbecued some steaks and ate lunch in the backyard. They made polite small talk and caught up on each other's lives. Everything was very cordial.

When the meal was over and there was a lull in the conversation, Ed decided to take the opportunity to tell his dad the reason for his visit. He took a deep breath and ran through his mind everything the therapist had told him about not being "confrontational", and speaking in a non-defensive tone, and using "I feel" instead of the accusatory "You did this. You did that." Ed had all the pop-psychology moves down. He was ready.

With heartfelt sincerity, Ed carefully explained to his father his feelings of loss, and the pain and sadness of his childhood, and the far reaching effects it had on his adult life. His father listened; never once interrupting. When Ed had finally said what he needed to say, he breathed a sigh of relief, leaned back in his chair and waited for his father's response; hopeful that his confession would bring them closer together.

Ed's father sat silently for a moment, and took a good long look at his son. Then he got up from his chair, glared at Ed and sniped, "So what?!" And walked back into the house.

Comments:

I guess sometimes you gotta test your hope against the facts in order to really deal with the reality of a narcissist parent.

I would never expect closure with a narcissist. Heck, I would never expect a conversation with one. The confrontation I had was about shifting positions of power and authority. That's all they understand.

At my dad's funeral I am going to say "he was a good man, and when good men do nothing evil thrives" then walk out on my MN brothers and family.

Well, I confronted my NPD mother, and I felt good about it. I did it for me, and it gave me a sense of closure. As long as you have no expectations, and you want to do it, go for it.

My beloved grandmother (who lived to be nearly 101 years of age, who was nothing whatsoever like her daughter (my N mother), and who was the one who convinced me to permanently walk away from my parents) told me a wonderful mantra: When you go, stay gone. No contact means no contact. Not for money, material goods, illness or death. These people simply are what they are, will never change, and will never be the kind of parents/family members/friends you need or deserve.

Shameless Narcissist Parent(s)

In the last post, I described the story of Ed who went on a long and arduous journey to confront his narcissist father. I must admit, when I first heard Ed's story, I burst out laughing and just shook my head in recognition. You see, about six months prior, I too had embarked on a journey of "great expectations" to confront *my* father who turned his back on me while I poured-out my heart and only faced me to groan, "Move on." Then he walked out of the room. He was so annoyed that I even had the *nerve* to bring up the past that he kicked me out of his home and I spent Christmas holidays in a hotel.

Like Ed's father, my father fired-off a two word missive; not even a full sentence. What's even more galling than getting rid of me because I committed the sin of thinking and feeling and questioning his delusions of perfection, is the book of quotations I found in his guest bathroom with a bookmarked quote by Oscar Wilde:

"Children begin by loving their parents; after a time they judge them; rarely if ever do they forgive them."

How's that for total hypocrisy!? Are you laughing? It's times like this that we really have to laugh and see the black comedy in the tragedy of life as an Adult Child of Narcissists (ACON). They sure as hell provide us with an excess of material to write about.

Though, we can sometimes see the dark humour in the narcissist's astonishingly deluded mind, it doesn't do much to relieve the intense frustration in dealing with them. I left the story of Ed open-ended in order to illustrate the fact that there is no reconciling with a narcissist, only resignation. We resign ourselves to the cold, hard reality that we will *never* obtain *the freedom* that comes with forgiveness because a narcissist will never repent. Their ego won't allow them to admit defeat. And despite all evidence to the contrary, they live their lives convinced they are above reproach.

We are never able to forgive the narcissist because the narcissist won't allow it. Forgive what? They didn't do anything wrong. They are not sorry about anything. Those are the rules of engagement: The narcissist is shameless so you must be spineless. Put up and shut up. Narcissistic abuse is a *crime in progress* that we never find *relief* from because the hypocrisy is never ending. If you have *any* kind of a relationship with a narcissist then you are being abused - period. Simply put: they get to act like assholes and we get to tolerate them.

Moreover, the shameless narcissist characterizes your deep need to forgive as "being stuck in the past" and makes *you* the guilty party by responding to your grievance with the accusations that *you* are guilty of "not moving on" and are committing the offense of not forgetting. You are also guilty of having a backbone and daring to defy God Almighty's omnipotence. I swear; the hypocrisy of it all is the most traumatic aspect of narcissistic abuse. It's so infuriating; it's enough to make you want to pull your hair out and run screaming into the night.

I'm convinced that narcissists act the way they do so we *will* start screaming and flailing about like a crazy person. That way, they can turn around and point the finger at *our* behaviour thereby projecting their sickness onto us. I remember when my dad told me to "move on" I did everything in my power to remain calm. I was in a frozen state of disbelief so it wasn't that difficult. The narcissist's warped behaviour can often leave us stunned. Did that just happen? Did he just say that? Afterwards, you have to shake-off all the weirdness.

There's another reason narcissists act the way they do. They know they can't possibly win any reasonable discussion, and a narcissist must always win. As diminished as their mental capacity appears to be, they know damn well they haven't got a leg to stand on factually. Sense, decency and reason are all on your side. So, the only way the narcissist can win is by ignoring you and or intimidation: a withering glare, a nasty snipe, criticism, righteous indignation, the evil side-eye, walking out of the room, running the vacuum, cranking some tunes, singing, whistling, and laughing at the TV - this type of childish behavior is just the narcissist's method to shut you the hell-up and drown you out.

What's worse are those whiny, snivelling narcissists who play the martyr card and moan, "What about *me*?!" "What about how *I* feel?!" ME ME ME ME. One thing for certain when dealing with a narcissist is that they will *always* redirect the conversation back to their favourite topic. Another thing you can count on is this: if you were to pull one, one millionth of the stunts on them that they have pulled on you, they would have had you "offed" long ago. For despite the fact that narcissists are missing the 'sensitivity chip' with regards to others, they have very tender feelings for *themselves*.

It's unfortunate that some of the people we have most longed to forgive are the ones that make it humanely impossible. Elderly narcissists have passed the point of no return long ago. So we write them off and move on with our lives. And, perhaps over time, our journey leads us to the point of indifference. That's the best destination we could ever reach, for the pitiful narcissists are unworthy of our hate.

Comments:

My narcissistic father is 90 years old now and will never change except he is more vulnerable now. Be good to yourself and lose all hate and resentment and try to feel sorry for them. It's no fun to be a narcissist and you miss out on so much. You never realize what you have... isn't that tragic? If you can actually feel sorry for them, you feel better and bitterness eventually goes. That's a state to wish for!

I find it interesting that Righteous Anger should be subsumed to "feeling sorry for" a Malignant Narcissist Parent(s). Additionally, those who grew up under MN abuse and respond with honesty and integrity regarding their feelings are then slapped with the labels "hate," "resentment," and "bitter." It is your choice as an adult to continue to collude in the parental "fantasy" of omnipotence (and potential for a genuine relationship) with a MN who is now "vulnerable" secondary to the normal process of aging. However, it is quite imperious to suggest "feeling sorry" for an a MN parent/Perpetrator who has sadistically abused their offspring throughout their lives is de facto suggesting the Sin of Sodom continue as well as the MN dynamics which result in inevitable continuing exploitation by the recipient of MN abuse. Further, through feeling pity for the Perpetrator the normal feelings of the Adult Child will magically morph into some "whatever" is delusional in that it is not reality based. What IS "tragic" is blaming the victim for their feelings subsequent to years of abuse and portraying such in the most negative possible fashion. Please read the entire Blog. Your comment indicates you have failed to grasp some of the most basic realities regarding MNs and MN Parents throughout the aging process: Unlike wine, they do NOT improve with age nor do they become less treacherous.

How is it that all the Ns know how to act all the same without having read or studied anything? How can that be, when it's taking a lifetime of learning for the abused by reading and studying everything we can on the subject and even then, I read something new and have another major revelation giving insight into the N's despicable behavior? Does anyone know?

Satan gives these fuckers all the same playbook at birth.

Narcs are what they are because they reject all interactive mutuality grounded in good will: mutual respect, mutual rights, mutual concern, mutual regard and especially the mutual obligations which exist in healthy human relationships. It's not what they have "learned". It's what they refuse to do, because ordinary human obligations are beneath their grandiose dignity.

They've learned what "works" and what "works" are the same tactics of a temper-tantrum throwing 2/3 yr. old with all the tenacity that little ones at that age/Stage of Development use to wear down or otherwise shut down anyone that opposes their agenda. Unfortunately, unlike little ones they never grow out of using these types of ploys to steam-roll the opposition, so to speak. They become very adept at picking up on verbal/non-verbal cues from others. It's not that they don't see; they just DON'T AGREE.

Since reading this blog, behavior that baffled me before now makes much more sense and I'm finally disembarking from the anger/guilt teeter-totter I've been on. All I want is to have my peace of mind.

Narcissistic Abuse and Isolation

Something that I have always heard from the narcissists in my life – the so-called Nfriend – is, "You're such a *strong* person." This platitude is met with a secret eye-roll. Of course I'm strong. I have no other choice but to be strong. When you are surrounded by narcissists there is absolutely no support. This is also a get out of jail free card for the narcissist. They can delude themselves into thinking they are a good friend by offering nothing and taking everything because "You're so strong." It's an excuse that the narcissist uses to justify withholding support of any kind because the sad fact is, they have none to give. Narcissists are anti-supportive. They are users. They are abusers. And they are always looking for ways to rationalize their cold-blooded reptilian existence.

It is impossible to have a reciprocal relationship with a non-human that lacks empathy and thinks only of themselves. Anyone who has survived a family of narcissists and a world of the same with their sanity intact is "strong" by virtue of the fact they survived a life being exploited, neglected and abused.

Being "strong" and surviving a lifetime of narcissistic abuse is fucking exhausting and it's what sends me into isolation. Sometimes I say to myself, "I hate people." But the truth is I hate the people I've known –

narcissists. Yes, I hate narcissists. I'm not going to mince words here. I loathe each and every one of them. My "lack of empathy" toward them is a learned response that I have gleaned from a lifetime of enduring their pathology. I don't give a flying fig about any of them and I hope they know it. They taught me how NOT to care about them.

In brief, here's what a relationship with a narcissist looks like for a non.

Being rejected and denied value as a person

Being degraded and having your self-worth and dignity as a person diminished

Being exploited and used for the narcissist's profit or advantage

Being terrorized by intimidation, control, coercion, and stalking

Being denied care, affection, and attention of any kind

Being dismissed, humiliated, manipulated, and belittled

Being violated by pathological envy, greed, and entitlement

Being plundered, pillaged and systematically destroyed

Narcissistic abuse tears at a person's self-worth and manifests in social withdrawal, anxiety, fearfulness, depression, self-blame and self-destructive behaviour. It results in feelings of guilt, shame, inadequacy and powerlessness. Is it any wonder that my coping mechanism of choice has been to hide from a world of narcissists?

An unsupportive world of narcissists is all I've known. And that hard reality is by far the most difficult thing to come to terms with about my narcissistic upbringing. I despise them for brainwashing me and training me into accepting the same abuse from their kind. This has done great damage to my life. If the narcissists from my "family" were the only ones I've known, I would not be writing about this dangerous species. It is a *lifetime* of enduring the cruelty of narcissists that has brought me here. And it has not been easy.

If I added-up the months that I've isolated from a world of N ghouls it would amount to years. I've lost *years* hiding from the abuse of narcissists. By isolating, I was essentially protecting myself from harm. And each and every time I gathered my resources, picked myself up and stepped back out into the N world, I have been knocked back down; each time harder than the last. I think the more one gets pounded down by narcissists, the more vulnerable one becomes and this attracts an even more vicious type of predator. Malignant narcissists are odious creatures that can instinctively sense victims who have been primed by their own kind.

One does not get "stronger" by experiencing a world of unrelenting abuse. It's a brutal cycle that causes unbearable shame and forces the victim to withdraw. The victims of narcissists - those so-called "strong people" - end up hating themselves for being reduced to a hostage of their pain and suffering while being *forced* to put up a brave front. And the vile narcissist is able to walk away as if nothing has happened, and as far as they are concerned, nothing has. Like sharks, narcissists injure and kill cold-bloodedly and keep on moving. It is always others that suffer, NOT the narcissist.

Why do we isolate under duress? What else can we do? We are normal people who have been placed in a pervert's warped world. We are normal people acting on normal human principles and having those principles play right into the narcissist's perverted premises. We are right side up, the narcissist is upside down. Being in a family of narcissists, having relationships with narcissists, and being surrounded by narcissists doesn't feel normal because it isn't normal to take abuse. It prompts us to fight or flee.

I've fought back and believe me I have been condemned for it. Why does this always happen to you?! What did you do to them?! You're so confrontational! You're so angry. Don't be so difficult! You seem fine to me. It's over, move-on! You're strong... take the high road! Don't give them the satisfaction. Say nothing! Just take-it and act like it didn't happen!

The merciless suppression by the rest of the world over the victim's efforts at self-defence is what really breaks us. Who is strong enough to withstand the abuse of the narcissists AND the jumping on our backs of everyone else who doesn't want to hear about it because it makes *them* uncomfortable. So uncomfortable in fact, that they must minimize the reality of our experience and assign the cause of the abuse to the victim by way of blame and pathology. They jump on us for fighting back; they jump on us for causing it; they jump on us for complaining; and they jump on us for being depressed. So the callous bystanders pile on and do to us what the narcissist couldn't achieve: they break our back and crush what's left of our most precious possession, our self-concept as a solid person. And this is how we become exactly what everyone wants to label us because no one has a strong enough backbone to withstand all that abuse. We become demoralized and retreat into a state of withdrawal and isolation.

Those targeted by narcissists long to be HEARD, but they are universally abandoned when they go in search for help, support, care and understanding. No one will ever get "it" unless "it" happens to them. That's why isolation - "fleeing" – is the safest way to recover from narcissistic abuse. It helps you avoid more abuse from a world of heartless bystanders who get irritated by your sad face and punish you for fighting back.

Those that have experienced it need no explanation.

Those that have not experienced it, there is no explanation.

Any way you slice it, enduring narcissistic abuse is an isolating experience.

Comments:

I was exclaiming "YES!" and "AAARGH!" as I was reading this post, and I'm actually not sure if it was out loud or inwardly.

If anyone else in our lives treated us with the tenth of evil that our "parents" did, we would not only be listened to, we would be encouraged to sue!

This post is exactly how I am feeling now. I recently went no contact with the evil that is my parents and brother. The worst part is that everyone wants me to just move on. If they were that bad it should be easy right?

I bawled hard reading this blog! It is the first time in my life that I have ever read the TRUTH in identifying ME in the torment and suffering I have literally endured with a very large malignant narcissistic FAMILY!

Your blog has been priceless in understanding my life which up until a few months ago I described as nothing short of a disaster. So many empowering changes have happened.

I think that when we isolate, THEY win. That's why it's important to keep pushing ourselves to be the people we would have been if not for them.

I have also gotten the "You're so strong" BS. Well guess what? I had no choice but to be strong. If I had a dollar for every time I heard this one! Seriously, for me it came down to be strong or die, so there was no choice over here. I suspect the same for the rest of our fellow ACONS.

I think isolating actually helped me. I was alone with my thoughts and could process my experiences without N interference or influence. That's how I started to get rid of them faster, and faster.

To the commenter who wrote: "A therapist once said to me, "You better watch it, people are going to take advantage of your good nature." I thought, huh?! Good nature?! Me?" You are not alone here – I had the exact same reaction. Good nature? Me? No way! It was drilled into our heads from such a young age that we were worthless, hypersensitive, mean, selfish etc. that hearing that is a shock to the system. Talk about mind control. It took me many years to de-program and accept the fact that I am a good person who is worthy of nothing less than love and respect. Though I'm still pissed that I was brainwashed for the better part of my life.

Never Let A Narcissist Into Your Head

The survivors of narcissistic abuse are not just *strong* people. They are *strong-minded* people.

I truly believe those who succumb to self-destructive acts or suicide have had a malignant narcissist burrow way too deep into their head, and this has led to their demise. I am not blaming the victim in any way. I'm just conveying the severity of the narcissist's mental torture. The narcissist is on a psychological killing spree designed to murder life: to leave their victim hollow and under their deadly control. What they do to us psychologically is equivalent to someone repeatedly smashing us over the head with a baseball bat. Not everyone survives this type of violence.

Our mind is our most sacred possession. And it's much too valuable to hand over to someone who wants to trash it – a narcissist. The gates to our mental garden should never be left open to anyone. My gate was kicked open at a young age, and the narcissists eagerly invaded and trampled my garden. It took years of undoing their destruction to rebuild it and nurture it back to health. I'm still tending to my mental garden and always will be. The narcissist's taught me a valuable lesson: don't let *anyone* into your head.

Our innermost boundary of privacy is our mind. We live there and it's our private property. KEEP OUT! Whoever wants in, wants to make a mess of it. So BEWARE.

You have the right to control what passes in and out of your mind. You own it. Your mind is yours alone so take damn good care of it. It's up to you to keep an orderly mind because you are the one who incurs the consequences of what lives there. You have a right to privacy. You have a right to think and believe what YOU want.

The narcissist is always trying to weasel their way into your head because once they've snuck-in they can control you. They gaslight routinely. They plant destructive messages and evil seeds of doubt. They belittle, criticize, embarrass and flatter. A confused, off-balance and insecure victim is easier to manipulate.

Do not let the narcissist snack on you mentally. If you give them a taste, they will devour you whole. Malignant narcissists are mental predators who carefully study their prey. They are always watching and listening to you. They badger, bait and trap you. Don't let out information they can use to exploit you. Don't let in information they can use to control and manipulate you. Hone that mental filter because the narcissist NEVER means well. And you can count on this: once you let them into your head, they will never leave. They're like mental tapeworms.

All malignant narcissists are inveterate snoops, busybodies, gossips and liars. They are constantly on a fact-finding expedition to pry information out of you. The information is *always* used to manipulate you; embarrass you; frame-you; damage your reputation; control you; blackmail you and come between you and the people and things you love. Zip those lips up tight. Play your mental cards very close to your vest and protect your borders.

The narcissist isn't about to give away all *their* personal information. On the contrary, the narcissist is guarded and their boundaries are very strong. The narcissist understands damn well that information in the wrong hands is a dangerous thing. But they feel *entitled* to know everything about you because they are *greedy*. Don't ever let them guilt-trip you into giving-up something they never would.

Malignant narcissists are pathological gossips. The essence of gossip is to dirty-up people. The narcissist wants to dirty-up *everyone*. Making others look bad makes them look good. They also make themselves look good by placing themselves ABOVE others as their JUDGE, and dumping their toxic projections onto others. Never believe anything that comes out of the narcissist's mouth. Their only form of communication is judgment, criticism, gossip, lies, slander, projection, manipulation and control. Never trust them with one iota of information on you (Read: VERY VERY SNEAKY). NEVER drop your guard at the N's *transparent* attempts at magnanimity. It's all a ploy to draw you closer so you'll be easier to attack and easier to pin as the fall guy for their scum of the earth dirty work.

Healthy, safe people are always direct in their interactions with you. Narcissists are NEVER direct. EVER. Controlling someone mentally means sneaking in and out of their headspace without getting caught. Malignant narcissists are slippery creatures. They slither into your mind hoping to dig-up dirt, and then slither out of your mind intending to spread the dirt. I would describe malignant narcissists as "slimy" mental perverts and voyeurs.

I've conjured up a couple of scenarios to illustrate my point.

Here's an example: maybe something hurtful and humiliating has happened to you. Maybe you found out your boyfriend is cheating on you. You would never tell the narcissist about this, but through the narcissist's predatory parasitic ways, she has gleaned this information on you, and you KNOW IT. The resulting conversation with the narcissist might sound something like this. The narcissist will say, "It's so sad when someone is cheated on and they don't even know it. God, can you imagine how embarrassing that would be?" I feel so sorry for people who are betrayed. What would you do, if it happened to you?" And the narcissist snake slithers in and out and around your headspace. The narcissist gaslights, humiliates and pokes at you in an effort to break you down so that you will confide in her. She salivates at the thought of obtaining more information to use against you.

Here's another example: you have bought a brand new car and you just love it. You don't tell the narcissist about this because *any* information the narcissist has on you just invites the narcissist inquisition. They need to know EVERYTHING. How can you afford that new car? Did you get a raise? Why did you buy *that* car? What deranged, abusive meaning can the narcissist ascribe to you purchasing a new car? Knowledge is power for the devious malignant narcissist.

Again, through their treachery, the narcissist has discovered that you bought a brand new car. They know the exact model. Instead of saying – like a normal person – "Hey, I heard you just bought a new SAAB." The narcissist will say, "You know I'm thinking about buying a new car. What do you think of the new SAABS? I don't think I could afford one. What do you think the down payment and lease would be?"

Do you see how slippery and slimy and deceitful narcissists are? They are the antithesis of up-front and honest. The narcissist is forever hiding. They are nefarious frauds, twirling their thin moustache, and peeking out behind their swirling black cape of lies. Exploiting people in this way reveals the contempt in which narcissists hold others. There is absolutely no reason for the narcissist to be shady and secretive, except to give themselves a narcissistic boost. They enjoy toying with people even if nothing significant depends on it because it makes them feel powerful. They lie and trick to amuse themselves. Successful head-games prove their superiority and the stupidity of others. It's the way the narcissist operates in the world. It's how they *think* they obtain power.

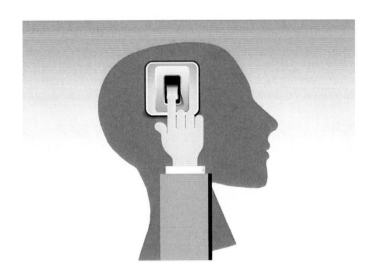

So you call the narcissist's bluff on the SAAB bull-shit. Remember, you know that she knows you bought a new car. You say to her, "Why do you keep talking about SAABS? Why the sudden interest in SAABS?" The narcissist explodes in a narcissistic rage. "Why the hell can't I talk about cars?! What's it to you?! What's your problem?! It takes two to have a conversation!"

"It takes two to have a conversation." Gag. This is a common line the narcissist uses when they're playing head games during a "conversation" and you make notice of their deception. Yeah right. A "conversation" is nothing but a game for them. In fact, every interaction with a narcissist is nothing but a game. And it takes two to play the game: a narcissist and an unsuspecting victim, an object – their chess piece. And we are the ones with a *problem* when we call them on their duplicity.

When I was younger, after hanging out with an Nfriend(s), I would sometimes wake-up a few days after the encounter pissed-off. Usually the N deposited a toxic message into my head, but the assault was engineered so subtly that it just escaped me at the time. It would usually take a few days, after the fact, to decode their destructive message because they always employed sneaky methods to confuse and disarm me at the time of assault. And, if and when I called them on it, in true N fashion they would deny, dismiss and evade, or say the standard, "You're too sensitive."

If you listen real carefully to what the narcissist says, you will find that their thinking patterns are entirely circular. They go round, and round trying to spin your brain into a state of confusion. They hope to make you so dizzy and disoriented that you will give into their demands, whatever they may be.

Narcissists drop shit in your head, they stir up trouble and they take the valuable stuff out. The harder it is for them to get in, move stuff around, and move stuff out, the better. Pay very close attention to your mental and emotional state when you are interacting with a narcissist. Your anger, irritation, confusion, or frustration is like a burglar alarm going-off and it should never be ignored. It alerts you to the fact that you have an intruder present. The narcissist needs to know at the point of entry that they have been discovered so they will stop doing their dirty work.

I remember having one of these annoying, anti-logical, circular conversations with MN sister. I politely tried over and over again to get off the phone with her. She was attempting, in a covert way, to break me down so I would offer to run an errand for her majesty. She was unrelenting in her efforts to get her way and I knew exactly what she was up to. I was not going to give-in to her scheme. She was incensed that she was unable to manipulate me and said, "You know. You sound irritated. Maybe you should take something for your moods. You might have a mood disorder." Ha! It would never occur to the narcissist that she is irritating. No. Never. She believes she is perfect. And once again, our natural reaction to the narcissist's skeezy personality means that *we* have a problem. It's the projection/gaslighting portion of their mental terrorism.

As an ACON (Adult Child of Narcissists) I'm done with intruders violating my headspace. It took me decades to exorcise the destructive messages that the narcissists dumped into my mind. I think that's why I am so adamantly opposed to analytic therapy for victims of narcissistic abuse. I came across two malignant narcissists in my search for answers and they *tried* to trash my mind. Just like all the other narcissists, they were warped weirdos, gaslighters and projection machines who were terrified of creative thinkers. What the hell gives *them* the right to enter my headspace?! The "Dr." before their names?! Fuck that! A predator is a predator. A con job is a con job. The so-called mental health profession is a PROFIT making enterprise and don't ever forget it. The bad ones are no better than the shady auto-mechanic who you take your car to, to fix a certain problem. The mechanic lifts the hood and tinkers around and creates another problem. You drive off with the original problem fixed, and then you have to bring the car back in to get the problem that *they* caused fixed. And it happens again and again. The shady auto-mechanic earns a living causing endless problems in your car.

The mental health industry is a business that thrives on vulnerable people, and it's filled with mental manipulators and mental rapists - narcissists. You have the right NOT to answer questions. You have the right to say, "That's private." You have the right to ask, "What gives *you* the right to ask me that?" The thing that I find so suspicious and dangerous about therapy is that this complete stranger has all this information on you, and you know nothing about them. It's not unlike what the narcissist does to you. Talk about an imbalance of power. It is only upstanding, healthy, safe people who will not abuse that power and they are more difficult to find than a trustworthy auto mechanic.

The best advice I ever got was at the age of 21 from a psychic of all people. He read my tarot cards and looked-up and me and said, "Stay away from your family. They're not lucky for you. They're crazy just not confined. Your mother is PSYCHO. She wants to get inside your head. She's very destructive. A brown haired girl, your sister, is extremely jealous of you."

How's that for cutting to the chase? How's that for practical advice? Sure beats the mounds of crap I let into my head from lousy books, support groups, therapist, and doctors. It wasn't until I discovered malignant narcissism that I had the "why" fully figured out.

I'm done with "psychologizing" myself. When you are suffering from the narcissist's mental abuse you *constantly* live in your head. You pick yourself apart. You question yourself. You try to figure out what's wrong with *me*? What did *I* do to make this happen to me? Fuck that! Why the hell did that car careen into that innocent pedestrian? The innocent pedestrian was just minding their business and crossing the street. The narcissist is no different than an out of control, fast moving SUV that is ready to run-over whoever doesn't get out of its way.

And what's with these people who spend years, if not decades, in therapy? Who are they? Woody Allen? They say, "My therapist thinks blah blah blah…" What the hell do *you* think?! Have you merely replaced the dependency of your controlling narcissist parent with a dependency on a controlling therapist who is buying a beach house with your payments?!

Anyone who wants you to repeat what they say back like a parrot is not to be trusted. They have ulterior motives. They are no better than the devious narcissist. Isn't the idea of therapy to go in for a mental tune-up or get help with a life issue and get the hell out? You are supposed to learn practical *tools* that you can apply to your thinking and behaviour and move on – hopefully – toward a healthier life.

If you let anyone into your mental sanctuary you are allowing that person to judge you, and manipulate you and decide what you think and believe. If you let a narcissist know what makes you tick, you are inviting abuse: you are giving them the right to control your mind. Pushed to its limits, you are giving the narcissist absolute power over you. Possession of you. Psychological murder is only one step away from physical murder.

Narcissists operate in the realm of the mind. They don't give a rat's ass about you. They are only interested in information they can use to manipulate, control, abuse, and exploit you. The narcissist's point of entry is your headspace. Block it. Barricade it. Fortify your boundaries. Figure out who you are and what you stand for. A strong mind means that YOU are in control of YOU. And it should give you great comfort to know that the narcissist hates impenetrable minds and are intimidated by them. No supply is given and none is taken. The starving narcissist moves on to feed somewhere else.

We are born a single consciousness and we should live and die a single consciousness.

But don't take my word for it. Only you have the right to decide what you think and believe.

Comments👣

I have changed a lot without therapy, and I am grateful for that and for your continuing posts, which are incredibly validating to me.

Love your blog!! I'm an Acon and what you say is right on. Ns mess with your head. I know when I'm around one because there is just a lot of confusion, stress and anxiety. I stay far away from them but sometimes they come to you. They are all over the place.

This is an important post, and thank you for having the courage to write it for the world to see.

Outstanding! I am an ACON, finally out of the pupae and looking around with blinking eyes in the sun and these are my feelings also. I have never felt I could trust a therapist, the imbalance of power has put me off even if I could afford it.

The ACON brain has been formatted to dovetail with their sickness and it takes an incredible amount of abuse for us to be fully aware of the toxicity they heap on us. The threshold is so high. It is all we know. Even after going no contact we struggle with guilt and feelings of obligation just about forever.

Wow, BRILLIANT!!! I just figured out in the last week or so that my Mom was a MN, but it was insane b/c throughout my whole life she painted my DAD as the MN, when she was the CRAZY one!! Makes me so mad that she distorted my head like that for almost all of my life.

Dealing with an N is a think on your feet challenge. That's why so many of us go no contact. When every encounter with your parent is a prolonged verbal chess match, it's just not worth it any more.

I wish that I could say that I am the only person in the world who has been affected/neglected/ abused by an N. These stories are brutal - it helps to know that I am not alone. I am so sorry for everyone here who has had to live in the Narc 'hell' created by these types of people.

This article about how to never let the narcissist into your head has made me feel safe for the first time in my life. I slept like a baby last night, knowing I can control the narcissists in my family. Now I know some methods to deploy that will keep me safe. Thank you for explaining the steps specifically.

Kudos on this entry! You did a great job explaining the subtlety of how they gather and use information against their target. And I love the name of the blog, perfect for what it's like to deal with people with NPD!

Good article. Yes my MN mother gaslighted and denied everything, she would deny even something she said 10 minutes earlier. I believe NC saved my life. My "mother" was literally making me sick. I couldn't sit there taking that devaluement anymore.

Both of my parents are Narcissists, as are some of my siblings. Like all of you, the horrors I have lived through can't even be described to a person who does not understand NPD. As someone else said, most therapists are not able to recognize NPD.

Abuse aside, who am I? Sadly, the answers have not come to me yet. I won't find out by going to a therapist, I can almost guarantee you of that. When I heard, "But she did the best she could do" from my very own therapist, followed by, "I wonder what horrible things she had to endure to make her this way" after I hit the roof and responded to the first comment with, "The fuck she did! The level of abuse that I suffered at the hands of this monster could hardly be considered anyone's best!!" I was done. Hopefully the answers will come in time.

Malignant Narcissists Get Worse With Age

Everything that characterizes NPD makes the narcissist impervious to change. So if you're holding out hope that a narcissist will one day see the error of his or her ways and make adjustments – Fogetta bout it!

And from what I've observed, they don't mellow with age. The malignant narcissist does not become a kinder, gentler, wiser version of its sinister self. Au contraire. The MN is always pushing the boundaries of bad behaviour and they only become more cruel, vicious and treacherous with time and opportunity. A lifetime of getting away with evil deeds makes them nastier and crazier. I would say that malignant narcissism is a progressive disorder in that the narcissist becomes more disturbed with each passing year.

Think Tony Soprano's (of the TV series *The Sopranos*) ruthless malignant narcissist mother Livia, who while lying in a hospital bed after suffering a stroke, continues to plot to have her son murdered. Tony learns of his mother's scheme and goes to the hospital planning to suffocate her with a pillow. But when he sees how helpless she is, he decides to mock her instead and says, "I'm gonna have a nice, long, happy life, which is more than I can say for you." Of course, in true malignant narcissist mother fashion, Livia is able to squeeze out the old evil side eye smirk. The "look" sends Tony into a rage and he has to be restrained by hospital staff.

I will never go anywhere near my malignant narcissist mother ever again. I am convinced that if I was to go to see her on her death bed, she would summon up her last bit of strength just to motion me over to her side, so she could whisper into my ears her last hateful words. And before I could reply by saying, "I hope you're packing sunblock because it's hot where you're going." The bitch would die with that smug, evil smirk plastered across her face. I simply won't give her the satisfaction. The last thing the old witch communicated to me – after 17 years without access to me – was an email that read, "Some people are NOT meant to live." Malignant narcissists are hell-bent on destroying the objects of their irrational malice right up till the bitter end and even beyond the grave.

Let's take a look at why malignant narcissists not only don't change, but become worse. Keep in mind, they have mastered a lifetime of this twisted way of being in the world, and are always pushing their warped behaviour to the limits.

All Malignant Narcissists are a case of arrested development. They live in the mindset of a child. Like a child, they know the difference between right and wrong but *choose* to do wrong when they can get away with it. However, unlike a child, the narcissist cannot be influenced by authority figures. The narcissist believes they are the ultimate authority on everything. They are determined to remain children who always get their way. And like all spoiled brats who control everyone by temper tantrums and bad behaviour they only get worse with the more they get away with.

Narcissists feel entitled. Like bratty children, they expect favourable treatment and excessive amounts of attention and adoration despite their unsavoury behaviour. They feel special and exempt from living as others do. They have no desire to grow-up. They feel entitled to remain a spoiled, foul natured, controlling child.

Narcissists are delusional. They refuse to confront reality. Like a child, they use illusions and distortions to maintain their fantasy about themselves and the world around them. And everyone is expected to play along. If you refuse to play your role in the narcissist's fantasy production then the narcissist child screams, cries, and stomps her feet declaring that something is wrong with you.

Narcissists are control freaks. They think they are in charge of the entire world, including how *you* behave and what *you* think, feel and believe. The narcissist is in charge and that means they are always right, and the whole world is wrong. It's *your* job to adapt to the narcissist's bad behaviour. Failure to comply with the narcissist's world view is considered an attack of their superiority, and *you* are considered difficult and *you* must make the necessary adjustments to appease them.

Narcissists are grandiose. They really believe they are perfect and there is nothing wrong with them. A prime example is my malignant narcissist sister stalking me on narcissist blogs, and reading about all the people who have been harmed by narcissists. Her response was, "Why should *I* have to act a certain way?! Why can't *YOU* just be complaisant?!" The narcissist believes it's *your* job to always please them. And if you don't do *your* job and acquiesce to all their demands then the narcissist feels deflated and they must re-inflate by diminishing, degrading and debasing you.

Narcissists lack empathy. A lack of empathy means they don't know what it *feels* like to be human. They are callously indifferent to people because they do not possess normal human feelings. They simply can't relate and are therefore unable to recognize how they hurt others. Narcissists lack the underlying compassion for others that keeps actions or behaviours more or less in check. So when they find themselves abandoned because they have hurt everyone around them, the narcissist simply denies, dismisses, and minimizes the gravity of their actions. Hurt feelings? What does that mean? No big deal. Narcissists are coldblooded.

The only so-called *feelings* the narcissist understands are their own. For example; the sting of a bruised ego; the frustration that comes with not being in complete control; anger from not getting their way; envy from wanting what others have; jealousy from not getting all the attention; fear of exposure; hatred of all their inferiors; pity for themselves; smug satisfaction.

Narcissists lack a normal conscience. Narcissists do not suffer the burden of a conscience, but they are not blind to social mores or the emotions of others. They know *exactly* what they are doing and they make a *conscious* choice to hurt others. That's why NPD cannot be used as a defence for crimes. Malignant narcissists know the difference between right and wrong but choose to do wrong when they think they can get away with it. They have absolutely no concern for anyone but themselves. As a result, they are dangerous and pose a threat to *everyone's* well-being.

Narcissists are shameless. Without a conscience, the narcissist is unable to process the feelings that make us want to alter our behaviour like shame, guilt, embarrassment, and remorse. They simply excuse, rationalize, blame-shift and project all their problems and bad behaviour onto you. Whatever shame sneaks into the narcissist's wisp of a conscience is simply dumped onto you.

Narcissists are pathological liars: If they're breathing then they're lying. Narcissists don't just tell lies, they *are* lies. They are the people of the lie. They hate reality because reality = the truth. The narcissist wants to avoid the truth about the world and everyone and everything in it. By disregarding the truth about you, themselves, the past, the present etc., the narcissist is able to maintain their delusions of superiority. Do you think a pathological liar is suddenly going to stop lying just because they are getting old? If anything, the narcissist's slander, projection, smear campaigns, character assassinations and false accusations become more vicious and bizarre over time. The load of lies that they have been hauling around, juggling and hurling onto others over a lifetime become so burdensome and complicated that they must go to greater extremes with even more outrageous lies to cover up the last batch of crazy they dished-out. Fair warning; most malignant narcissists end up visibly demented in old age. I say "visibly" demented because often it isn't until then that others cannot ignore what we have always seen.

Narcissists are incapable of introspection. The narcissist maintains their delusions of superiority by constantly dodging reality. They refuse to take a good look at themselves because the feedback would not flatter them, and the narcissist must always *appear* good, even to themselves. They are incapable of looking inward and learning from experience, and instead opt to live in a state of denial. If you think your silence will send a malignant narcissist into deep thought about the relationship and their part in it, think again. The only thing the narcissist will be doing is stewing in hatred for you and pity for themselves.

Do not think for a second that a narcissist will cave to your pleas of compassion and understanding. They will NEVER understand you, and they do not possess an ounce of compassion. A narcissist will NEVER say, "I'm sorry." Or "I was wrong." EVER. It doesn't matter how trivial their mistake or how grave their crimes, they will NEVER cop to it. A narcissist will NEVER admit defeat. They are perversely willful.

The narcissist may shed crocodile tears and pull-off childish drama in order to manipulate you and divert your attention away from their wrong doing in order to get their way, but they will NEVER apologize. Don't buy their act.

Narcissists are an alien sub-species and they don't operate under the norms of human principles. They are incapable of change and you are wasting your precious time if you believe otherwise. The regular narcissist is uncritically self-satisfied and remains set in its ways, and the malignant narcissist becomes more vile and corrupt over time. Either figure out a way to deal with the regular narcissists as they are, or do not deal with them at all. Don't go near malignant narcissists. They are unsafe for human interaction.

Narcissists don't know what it's like to be human. Being human means being able to feel love and suffer the agony of loss. It means finding meaning for our lives. A meaning that connects us with something real beyond ourselves. Narcissists don't look beyond themselves. They simply inflate their egos to find meaning in life.

But we normal people know that part of the human condition is about transcending the ego. We learn the most difficult lessons in life the hard way. We suffer from our mistakes, we acknowledge them, and knowledge becomes our own and we make changes. We experience the process of turning all of our experiences, good and bad, into something more for our growth as a person. The meaning of life has value and it influences every choice we make. It influences how we treat our fellow passenger. It involves faith of some kind. We understand that transcending the ego is difficult and scary because it entails going into unknown territory, feeling, doing, and relating in ways contrary to our past habits, our old attitudes and identity, and overcoming the handicap of our abusive upbringing.

Everything is lost on the malignant narcissist. Life has no meaning to them beyond their own selfish needs. That means *nothing* beyond the narcissist influences the choices they make. The narcissist is incapable of turning their experiences – both good and bad – into something more for their growth as a person. Malignant narcissists NEVER evolve as people. They only become more twisted and convinced of their warped way of being. Delusions, immaturity, lack of empathy, lack of conscience, shamelessness, grandiosity, control freakism and the inability to introspect stunt them and corrupt them. As time passes, they become more deeply entrenched in their pathology.

Life has no value to the malignant narcissist beyond their wretched selves. That means you have no value to the narcissist other than what you can supply to feed them. Don't let them hold you back. Keep on moving forward and leave them stuck behind in the murky depths of hell that they call home.

Comments:

You are absolutely right. They *do* get worse, they get even more rigid and fucking batshit crazy as they age. There will come a point where the mask doesn't just slip--it drops on the floor and shatters. The brain-to-mouth filter is removed and the overtures of pretending to be "normal" or even care disappear.

Nparents are worse and have gotten meaner as they've aged. I really believe that people can only hide their true selves for so long and then the real person finally comes out for everyone to see. But not everyone will see it because denial still exists among the narc appeasers.

Lots of wisdom here, Lisette. I think you hit the important issue, which is that for practical purposes there is little difference between a MN and a sociopath or psychopath. I think for those of us who need confidence that we are not the moral monsters for deserting the "weak" parent, and it's perversely more comforting to know that we're running from a psychopath than a mere turbo-narcissist.

Not only do MNs get worse with age, they remain unrepentant for all the wrongdoing and grief they've ever caused, even on their deathbed.

MNs are hideous in their old age. Aging for them seems to be a time where their life of nasty deeds seems to come back to haunt them. They are decrepit and hideous creatures.

You summed up perfectly what I came here looking for that I feel relieved beyond belief. That this wretched narcissism is so real and that people like you have experienced it to this terrible degree left me reeling. I thought I was losing my mind. Thanks for the insights. Though I remain deflated that I was too slow to figure it all out all these years and waited much too long. My phone is now disconnected to this bitch and I will remain off the hook and free!

They can take mine with them and my NM mother. Hope they choke on their own poison!

Death to a malignant narcissist is the ultimate opportunity to be the center of attention, before a captive audience, and do the most lasting damage before the curtain comes down.

I am realizing my mother is a MN. So much is making sense I'm reeling from it all. I'm ready to be done with her CONTINUAL abuse to me even now. Screw it! I'm done! My shock and depression at what I'm learning is made better when I KNOW now, that I'm not ALONE!!! Thank you all! And thank you blogger!!!

I plan on doing the ultimate, and simply and completely, ignoring my N parent for the rest of her life and most certainly her death. I'm an only child, a grandmother myself-and over time the blindfold slipped from my eyes-I see who I really am, and I see her for what she is. I have decided that any family member that seeks to give her information about me-or give me input on my choice about absolutely not acknowledging her existence or demise-will likewise be on the no contact list. I am filled with contempt for the thing that tried to destroy me from the moment of my birth.

My God I am so disgusted by what I have learned. I feel like torturing my MN mother with harassing phone calls, and take her down till the old bitch dies. Slowly.

NARCISSISTS ARE PARANOID

Some say narcissists are paranoid because of their delusions of grandeur: they see themselves as so dang important, and powerful that they feel their inferiors (the rest of the human race) are out to persecute them just for being so awesome. I don't buy that theory. In fact, the most grandiose narcissist I know – my father - is not paranoid. He's delusional alright, and so pathologically self-absorbed that his self-absorption makes him dense. If someone fed him some tasty narcissistic supply, he could be conned in a New York minute. If a room full of people were watching him and bad-mouthing him in murmurs, he would think that he was being admired. He lives in his own world and it's called Awesomeville. He is so self-absorbed that he can't even recognize his own children.

Once N father drove me to a store and waited in the car while I did about 15 minutes of shopping. On my way back to the car, he watched me as I walked down the street. Eventually I got to the car and stood at the door waiting for him to pop the lock. He just sat there, staring straight ahead. I tapped on the window and startled him. He *finally* "recognized" me and opened the door. When I got inside the car he said, "I was watching you walk down the street, but I thought to myself, that's not Lisette."

When we were at my Grandmother's funeral, my sister was walking down the aisle to be seated. N father turned and watched her the entire time. A minute later he said to me, "I wonder if your sister is going to show-up." I said, "She was just seated." He said, "Really?" I said, "You just watched her walk down the aisle." He looked confused. I said, "She's the one with brown hair, and she walks with a cane!" "Oh yes, of course." said King Oblivious. His self-absorption is mind boggling. The man is fixated on himself 100% of the time.

From what I've observed, I don't think grandiosity is the reason for a narcissist's paranoia. N father is way more grandiose than MN mother and MN sister. Or, maybe it's just a different kind of grandiosity. They all believe that everyone is as obsessed with them as much as they are with themselves, but in N father's mind it's about admiration, and in MN mother and MN sister's mind it's because people are out to get them. N father may have delusions of grandeur, but he's not paranoid because he's not a predator. He doesn't deliberately go out of his way to harm others. The harm N father has caused is by neglect, callous indifference, extreme self-centeredness, pathological superiority, demanding adulation and attention and denying regard of any kind (even facial recognition!!) to those near and dear. His children may dislike him, but he has not caused any strife in the world at large. And because he has no real feelings for his children – those he has hurt – in his mind, he is nothing less than perfect. His kids have no significant meaning in his life. He just doesn't care about them one way or another. The man is an island, and it's called FANTASY ISLAND!

My point is that predatory malignant narcissists come by their paranoia honestly. They have earned it. They are out to cause chaos, and wreak havoc. They are addicted to the power high they get from destroying others. They have "deliberately" harmed others and they know it. So they lie, gossip, slander and malign to cover their tracks. They constantly have to watch their backs. They live in constant fear of exposure, their victims speaking-out, exchanging stories, or digging-up dirt on *them*. Think about the psychic energy that must go into maintaining all those lies! Malignant narcissists are suspicious of everyone because they don't have an honest bone in their body. They are so filled with ill-will that they believe everyone is the same way. MN sister has lived in a bubble her entire life. She is so protected, pampered, and sheltered that she has never really had to deal with the assholes of the world. Yet, she hates people because she thinks the worst of them: that they are like her - malevolent.

Malignant narcissists have victims that don't just hate them, they hate their f*cking guts! Even peace loving types will end-up absolutely loathing a malignant narcissist. These MNs incite in normal people, a source of hatred so potent and so foreign that it's hard to believe we could ever feel that way toward another human being. But we all know malignant narcissists are far from human.

MNs have every reason to be paranoid. They mess with people's minds so they believe everyone is messing with their mind. Their first name is LIAR so they believe everyone else is a liar. They stab people in the back so they believe everyone is stabbing them in return. They cheat everyone so they believe everyone is cheating them. They steal, pillage and plunder and live their lives as vindictive and malicious frauds. How could they not be paranoid? Malignant narcissists are like grotty Pirates. Pirates are thieves driven by greed and a violent sense of entitlement. They take whatever it is they want, they have lots of enemies, and are always at war, and on the move. Everyone is an adversary to the malignant narcissist. They are on the run from the reality of their wretched selves. They are on the run from exposure. They are on the run from getting what's coming to them. This makes them paranoid. Ever see a MN have an over-the-top reaction to the tiniest slight? When a MN feels snubbed it signals so much more to their fraudulent selves. It incites their paranoia: What do they know?! What have they heard?! Who are they talking to?! What are they saying about ME, ME, ME?!

The first time I was confronted with MN mother's evil, was also the first time I was confronted with her paranoia. I was still sleeping in a crib, so I guess I was still a toddler. I awoke from an afternoon nap to find a rat crouched against my bedroom wall. The creature terrified me. I was so small that the thing appeared to be half my size. It was hideous. It looked as if it was ready to pounce at any moment. Unbeknownst to me, the little beast was dead. I screamed at the top of my lungs for my mother to come to my rescue. My bedroom door was slightly opened so I knew she could hear me. I cried and screamed, and wailed and rattled the bars of my cage like a wrongfully accused prisoner fighting to break free. I was panic stricken, and feared the hairy beast would crawl-up and into my crib and attack me. MN mother ignored my cries for help for what seemed like an eternity. FINALLY MN mother appeared, pushed my bedroom door open and looked at me with contempt. Anticipating a rescue, I jumped from foot to foot and held my arms out for her to whisk me away to safety. She sighed. Patted her hands on her apron and reluctantly moved forward. I reached out to her, hoping that my outstretched arms would reach her sooner and get me out faster. MN mother picked me up, and was about to lift me out of my crib when she spotted the rat. She squealed. Immediately dropped me back into my crib. Quickly ran out of the room, and slammed the door shut behind her. Now I was trapped all alone in the room with the scary hairy creature without a source of rescue. I was terrified and screamed and cried for what seemed like hours. I still remember how swollen my cheeks were, how my tears burned down my face, and how exhausted I was from wailing my little lungs out. I'm convinced MN mother started vacuuming to drown-out my cries of terror.

When my Dad finally came home from work he carried me out of my crib and brought me to me the safety of my parent's bedroom. I remember sitting on the edge of the bed with him and sobbing and whimpering while he held me on his lap and rocked me back and forth. MN mother appeared at the doorway with that little smile on her face. I was young – probably couldn't even talk – but I knew she was delighting in my trauma. She sat down beside us, and giggled and cooed, saying things like, "Awe. It's ok." Then she reached out to take me in her arms and I quickly pulled away, grab onto to my father for dear life and cried harder and louder. My adverse reaction to her – in front of my father – enraged her. She was such a fraud "mother" even to her husband that she couldn't tolerate an innocent baby unwittingly exposing her. My Dad must have wondered why I didn't want her touching me, and I have no idea what she told him. All I know is that she was furious that in the presence of a witness, I recoiled in horror to her affection. She was fuming that the gig was up, and a baby had her number. The vile evil bitch was threatened by a harmless baby – me. She stood-up and sent me a withering glare that said, "You keep your mouth shut or you'll be sorry." And that was the beginning of the bitch's paranoia.

The most telling thing to me (even as a little one) was not MN mother's selfish instinct to save her own skin and sacrifice her young, or that she herself was dangerous, it was the fact that she was an utter fraud, and that she was threatened by me because I knew she was bad. It was this unspoken law of SILENCE of who she REALLY is that she laid down that day. Now an adult being threatened by a toddler who can't even form full sentences is really kind of comical. But I think the dead rat experience demonstrates just how deep the MN's paranoia runs. These psychos churn-out countless victims and live in panicky fear of exposure.

And so the story goes... the nasty, evil bitch has been paranoid of me "talking" ever since. Growing-up under her roof my privacy was constantly violated, my bedroom was ransacked, and diaries were read. When I had friends over, I was spied-on through windows, doorways, and the intercom system. Telephone conversations were monitored, and on and on and on. Talk about paranoid. The thing is, I had better things to do than spend my time talking to my friends about that bitch. I couldn't care less about her. And the last time I saw her, 21 years ago at Christmas, we got into a blow-out and the first thing she whimpered was, "I can only imagine what you tell your friends about me." That was her main concern: her false image. I had seen her maybe 10 times in the 7 years prior to that Christmas. I lived at the other end of the country and she didn't care if I was dead or alive in that time, her only concern was what I might be saying to my friends about her – complete strangers that she never met and would never know.

MN sister is the exact same way. I'm her primary target. I know what she is capable of. I've seen her with her mask off, and she knows that I hate her guts. So she lives in paranoid fear of me "talking". That's why she spreads gossip, lies, and slander about me. That's why she needs to know my every move. It's a precautionary tactic to discredit me – her victim – in advance. MN mother and MN sister have so much to hide, and so much to be paranoid about. When will these MN fools ever learn? The only thing they should be paranoid of is their own stupidity. Their grandiosity (that they are untouchable) along with their delusions get them in a heap of trouble. And their silencing tactics only backfire on them.

Malignant narcissists become more paranoid with each passing year. The older they get, the more harm they have caused, and this means more enemies. The favourite weapon in their arsenal is gaslighting because it's a way to deflect their paranoia onto others. MNs want everyone in their pathological space to be just as paranoid as they are: don't trust outsiders, people are sneaky, no one wishes you well, be suspicious, never let your guard down, live in fear and be ready to make a pre-emptive strike at the first sign of disobedience.

A few years ago, I had the misfortune of renting in a building managed by a MN husband and wife. Yes, MN couples exist, and they are hideous. I swear you could sniff out the dysfunction in the place the moment you entered the lobby. It had the strangest vibe, it was tense. Before I even knew what was going on there, I sensed that I was being watched and I had a feeling that the tenants were living in fear. The couple – let's call them Mary and Ed – were in their early 70's and had been onsite managers for about 10 years. I moved into the building during the last couple of years of their reign of terror. Mary and Ed were textbook malignant narcissist bullies, TOTAL predators, TOTAL control freaks, TOTAL liars and TOTALLY paranoid. They had abused, harassed, stalked, and violated the rights and privacy of countless tenants over the years and they lived in absolute fear of someone coming back to exact revenge. In fact, they lived in absolute fear of ANYONE exposing them for what they are: scum of the earth.

I could write a book about Mary and Ed's malignant narcissism and how it infected an entire building, but for now I'll just give a few examples of their blatant paranoia. Keep in mind; they were just bad people, period. Ed and Mary were rotten to the core and they needed to do everything in their power to counter that reality, and stop the truth from bubbling to the surface: sort of like someone trying to cover a huge festering zit with a lot of concealer. The puss eventually seeps through. So Mary and Ed controlled their pathological space – the apartment building – like a prison camp. The inmates were on 24 hours surveillance. There were video cameras at the front and back of the building, in the laundry room, and in the hallway to the management office. Ed and Mary watched and monitored the tenant's every move on the monitors in their office and even had three monitors in their apartment so they could keep an eye on their prisoner's comings and goings. One evening a friend of mine dropped by with a couple of empty boxes for me. I buzzed him into the building, and as soon as he was inside, Mary poked her head out her door and sniped, "What apartment are you going to?" I ended-up coming down to the lobby to meet him so when Mary saw me she said, "Oh." and quickly pulled her fat head inside. Though, it goes without saying that she continued to watch us on one of her many monitors.

Ed and Mary hand-picked certain tenants to abuse and harass and would print photographs of them off the surveillance system and hand them to them just to let them know they were being watched. Unfortunately, all the people they abused on the sly thought that they were alone. They even posted photos of people (who had just moved-out of the building) in the elevator, circled their heads and wrote a caption saying they *illegally* dumped a large piece of furniture outside and urged tenants to "Help us find the offenders." They constantly went through the building's trash container, and spied on tenants through the mail slot in the apartment door. After I saw them doing this, I ended up blocking my mail slot in the evening so they couldn't peer in, or listen in.

Being malignant narcissists Ed and Mary had no respect for other people or their boundaries. They felt entitled to do as they pleased because in their warped minds they were King and Queen of the Castle and everyone else – the tenants that they owned – were nothing more than their objects to control and manipulate. They even sent out a form to all the tenants asking them to list any medication they were on. They said it was for the tenant's own good – in case of an emergency. What an absolute crock of shit and a violation of privacy! It was just another way for them to glean information about tenants to use against them and gossip about. Sadly, I'm sure some of the naïve elderly folks complied.

These MN freaks abused, harassed, slandered, gaslighted and terrorized their targets on the sly, but put on an over-the-top performance of Christian do-gooders and neighbourhood vigilantes to all the other tenants. But everything they did to vaunt themselves was tainted with paranoia. Because they were so dishonest, nasty, vicious, cruel, dangerous and bat-shit-crazy they wanted to make everyone else look that way.

For example, one time they took a photograph of a fellow in the neighbourhood with mental health issues who stood outside a bank and asked for change. They created a type of WANTED poster with his photograph and a caption that read: "Stay away from this man. Don't give him any money. He was too aggressive with one of our tenants. He is mentally ill and dangerous." They posted the WANTED poster in the elevators and all around the building. Hmmm. Projection much?

Another time, there was a news story going around the city about a man who was targeting elderly people in a hospital miles away, and stealing their jewellery. Ed and Mary salivated over that news story, and photocopied the newspaper clipping and posted it in every crevice of the building to incite fear and paranoia in the elderly folks in the building. But here's the kicker. I was targeted by those low lives because I was vocal about their bull-shit, and you know what they did? They snuck into my apartment, moved a few items around, and stole my favourite ring. No wonder they eagerly lapped-up the jewellery heist story. Ed and Mary were KARAZY, cons and frauds and criminals and they went out of their way to point the finger at everyone else. They even posted articles about corrupt politicians in the elevator. Talk about trying to cover that zit! And when there was a break-in in the neighbourhood, they slipped a frantic, paranoid notice (written in 24 points, caps, and bolded) through every tenant's mail slot that read:

"There has been a break-in in the neighbourhood. Our building is not IMMUNE. Always lock your door, turn on your lights, play the radio and close your drapes… even when you are not home!!!"

And the note came with a little cartoon of a cop blowing his whistle.

It was easy to see who in the building was infected with their paranoia because after that notice some tenants always had their drapes drawn and their radios on. I also think it was a way for Ed and Mary to monitor who was under their absolute control. So on the sly, these vile MN maggots abused, terrorized and harassed the living shit out of anyone they thought was vulnerable, or tried to bully into submission those they believed were on to them. During the height of their attack on me, they posted a Christian love-thy-neighbour message in the elevator. It was truly nauseating! It said they "loved" THEIR tenants, and *their* tenants meant the world to them. They "care" about everyone, and will always look-out for *their* tenants.

Barf! Pass the puke pail! It's only *really* bad people who make a *really* blatant showing of being good.

Ed and Mary posted their propaganda in the elevators on a daily basis. This included rules, regulations, idiotic jokes and puns and newspaper clippings on their political views and religious leanings as well as obituaries of people they didn't even know. They always used a massive bold, capped font for their names. They made me sick! So one day I decided to test the level of their paranoia. I took a tack from the bottom right corner of their propaganda, and moved it slightly so it stabbed Mary's name. Low and behold, less than an hour later, that particular sheet of bull-shit was replaced with a fresh one. Yep. Ed and Mary, the MN maggots, were so paranoid they noticed a tack being moved. And they were not having an extra puncture mark in their pristine marketing material. I'm sure the movement of the tack sent their paranoia into a tail spin. Who would do such a thing?! Who would stab a tack in Mary's name?! The horror!

Okay. Long, long story short. Malignant narcissists are PARANOID because they are imposters. They live double lives. They wear disguises, and they need to continually dodge the light of exposure. THAT. And the very real fact that they have enemies. Paranoia is the malignant narcissist's WEAKNESS. And I for one am damn glad that they are paranoids! It doesn't take much to trigger their fear.

MN sister's dirty little secret is that she is a hoarder. Yes. I could sign her up for that show *Hoarders* on A&E; notify all her neighbours, the building management, city inspectors, and the fire department… Or, I could just plant a seed and leave the rest to her paranoid mind. I could say to the crazy bitch, "You know, your hoarding is a fire hazard, and a danger to everyone in your building. Maybe they should know about it." Those simple words would be enough to incite her paranoia. When she saw her neighbours she would probably think that they were looking at her funny, or talking about her. She would live in paranoid fear of what they "might" know.

So in closing: Hey Malignant Narcs, YOUR PARANOIA will destroy ya!!

Here's a sweet revenge fantasy from ANON. It's one that plays on her MN mother's paranoia, and it's EXACTLY what I dream of doing to Ed and Mary.

ANON said….

"I've noticed that making us look like the crazy ones is a pretty common tactic among MNs. The way that you say that you would love to drive them over the edge, and terrorize them...believe me, I have very similar thoughts. One recent (and tamer) thought that I had was to hire a PI to stalk the living shit out of this bitch. The PI would be given clear instructions: NO undercover anything; make your presence known. Follow this bitch around with a video camera, or pull out a camera and pretend to take pictures. Follow this bitch from this state to the next; wherever she goes, you go. I would continue this long-term, until she was afraid to leave the house. Maybe after that, I'd stop for a while, and when she felt secure and started venturing out again, I'd sic the PI back on her ass! Welcome to the world of psychological torture bitch!!! How are those PTSD nightmares treating you? Jumpy much? LOL Whew!"

COMMENTS:

I hate your mother. Hugs. Big big hugs.

I am also horrified by the--what shall I call her? ---The "mother character" in the rat story. Your narrative creates such poignant images in the mind.

It takes little effort to do the right thing. So it has to be a buzz for them to fuck us over. It's the only way to explain it. To work harder to put you in a more compromised situation. That's as chicken shit as it gets.

How hard would it have been for your mother to grab you and leave the room when you were crying because of that rat? What an evil, selfish bitch she is! Wouldn't it be awesome if she got sick, and put into a nursing home where SHE got left in a room with a rat? Hopefully it will be alive and really, really hungry.

I read today that paranoia is more so evident in the low functioning MN, the more paranoid they are the lower functioning they are.

Hmm...I'm also paranoid of people, but because I grew up with MN's....

It's not paranoid to be watchful and cautious. The narcs trained us to discount our own feelings and perceptions and accept abusive/malicious/exploitative behavior as normal. It takes time to undo narc programming. Lots of time.

Be as paranoid or as untrusting as you need to be. Trust should be earned. That's something a narc of any stripe does not want you to know.

The more Malignant they are, the more paranoid they are because don't cha know, it's *all* about them. Almost ALL the ACONs I have come across have been stalked in some form. C'mon, WTF? WHO does this shit? This isn't remotely *normal*, Folks. But most people aren't anywhere near as paranoid as they are or equally as importantly, have as much shit to try to cover: A life-time of "If I'm breathing, I'm lying" leaves an incredible dung pile and the older they get, the higher the crap pile gets. Then, the more the paranoia increases exponentially to all the evil crap they've been involved in throughout their lives. Herein lies the lack of conscience.

These MNs are truly living in a whole separate reality and I really can't explain it any more clearly than Lisette does. In all its permutations, these MNs are just disgusting, "un-treatable" and unredeemable piss-poor excuses for a human being. But, hey, that's just my opinion.

My evil mother has always been the most paranoid person I have ever known in my life! From the time I was a little kid, I remember her always thinking that someone was plotting and planning to "get her." As an adult, I could clearly say, "Bitch, you aren't important enough for anyone to waste their time", but as a child this made me protective of her in some weird kind of way.

NARCISSISTS ARE GREEDY

DO NOT FEED THE ZOMBIES

One of the most disgusting characteristics of malignant narcissism is insatiable greed. Add to the Narcissist's gluttony, an appallingly stingy nature, and you've got one revolting creature. They are parasites, scrounges, users, moochers and vultures of the human race. Narcissists are always on the make, always on the take, and always at the ready to swoop in and sink their filthy claws into whatever they can get.

It's safe to say ALL narcissists are exploitative and opportunistic and they are all cheap and greedy, but not all narcissists are cheap and greedy in the same way. For example, the lesser narcissists (non-malignant) are not always free-loading leeches, hunting and scavenging to get a hold of your property, material possessions and "stuff." They've got their own stuff, but their greed drives them to make sure it is always bigger and better than yours. Some narcissists spend to impress. They lavish others with expensive gifts, always pay their way and often "treat" others. But these same narcissists, who appear to be gracious and even generous at times, selfishly crave, grasp and hoard all the available attention, all regard, all emotional support, all the care, concern and adulation they can drain out of you without giving you a drop in return.

A narcissist is selfish and withholding by nature. They don't *really* reciprocate. They don't know how to share, and they never "give" out of the goodness of their heart. They are the original even-steven, tit for tat, and they keep track of all they "give" out, and make damn sure that more comes in than goes out. To a narcissist, "giving" is an investment and often a covert form of manipulation. They give a little and expect a huge return in the form of "narcissistic supply."

Malignant narcissists are the original career thieves - what's in it for me? What have you done for me lately? What can I get out of this situation? They suss-out everyone for their potential "use value." They are greedy for EVERYTHING. ALL OF IT. ALL. THE. TIME. Malignant narcissists want to get their grubby paws on your personal property, they want to steal your material possessions, they want to rob you of your money and livelihood, your home, your relationships, your good name and virtues, and they want to take away the things you've worked hard to attain such as your accomplishments, talents, and skills. The grubbing malignant narcissist wants to snatch ALL your valuables, AND they want to pilfer your time and energy, and exploit you for attention, care, concern, support and regard, AND they want to obliterate your mental, emotional and physical health in the process. Sound like a good deal to you?

Narcissists truly don't see themselves doing anything but getting (they are revoltingly stingy) and they don't see anyone else doing anything but giving... to THEM. Greed is the driving force behind malignant narcissism and it relentlessly fuels all their destructive and despicable behavior and makes them predatory.

A Narcissist's need to "have it all" invests him with a spirit that is hostile to the needs and wellbeing of others.

If you feel a compelling need to have all the dollars in the world, no matter how many you get, you will compete with others for every single one; and if you see a dollar in someone else's hand, you will want to take it away. Just because he has it.

118

*That makes you an adversary of everyone else in the world. It
makes you view the possessor of the dollar as a predator views prey.*

*Therein lies the "malignance" in malignant narcissism. So
narcissists are desperate to keep its presence a secret. That is why
they invest so much energy in the false image of themselves they
carve out with everything they say and do.*

*Indeed, every predator must find some way to stalk its prey without
arousing suspicion.*

Kathy Krajco "What Makes Narcissists Tick" page40

It makes no difference how much bounty is bequeathed upon the
malignant narcissist. They can be spoiled, pampered, protected, privileged,
supported, loved and admired etc. But, since they view everyone as an
adversary, enough is NEVER enough. So, it would seem, the actual dollars
- no matter what form they come in - are of no consequence to them.
I'm convinced it's the game of *keep away*, and the destruction they heap on
their target's life by stealing it ALL that gives the malignant narcissist the
real thrill. Getting it all = power. Power = superiority.

A narcissist's greed has nothing to do with necessity. It's all about want. If
a narcissist wants it they feel entitled to it. It's about acquisition and
consumption. It's about competition and winning. The narcissist doesn't
give a damn that she hurts others in the process of getting what she
wants. Indeed, when it comes to malignant narcissists, their greed seems
to be motivated by the fact that it will hurt others. For example; the
malignant narcissist sibling with Power of Attorney who drains the family
estate before the parent dies. The MN isn't doing it just for the money;
she doesn't "need" more money. She has tons. The malignant narcissist is
stealing, spending and wasting assets in an effort to deplete the value of
the estate and thus screw her sister out of her inheritance. Deciding the
amount of her sister's inheritance makes the malignant narcissist feel
powerful because it means she is in control of the quality of her life.
Seeing her sister get less than was intended, and knowing her sister will
suffer as a result, gives the MN more of a thrill than rolling in all the cash.

Here's another thing, the malignant narcissist's lust to have it ALL, every last drop of it, is so strong that it is excruciatingly painful for them to see anyone get anything. The way they see it; if they're not getting all of it, someone is getting some of it, and just the thought of that incites their malicious envy. Life is a zero-sum game for the malignant narcissist. In order for them to win someone else has to lose. It's not enough that they get it all; they go out of their way to make sure you get none and what little you do have is taken away.

A narcissist's greedy and miserly nature is no small matter. It's a symptom of hostility towards others. It is an incredibly dangerous aspect of their personality and one that we should be especially cautious of. What starts out as a nasty kid stealing her sibling's Christmas gifts, escalates in time to a nasty adult stealing her sibling's inheritance. A person of strong moral character is neither cheap nor greedy. Greed is a red flag of malicious people – narcissists – and a sure sign that there is more ill will to come.

A "Cheap & Greedy Narcissist Combo Platter" *always* comes served with *many* poisonous side-dishes. No, you do not get to "choose" your side-dishes. All of the items on the following menu come with your toxic narcissist. NO SPECIAL ORDERS!

ENTITLEMENT: All narcissists believe they are special. And because they are so special they feel entitled to preferential treatment, privileges and indulgences. Indeed, they EXPECT others to gratify them at all times, but are not concerned with gratifying anyone else. EVER. Narcissists feel entitled to exploit others without any interference or any trace of reciprocation.

Since day one, MN sister has had a pathological sense of entitlement. Her EXPECTATIONS about what she's "owed" boggles the mind. When we were still in high school she told me that she wanted to start a video company but first "needed" to get a steadycam. I asked her how much a steadycam would cost, and she told me nonchalantly, "$30,000." I said to her, "Where are you going to get $30,000?" She snipped in a matter of fact one, "Dad." I was floored. I didn't even expect to get tuition for University, and this greedy bitch felt entitled to $30,000 for a camera that she wanted for a stupid pipe dream. And yes, her business ventures, nothing more than vanity projects, were all failures and "Dad" footed the bills. Again, all it requires is a simple "want" for the narcissist to feel entitled.

As for reciprocation, some more socially astute narcs, on the *rare* occasion, are capable of presenting a shabby facsimile of it. These narcs are fully aware that they have been taking and taking for a long time, and if they don't step-up with a "gesture" sometime soon, the gravy train is going to end. In other words, they are going to lose a generous friend and an easy mark.

For example, you have a new acquaintance that is a narc – let's call her Miss Greedy Guts – she is conveniently *always* short on cash and can never pay her share. So after treating the narc to countless coffees, drinks from the bar, a few meals and many car rides out of your way to take her home, the narc says she wants to take you out for lunch and asks you where you would like to go. Well, you're just floored at the narc's "seemingly" generous offer. You didn't think she had it in her, and maybe, just maybe you were wrong about her. So you tell the narc that you're craving a good burger and suggest an average priced restaurant that makes an amazing burger and fries. The narcissist says, "Well… maybe… I'll call you tomorrow to confirm." The next day the narcissist calls you to confirm the lunch date and asks you to meet her at a sushi bar. Now the narcissist knows that you had sushi recently and you are not even a big fan of it. But of course, the narcissist loves sushi and the narcissist is CHEAP. So you reluctantly meet the cheap, selfish, self-serving narc at the sushi bar of her choice: the grossest place in town. It has a quickie lunch special and no tables or chairs. You have to stand-up at this dive and eat your sushi over a counter. Plus, because the place is so small it stinks. And you are completely turned-off your food when you notice that the guy rolling the sushi has alarmingly hideous sausage fingers!

Time and again, the narcissist's offer to reciprocate is a horrible experience, but the narcissist doesn't think so. The narcissist now thinks they are ENTITLED to continue exploiting you without any reciprocation for months to come, and they actually up their demands. When you put your foot down and set boundaries, the ungrateful malignant narcissist gets pouty and petulant and mean. You end the acquaintanceship and the narcissist slanders you to others calling you "negative." Negative to a narcissist means you refuse to cave to their every whim.

IMMATURITY: Narcissists have not matured past the psychological mind-set of a child. And like a child, they believe the world revolves around them. Children live in a constant state of need and want and take. They are in a constant state of hunger and they EXPECT to be fed and cared for by others exactly when they want, without giving anything in return. So does the narcissist. They are big babies who have never learned how to share. All they know how to do is make sure their wants are met and they do this by sulking, and becoming angry and contemptuous and throwing nasty fits and temper tantrums to get their way. The narcissist wants it ALL, and they will whine and cry and scream and make your life miserable if you don't capitulate to their every greedy demand. Like children, narcissists are perversely willful. They will not let-up until they get their way.

ENVY & COMPETITIVENESS: Narcissists want to establish their superiority over others through competition. Rising above others reinforces their self-esteem making narcissists feel more desirable and worthy of admiration. They create rivalries where none exist. "I'm better than you." "My so and so is better than yours." Narcissists feel that unless they are better than everyone else, they are worse than everybody in the whole world. All of the narcissist's activities are geared toward winning the competition which is always at the back of their minds. Their opponent usually has no clue they have been entered in a contest.

Malignant narcissists are GREEDY PIGS who instinctively sniff-out opportunities. They exist in an obsessive state of seeking an advantage, securing a gain, compulsively acquiring and hoarding and *preventing* others from obtaining. They are extremely hostile and envious toward anyone who has anything they want. Getting it all = WINNING. In the malignant narcissist's deranged mind, satiating their greed is an achievement; a victory that puts them ahead in the game they are always playing.

Bad intentions lurk behind *everything* a malignant narcissist does. Even when a narcissist pretends to reciprocate, the person at the receiving end of their deed is the one who pays. In the case of Miss Greedy Guts, she *never* would have chosen the restaurant I wanted to go to because that would be too much like sharing, and sharing would mean she didn't "win."

The malignant narcissist also criticizes what is generously offered and available, and blames others for failing to provide enough. They are the real deal when it comes to ungrateful brats.

Christmas, over 20 years ago, is the last time I saw MN mother and MN sister. I had avoided them and their pathological space for 5 years so MN sister's all-consuming greed, and MN mother's extreme stinginess was very noticeable. I have many more examples to come, but the one that stands out for now is when my brother and sister and I all received a $500 cheque from N father for Christmas. I honestly didn't expect anything from him that year. I said to MN sister "Isn't it nice that we all got some money?" She was visibly irritated and huffed, "I was hoping to get a $1000."

GREED is not a secret vice of the MN sister and she is now a full-on hoarder who has to tunnel her way through all her ill-gotten gains to move around her condo. Her patio, with a million dollar view, is covered in junk. She has been leeching off N parents all her life, and is still on the take, be it furniture, TVs, computers, printers, telephones, mattresses, decorative items or even boxes, electrical cords, or clunky sports equipment she will never use. She takes not because she needs it. She takes to prevent others from having it. Preventing others from getting something that might bring them comfort or make them happy, to this sick bitch, means that she is in CONTROL = POWERFUL. She takes to feed her bloated ego.

SUPERIORITY: Narcissists are not concerned with what they have because they enjoy it, but because it makes them feel superior. They feel comfortable around people only if they feel superior to them in some way, either because the other person has less than they do, or because the narcissist has beaten them in some covert or overt contest. Every greedy evil deed, miserly act, and selfish withholding manoeuvre is motivated by the narcissist's constant need to regain superiority and stay on top. In other words, stockpiling and controlling *all* resources means they are WINNING!! And winning makes them feel superior. The malignant narcissist doesn't simply want a *portion* of the good stuff; they want your share too. And they will stop at nothing to get it.

CONTEMPT: Exploiting and stealing from people reveals the contempt in which narcissists hold others. All narcissists are cold and calculating, and as they see it, EXPLOITATION of some sort is necessary to continue to project a superior self-image. Their need to exploit others stems from a general lack of empathy and manifests in a dismissive attitude towards other people's feelings, wishes, needs, concerns, standards, personal property and boundaries. The irony here is that when you appease the narcissist by giving into their greedy nature, they become even more demanding and contemptuous of you. They see you as an easy mark and they EXPECT more and more, and if they don't get it, they become dangerously hostile and impossible to placate.

Contempt is the biggest issue at play when it comes to the malignant narcissist's stingy nature and greed. They have zero respect for others and their property. This contempt is an off-shoot of their superiority and covetousness. They believe they are deserving of everything, and you are deserving of nothing. So if you have *anything* they feel entitled to they will either steal it from you, denigrate it, or both. MNs are thieving scumbags who will plagiarize your writing, grab your brand new hat off your head, wear it and walk away. They will "borrow" you favourite DVDs and never bother to watch them. When you ask the MN to return what is rightfully your property, your request is met with narc rage and disdain for what they stole from you, but refuse to give back. Of course this is all an intimidation tactic to make you back down. Narcissists are selfish, spoiled-rotten brats and their game of "give me!" and "keep away" never ends.

The greedy, thieving narcissist's twisted idea of "giving" is allowing you to give to *them*. I once offered to help a narcissist move and the way he responded to my offer was as if he was doing me some great honour by allowing me to help him. Narcissists *always* place themselves in a lofty position above us mere mortals. In their deluded minds, our job is to reinforce their narcissism by lavishing them with gratitude for using, abusing and exploiting us. And if you don't reinforce their narcissism, these douchebags become incredibly hostile and contemptuous. The malignant monsters growls, "What's do you care about a cheap hat?!" "Why do you care about obsolete DVDs?" "Your creative ideas are crap, and you're a bully for expecting credit!" Of course, they covet the "cheap" hat, the "obsolete" DVDs and the "crap" creative work so much they refuse to give it back to its rightful owner. They covet it not because they value it, but because you do. Don't expect anything in return from the greedy, selfish, stingy malignant narcissist. To them, you are merely a provider of supply, and supply, to an effed-up narc, could simply be a feeling of smug superiority for stealing from you, frustrating you, and defeating you in a personal interaction, as well as CONTROLLING your property, under the delusion that they are also CONTROLLING you.

I have walked away from a long inventory of property stolen by narcs. A small price to pay to get those vultures out of my life.

LACK OF EMPATHY: Malignant narcissists have no capacity to empathize with anyone, so nothing restrains them from seriously harming others. In their quest to satisfy their greed, they cause a lot of loss and suffering and grief to others.

Narcissists don't care about you… AT ALL. They don't even know you. The only reason a narcissist will even look at you is to see themself in your reflection. They don't know who you are, or what you like or want. This makes narcissists terrible gift givers. Even if you tell them what you would like, the narcissist purposely denies you. Giving you something that would make you happy means that the narcissist is giving you positive regard, and the stingy, selfish narcissist can NEVER do that. They hold you in too much contempt, and they would not feel superior if they were sharing and caring and acknowledging you as more than an object to exploit for supply. To the narcissist, reciprocation in relationships = LOSING.

I had an N friend whose elderly N mother used to make weekly trips to the dollar store. This old bitty accumulated quite a stash of cheap junk and the N friend always relied on her mother's stash for presents. This N always had a "gift" for every occasion, but they had dollar store written all over them. I know for a fact, that this N never actually took the time to go out of her way to buy a specific gift for anyone; she just rooted through her mother's hoard. This narc was always trying to make herself look thoughtful and generous by giving-out useless dollar store gifts, but when it came time to give something that you *really* needed, like one night on her sofa because all the affordable hotels were full, and your plane was leaving in the morning, she would callously DENY you.

The pleasure for this narc was in knowing that you were in a bind, and it was going to cost you in terms of stress and inconvenience, and you would have to scramble to find a hotel and then pay through the nose for it. Denying something that was so easy to give made this narc feel powerful, and it demonstrated how mean and stingy and withholding she actually was. "I wouldn't worry about $250.00 dollars." She groaned. When I later asked her why, given my situation, she would not even give me one lousy night on her sofa, she angrily snapped "Did you ever think about MY situation?!" This narc, who I had known for 20 years, had no "situation." She was a big, spoiled, over-grown baby who lived a cushy, stress-free, pampered life. She was just a narc. It was all about her. Seeing other people suffer made her feel good, and having a hand in their suffering made her feel even better. Another thing I have noticed about these narcs is that they have zero respect for other people's money. They are stingy beyond belief with their own money because it's important just like them, but when it comes to other people's money they adopt the nonchalant attitude of "It's only money." Funny, the only time I have heard that phrase slither off the tongue of narcissists was when it was *my* money or someone else's that was being spent.

AMORAL/CONSCIENCELESS: Narcissists use deception, mind-control and manipulation to get what they want. So where there is greed there is fraud. Narcissists have no principles other than what works for them, and because they have never developed a conscience, they do not feel guilty for ruthlessly exploiting vulnerable targets. They are hustlers, opportunists, people on the make, always ready to take advantage of a situation and callously use people without the slightest thought to their welfare. Narcissists think nothing of taking whatever others have to offer, and leaving them disappointed and rejected. Indeed, the downfall of others gratifies the malignant narcissist's sadistic cravings. They must *always* frustrate, out-wit, or defeat others in personal relationships.

Greed and stinginess is a red-flag of poor character. I'm not talking about people who are thrifty and good at managing money. I admire those people. I'm talking about the insatiable hunger of the greedy narcissist who wants and wants and takes and takes because enough is never enough. I'm talking about the predatory nature of malignant narcissists and their need to always gain more regardless of the cost to others.

All the riches in the world, especially the ones you can't buy, will never fill the hollow soul of a malignant narcissist. So don't waste your time trying to plug their bottomless pit. Malignant narcissists are human predators that live in a tit-for-tat world. They use their prey as a measuring stick to gage how good they feel about themselves. This means they must always gain a base advantage over others no matter how disreputable. This makes them dangerous. This makes them thieves. This makes them criminals.

When you truly understand what bubbles beneath the surface of the narcissist's insatiable greed - contempt, superiority, lack of empathy, lack of conscience, immaturity, malicious envy, opportunism, entitlement, predation, control, sadism and the need to win at all costs – why would you want to drop *anything* down their big black hole? A narcissist once remarked, "I don't think I will ever be happy, no matter how much I get."

I say we starve them all to death.

COMMENTS:

"...their greed seems to be motivated by the fact it will hurt others." *EXACTLY. It's not simply enough to take from others, but to ruthlessly destroy them in the taking. I believe it's the annihilation of their targets, the scorched earth policy of War that separates them from the more garden-variety Narcs. The MNs will track you to the ends of the Planet with their hell-bent destructive agenda.*

In my opinion the worst thing that these disgusting people try to steal and destroy so mercilessly is your soul.

It almost seems like you interviewed my evil-ass mother to write this post...Guess that's probably not necessary because they're all the same.

My kid sister has put me onto this MN information that describes our Mother to a T. I have cut off relationships with her many times over the years as I was very aware of how she could manipulate me and get me to do things I did not want to do or say. I have 9 siblings and she has delighted in keeping us all mad at each other and no one could every say why.

I thought it was "just" my cruelly evil family, until I found and came here! I am relieved to finally even have a name for what's been going on and identifying exactly what's wrong with THEM... and the abuse I have been silenced, suffered and endured for YEARS because "they're family"!

Argh! The non ACONs who repeatedly say that the narcissists can be fixed!!! That belief is what we have to shake more than anything! They're broken as humans. Broken broken broken, with the sharpest of edges and the deepest of self-pity and the hole that gets filled by their victims' destruction.

The Malignant Narcissist is a Snoop, Spy, Busybody and Gossip

For people who are incredibly self-obsessed, narcissists are very nosy about others. But theirs is not an idle curiosity; it's the instinct of a predator. Narcissists are habitual snoops, spies, busybodies and gossips. They are always trying to dig up dirt that they can use to frame, blackmail, hurt and humiliate others. They will use information, *any* information they have on you to come between the things and people you love.

Getting dirt on others makes malignant narcissists feel good… *really* good. They salivate over a juicy piece of gossip. They get a drug high from hearing about another's failures and indiscretions. They are energized by people's pain, sadness and misfortune. Pretty sick, eh? But what do you expect from people who contain zero genuine goodness within? How else is a vicious, cruel, morally bankrupt liar supposed to feel good about themselves? Doing actual good and being good is not an option for them; it's simply not in their nature. But being actively bad and doing bad IS in their nature, so they are very skilled at digging up dirt and spreading it while not incriminating themselves as the sly and devious creatures they are.

Malignant narcissists go out of their way to snoop and spy and meddle in other people's lives because dirtying up others is priority number one in their campaign to "appear" good. By sullying you and your reputation they get to look good by comparison. Remember; they don't care about being good. Appearances are all that matter to the malignant narcissist. They truly have nothing nice to say about anyone whose back is turned. But to your face? Well, we've all witnessed their nauseatingly effusive displays. I contend the more they gush over you, the more violent the hatchet job behind your back. So beware. Gathering intelligence on you, controlling the data and spreading the misinformation is how they push you down in the gutter and elevate themselves to lofty heights.

Malignant narcissists need to dirty-up others to feel good on the inside and appear good on the outside – this is what makes them predatory. Here's some things I've experienced while the malignant narcissist is on a not so covert fact finding mission: I've been watched and monitored through building surveillance cameras and had my photograph printed off the system and handed to me; I've been spied on through the mail slot in my door; I've had telephone calls intercepted and listened in on; I've been eavesdropped through a home intercom system; I've had personal journals and letters read and my mail opened – banking records, credit card statements; I've been cyberstalked and followed, and had my home invaded illegally. As a result of the trespassing, I also experienced theft and Charles Manson style gaslighting that is so subtle you can't even accuse someone of it without looking paranoid. For example, an item that was in my bathroom was moved under my kitchen sink. In each case, the spying, stalking, watching and monitoring was done in anticipation of exposure – I was talking and the narcissists wanted to silence me. Who's going to believe the perceptions of someone these evil fucks parading as "concerned" citizens insist is mentally disturbed? Therein lies the rub. Narcissists snoop and spy and pry and prod because they are paranoid, but they are quick to project their paranoia onto you when you confront them on their intrusion.

In addition to making themselves feel better and appear better than you, the malignant narcissist's obsession to know all the details of your life – aka, have dirt on you – serves a couple of other purposes. One is they get to project onto you. Projection is the same as dirtying you up, but different. Projections are blasts of unwanted information the narcissists receives about themselves. Unwanted information they spend a lifetime repressing and denying. When this information reaches the level of consciousness they have to quickly dispense of it, and that means smearing it onto you.

For example, the oh so superior malignant narcissist who is greedy and selfish and has to have it ALL while you get zero, is sitting around in her living room buried beneath her ever-mounting hoard of computers, TVs, electronics, furniture, etc. and she hears you bought a new watch. Well "watch" her go off on a tangent about how selfish, spoiled and vain you are. "Who does she think she is buying herself a designer watch?!" It doesn't matter if you have been saving for the new watch for months and you paid for it. The fact is, the narcissist will use that titbit of seemingly innocuous information about you, attach a self-serving assumption to it and bend the narrative to support that assumption. That's why their need to know anything and everything they can on you is so important to the malignant narcissist. They are constantly trying to frame you. They make themselves "appear" good by making you appear bad.

One of malignant narcissist's weapons of choice is the phone. They can hold people hostage on the phone for hours and HOURS while they dig up dirt, make up lies, spread false information, come up with amateur diagnosis, analyse, criticize and pass judgment about every aspect of you and your life. Believe me, the telephone or any means of communication is a loaded gun in the hands of a malignant narcissist. Too bad there are so many stupid idiots that listen to their tripe. Don't these fools realize they are next in line in the MN firing squad?

Finally, the main reasons malignant narcissists are snoops, spies and busybodies are power and control. Malignant narcissists are relentlessly aggressive and ruthless – they are dictators, tyrants and bullies. They build a power base through communication strategies and its effectiveness is in proportion to the amount of control it allows them to exert over others. Amassing Intel on everyone about anything and everything makes them feel invulnerable. If they are in complete control of all the information they can spin it and disseminate it any way they choose. They are the gatekeepers of the all the secrets and lies and this gives them power over others. Their compulsion to triangulate their relationships fuels their power as they become the spokesperson between people they have intentionally come between. It's the whole divide and conquer thing.

Malignant narcissists see all of life solely in terms of power and its exercise. Rather than help those who are struggling or less strong, they take advantage of whatever weaknesses they perceive in others and disempower them more so. Weaknesses they hunt for through their spying, snooping around and marathon telephone conversations. And because the malignant narcissist's power is most effective when they make it their business to have what others need, they will attempt to control such necessities of life as food, shelter and security so that people must do whatever they want. Of course, one of the primary needs of people is money, so having a lot of it becomes an even higher priority to them because they regard money as power and a means to exercise control.

Malignant narcissists also may simply use information to advance their interests if someone fails to move first. For example, they hear you found a good deal on a car and are considering buying it. Well, what a surprise when the narcissists you haven't spoken to in months, rolls-up in that new car you were going to put an offer on.

Bottom line; malignant narcissists see the world the way a chess player sees the board – everything is merely a pawn to further their ends. That's why it is so important they have no access to you and know nothing about you including any of your weakness or vulnerabilities. My batshit malignant narcissist sister is a shut-in who lives her life over the phone and the computer and the amount of destruction she has wreaked on the lives of others through the telephone, computer and fax machine is stunning. Malignant narcissists do not wish anyone well. They are socially destructive and all their communication strategies are an act of war. That's why any information in their hands is a very dangerous thing.

Comments:

Excellent, ruthlessly honest article. Spot on. Thank you

Even to this day I have to tell myself that this behaviour isn't normal, but I've seen it all my life. I'm so used to it.

I think another reason they are such greedy information gatherers is because they feel (superior beings that they are) that they are *entitled* to know anything and everything - even about total strangers (who they will then slice to shreds with their vicious tongues). These creatures are truly beyond the pale.

My mother made your loss of privacy into a backhanded way to gaslight you.

I lived across the street from a completely fucking insane malignant narcissist for four years. This crazy bitch was OBSESSED with watching everyone all the time and letting them know it.

"They are energized by people's pain, sadness, and misfortune." That's got to be why NM always loves to tell about the horrible things that are going on in the lives of everyone she knows.

I think I saw a comment about using humour to camouflage the nasty business of surviving life with an MN parent. I have that in spades. The truth is that my mother rained untold grief and some very unfunny situations down on all of that she inflicted herself upon.

You really know how to put all the words together well in describing these psychos. This is exactly how they are.

You must have seen Hell very closely to write so well about it. The injuries these people provoke onto others are beyond imagination for those who were never victim of a N. I had no idea such demons existed until I met one. And the worst thing is (well, one of the worst...) it's so hard to explain the kind of pain they inflict. I for one could not - and still can't - tell how deep I have suffered. Thank You for putting words on an ever open wound.

A Birthday Gift from a Malignant Narcissist Mother

Today is my birthday so I thought it would be fitting to write about the last birthday "gift" I ever received from MN mother... the FINAL one.

First off, I'm not big on celebrating my birthday. I'm in my forties so when another one rolls around it's – Damn! They are happening way too fast! I really wish I could slow it all down, or better yet, go back in time. When will someone invent "The ACON Time Machine" so we can go back with the knowledge we have now and CHANGE things? All I know is that my life has been a hell of a lot harder than it should have. All I know is that if I had knowledge of NPD 10, 20 years ago... hell – All MY LIFE – I would have dodged a ton of bullets and things would be different. Alas, I cannot go back in time or change the past. The evil narcs have come and gone, and the important thing is they stay gone.

I have been NO CONTACT with my malignant narcissist mother for about 26 years. Technically it may be a year less as there was a phone call

135

here or there, but I haven't actually seen her evil ass smirk – up front and personal – for 26 glorious years. I might not even recognize her if I ran into her. Prior to going NC, there wasn't much of any contact. I rarely ever saw MN mother or MN sister and then I moved to the opposite end of the country and they didn't know my exact whereabouts for a while. They didn't care if I was lying dead in a ditch somewhere. They were just thrilled I no longer lived in the same city as them. In their minds, I was just as good as dead, I had evaporated, fallen off the face of the earth and that was fine with them. Even though the gruesome twosome ganged-up on me and bullied me together, they were extremely threatened by me and insanely envious of me… just for existing.

At some point after I fled my "home" base, I made contact with the two MN bitches and any communication that followed was always initiated by me. In other words, the only time I heard from them is when "I" reached-out and made contact and they decided to respond. They are far too superior to ever make contact first. I was but a lowly foot servant to their Royal Highness' which meant the onus was always on me to make kind offerings and gestures and the Queen bitches would then decide if they would grace me with a response. In retrospect, I wish there had been no response because all I got from this evil pair was the Cinderella treatment.

So I was living at the opposite end of the country in a big city where I had no roots, and I continually found myself having to move because of crazy roommates and one bad living situation after the other. I mean BAD, DANGEROUS situations. The contact I had with MNM and MN sister was intermittent because I always had to initiate, but they generally knew my address and phone number. I had not received a birthday card or gift from MN mother since I was on my own - about 6 years. And I had NEVER received one red cent from her… EVER.

Around this time, I was in contact with MN sister. I spoke to her long distance and informed her that I had just moved-in with a friend because of yet another shitty living situation. Back in those days, when you shared a residence, you shared a phone number, so when you moved your number changed. So MN sister had all my updated information, including my current address and telephone number. I suppose because of my recent contact with MN sister, MN mother perceived me as being obedient and friendly to the FREAK, and decided to reward me by acknowledging my birthday.

I get a telephone call from MN mother wishing me a happy birthday. I say thank-you, and she asks me if I received her card. I tell her, no. I never got the card. She then gets that "tone." You know the MN tone? Even though I can't see her, I knew she had that evil smirk plastered across her face and her eyes were all glassy and squinty. She says in a mocking sing song voice, "Yes you did." I said, "No I didn't." In that slimy MN tone she persisted, "Of course you did. You got my card." She was teasing me like the bully she is in a nah-nah-nah-nah kind of way, and the nasty bitch was getting a hell of a lot of pleasure out of it. Finally, I got upset and shouted, "I didn't get your card!" With an indignant - humph! - The haughty MNM sniped, "Well you cashed the cheque!" Again, I told MNM that I NEVER received her card, or cashed a cheque, and asked her what address she sent it to.

Turns out the demented MN bitch sent my birthday card to a place I had lived in 5 apartments ago. In other words, two years ago. I had been through hell trying to find a safe place to live and nasty MN mother sent my birthday card to a house that I lived in when I first moved to the big city. A house that I had to move out of because my crazy roommate – an old perv with a toupee – was spying on me and another female roommate. This crazy fucker climbed a telephone pole to look into my bedroom, and he climbed the roof of the house to peer in on my roommate. I have to say it was funny as hell when we heard him sliding off the roof of the house and crashing to the ground. We found him a crumpled mess in a bush with a lopsided toupee.

I told MN mother that I hadn't lived at the address for years. She said, "Well SOMEONE cashed the $50 cheque I sent!" Given my roommate, it didn't surprise me that my mail was violated. His brother owned the house and he wasn't going anywhere so it had to be him. I informed MN mother of all of this and the conversation ended. She still didn't believe me.

About a week or so later, I received an affidavit in the mail from MN mother ordering me to sign it. She had gone to her bank AND a lawyer to get her measly $50 bucks back. The bank was negligent, and would reimburse her, but in order to get her lousy $50 back I had to sign the affidavit to confirm that the signature they accepted wasn't mine. I promptly and dutifully signed the legal document and sent it back to her. In the meantime, I spoke to MN sister on the phone and casually remark, "I can't believe mom sent my birthday card to that old address." MN sister screamed, "Lisette, you should just be grateful she sent you a card at all! It's not mom's fault YOU move all the time!"

MN mother received the affidavit, and the bank reimbursed her $50. A couple of weeks later I got a belated birthday card from MN mother but…. NO CHEQUE. MN mother called me and asked me if I received the card. I told her yes, and asked if she had included a cheque? She snapped, "NO." I never asked her why. And that was the last birthday present I ever received from MN mother - an affidavit. I went no contact with her later that year. I remember at the time feeling really brave for even asking her about the cheque. I knew she hadn't included one, and I knew how cheap she was but I wasn't going to let her get away with that petty stunt without saying a word.

To put this all in perspective, about 6 months prior she bought MN sister a brand spanking new condominium. MN sister had gone from the luxury of MN mother's townhouse to the luxury of a sweet condo. No shabby rentals or dangerous living situations for MN sister. No, of course not. $50 versus $150,000. Hmm, something is off here. So the ONLY time MN mother ever sent me money, I didn't even get to keep it. She stole it back. And what's odd about the whole thing is that MN sister sent a birthday card to me at the correct address before I heard from MN mother. I'm convinced MN mother sent the card to the wrong address on purpose, or malignant narcissist sister gave her the wrong address. They both had my correct phone number so it's quite a mystery as to why my address got botched. It is likely MN mother just didn't give a damn, and never kept track of where I lived. Anyway, come hell or high water, the stingy bitch was not going to give me a dime. Yes, she would bend-over backwards to deal with the bank and lawyers and legal documents and postage and signatures in order to get a lousy 50 dollars back, because $50 is important to her. 50 dollars has value. And her going to all that trouble to take that money back AND KEEP IT, is an egregious display of how selfish and self-centred she is. It's also a remarkable demonstration of her abuse. She took away the $50 birthday present and kept it for herself to let me know I am worthless to her. I'm not even worth a meagre 50 dollars. Giving me that blood money would be showing me a smidgen of regard and malignant narc parents do not want to EVER show their children any regard. The narcissist's goal is always to let you know every day and in every way that you are worthless. That you have no value. Giving a gift and going to ALL THAT TROUBLE to take it back shows that it PAINS her to give me anything. Malignant narcissist mother is a stingy, sadistic, vile witch. When she dies she should leave me a note saying, "Sorry" AND her entire estate as damages for pain and suffering.

Malignant narcissist mother's utter contempt for me, or any occasion that celebrated me, was a running theme throughout my life. And since we're on the subject of birthdays, I will tell you about my sweet 16.

My birthday fell on a Friday. There was no celebration in our house, no nothing. That evening, the malignant narcissist mother and I were left alone sitting at the dinner table finishing our meals. In two hands, she held a stake bone at her mouth and was chewing away like a wolf. I could have sworn I heard her growling. The doorbell rang. My friends had come by to pick me up. I was about to get up from the table to greet my pals, when MNM reached with one hand under the table and pulled a bag off her lap and slapped it down in front of me. She didn't say a word, and went back to chewing on her bone. It was a paper bag. No birthday card. No birthday wrapping. I opened the bag and inside was a little purse. So not me. I was a tomboy and I was not into purses, none of my friends were either. We just put our bonne bell lip gloss and combs and whatever else in our pockets. Back then, purses were not cool. I thanked MN mother for the purse and asked if I could leave to go hang with my friends. She grunted, "Yeah." I tossed the purse in my bedroom, and left for a night out with my friends. I never used the purse. Not once. It was a thoughtless "gift" and I believe that was the point.

MNs are incredibly petty, irrationally stingy and terrible "conditional" gift givers. I have never received anything from a MN that wasn't a thinly veiled insult or a kick in the face. The malignant narcissist mother didn't know who I was because she had no interest in knowing me. Her inappropriate gifts reflected her "You don't matter! I don't give a damn about you!" attitude toward me. In fact, her thoughtless gifts were nothing but an abusive message to me.

If ever there is a time for a narcissist to demonstrate their utter contempt for you, it's during your birthday, a time when normal people celebrate your existence.

Comments:

I've been flooded with memories about this. I never made the connection fully before about those invariably unfitting presents and narc parent's hatred.

I had lots of the same types of experience: N's making me work so hard for a gift that wasn't really a gift at all or that never actually materialized or buying me something that NSis or GC Brother wanted or making sure I saw how much less they gave me than my sibs or, my personal favorite, buying themselves something new and then giving me the old item their new stuff was replacing for them. Like I was a human thrift store drop box.

I always got the "you're special, blah, blah, blah" cards. Then to top it off, it always had love, NM and NF. It's always a freaking game to these losers. They really are warped.

Ohhhh, the stories, the untold stories of the "Art of the Fuck YOU Gift" courtesy of these POS. There's a million ways to make your kid "bend over for it" regardless of their age just as there are millions of MN's, but their stories are consistent theme wise and are the true stuff of MN Parental Legend.

The fuck-you gift indeed! An unfitting gift that you can never use that they never intended for you to keep and that they only gave to you to either steal back or make you feel bad. Every "human" interaction is about power and control for malignant narcissists!

MN's are such bad gift givers. I'm relieved to not get them from my mother anymore.

Narcissists suck at gift giving, that's a given. My mother would give me shit like pens and paper - stuff she'd randomly steal from work then wrap up in a brown paper bag (that's right, she'd recycle a paper bag to turn it into wrapping paper).

I swear, no matter what I read about these people, I will never be surprised.

Here's a Birthday card for my MN mother ...Outside - "It's hard to find the words to express what I feel inside..." Inside - "But 'fuck you' would be a good place to start." Love, Your Daughter the Scapegoat.

I spent most of my life wondering why my family could always find "the perfect" gifts for each other but that mine were always terrible and seemed cheap. It has taken me until today, at 58 years old to realize that the gifts I received were crappy because the gifters deliberately meant them to be crappy.

I could so relate to your birthday story. Birthdays were an awful time, because we were reminded of how insignificant we are to our own parents.

Oh dear, birthdays were the worst time. And like the naive daughter desperate for a normal life I was, I always hoped THIS year will be different.

THE DANGERS OF MALIGNANT NARCISSISM

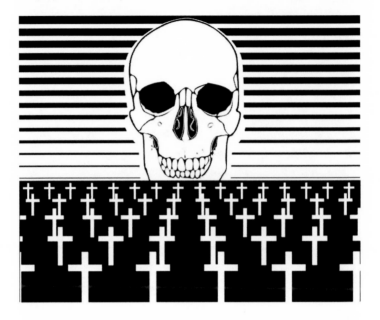

For many people, the word "evil" conjures up something in the spiritual realm. Although I believe malignant narcissists are morally, emotionally, and spiritually bankrupt, my use of the word "evil" is not in a heaven and hell sense, or a god or the devil kind of way - it's just the best word to describe these "people."

It's potentially deadly is to go through life refusing to believe these evil "people" could ever be a family member. The disturbing reality of malignant narcissism can be very difficult to accept, but there are dire consequences for allowing one of these "people" to remain in your life. I have received one too many emails from readers who are on the run, living in fear, and being stalked by a malignant narcissist parent(s). The MN is no longer just a threat to their emotional and psychological health, but a dangerous threat to the very fabric of their existence; including their physical safety. Their stories are Cautionary Tales of law enforcement, lawyers, detectives, restraining orders, suicide attempts, anxiety disorders, PTSD, financial ruin, job loss, kidnapping, ransoms, blackmail, slander, harassment, hiding out in hotel rooms and the list goes on. This stuff is real. I know. I've lived it. There is no rock bottom to the level of malevolence in a malignant narcissist.

Malignant narcissists are so gratuitously mean, calculating, spiteful and malicious, and all without motive. They methodically and systematically go about destroying their victim's life by wreaking havoc that is so severe, the damage is often irreparable. That, to me, is far more sinister than simply picking-up a gun and blowing a person's head off. If you let a malignant narcissist near you, at the very least, you will live in constant fight or flight mode and this state of being is so taxing on the nervous system that it could cause other life threatening illnesses. Kathy Krajco's article "Self-Preservation Under Narcissistic Abuse" clearly illustrates the dangers of malignant narcissism, and how narcissistic abuse is indistinguishable from psychopathic behavior, and why it is so critical to sever all contact with these monsters. One of the key points of Kathy's article is: *the ultimate narcissistic high is to demonstrate absolute power over the victim by somehow making the victim offer themselves up for abuse (bend over for it)*. This is the kind of power that psychopaths lust after. This is the type of power my MN mother and MN sister want over me.

So, to be blunt, it you are in a relationship with a malignant narcissist then you are sacrificing your SELF for the narcissist's sadistic pleasures. Believe me when I say; you can *never* have a relationship with a malignant narcissist unless they are in absolute control, and that means you are their subservient whipping horse. I don't care how the narcissist dresses-up the abuse, or how fancy the façade of their sadism, or how crafty and cunning their crimes. The reality is this: malignant narcissists are only in relationships with people who allow themselves to be abused and exploited in some way. The art of narcissistic abuse is about the skill of manipulating the victim into offering themselves up to abuse.

In this way, the malignant narcissist's mind-set is no different than a psychopath. The narcissist's greatest victory is to abuse, and abuse, and abuse, and have their victim come back for more. It brings to mind the comedy *Animal House* where the fraternity pledges bend-over for it and shout, "Please sir, can I have another!" while the head frat boy whacks them on the bare ass with a paddle. Talk about degrading. But this is no

143

comedy. This is real life, and this type of sick sadistic power rush is what the malignant narcissist wants and needs. Though it doesn't have to look like the scene from the film *Animal House* for the narcissist to satiate their craving for power over you. And remember, the level of abuse escalates with every opportunity.

I was going to title this post "Sadistic" Malignant Narcissists are Psychopaths, but that would be redundant. ALL malignant narcissists are sadists, and this is why they are indistinguishable from sadistic psychopaths. ALL malignant narcissists are predators, in that they go out of their way to deliberately inflict pain and suffering. The more they hurt others, the better they feel.

Malignant narcissism is about sadistic, twisted malice. They might not leave bloody body parts lying around but they do things so abhorrent, so depraved, and so diabolical that in many ways they are more dangerous than the out of control psychopathic serial killer. For example, it's far more gratifying for the malignant narcissist – and much safer – to murder someone by driving them to suicide. That's absolute power. That's the ultimate narcissistic high. And it's so much more aggrandizing to the narcissist than plain old fashioned murder. Besides, the malignant narcissist probably feels above the actual act of murder. What they get off on, is having so much power over another person that they can "will" their victim to do the killing for them. Or, they drain the victim of their life force leaving them a hollow, walking dead Zombie. How's that for God-like power? Taking life without getting your hands bloodied takes real skill in mind-control and manipulation, and it's much more satisfying knowing you will never be viewed as a lowly murderer.

It's all about power for the malignant narcissist, and it's not about power for good, it about power for evil, or power for its own sake. Like the psychopath, the narcissist's drug of choice is POWER and CONTROL over others.

I know all about this. I've lived it. My malignant narcissist mother attempted to psychologically murder me by using covert *suggestions* that I commit suicide. I swear I would find her far less dangerous if she came at me with a butcher knife. There is nothing more sinister, more sadistic or more NARCISSISTIC than someone deluding themselves into thinking they are so powerful they can control their victim into carrying-out their own murderous impulses. A malignant narcissist trying to manipulate their victim to suicide is also the ultimate in PROJECTION! They try to sneak their homicidal obsessions into you by way of self-masochism. The MN bitch's evil plan didn't work on me. She only proved herself to be more of a threat so I stayed farther away. But all too often it works.

Malignant narcissists crave POSSESSION, and ENSLAVEMENT of their victim. ABSOLUTE POWER over another is NIRVANA for the narcissist. They live for the kind of power where they usurp the victim's will to the extent that the victim serves themselves up as an object for the narcissist's sadistic pleasure. This is god-like rush of grandiosity is what the malignant narcissist is always chasing. It's the ultimate form of degradation of the victim, and the ultimate power high for the narcissist. Malignant narcissists are sadists. They enjoy your pain. We've all seen that little smile and evil smirk.

Never forget that malignant narcissists, like psychopaths, *elect* to switch the conscience and empathy button to off for everyone but themselves. And I mean everyone. Even their own children and even their own parents. I know for a fact that neither my malignant narcissist sister nor malignant narcissist mother give a damn about each other. One would think these two bitches are the other's biggest supporter and protector, but at the end of the day, they are malignant narcissists.

EVERYONE is just an object to the malignant narcissist, including their fellow malignant narcissist counterparts and accomplices. Not one single motivation of the malignant narcissist is concerned about anyone else's well-being, including their beloved "Golden Child". Malignant narcissists are absolutely incapable of the true emotion of love and compassion for any other human being. So if you think the malignant narcissist parent loves the golden child, think again. From where I sit, the malignant narcissist sees the golden child as nothing more than an "object" of narcissistic supply. So if someone threatens their supply, it may seem like they are out to protect the golden child, but in reality they are just protecting their own image. The MN parent may go out of their way to dote over, and promote the golden child but all they are doing is doting over, promoting and protecting their human extension.

Malignant narcissists wish no one well so the only way the malignant narcissist will show simulated affection for you is if the malignant narcissist has internalized you as an object of "special" narcissistic supply. Scapegoats have been internalized more as a tool for the narcissist to use and abuse as they please. But everyone is an object to the narcissist; it's just a matter of what type of value you hold. For example, a lowly tool (the scapegoat) that is available for cruelty, exploitation and abuse provides an amazing power high to the narcissist and is extremely valuable, but is held in contempt. The object of special narcissistic supply that can glorify the narcissist's fragile *image* is also extremely valuable, yet coveted and protected. The malignant narcissist does not want to lose either of these objects. They both satisfy very significant narcissistic needs. However, the narcissist is going to take much better care of a Mercedes than they would a screwdriver. And, if the MN parent treats their child as both, they will degrade the child and aggrandize the child, and they will have created one

146

messed-up psyche. I refer to my MN sister as my MN mother's Franken daughter. This is a fact, and it is one that in many ways tastes like sweet justice to me as far as the malignant narcissist mother and sister are concerned. I *understand* they don't love or care for one another. They are not capable of loving or caring. They are malignant narcissists. They desperately need one another, but need is not love. They are dependent on one another, but dependency is not love. The view each other as narcissistic supply to feed on and as tools to exploit and abuse for their own selfish needs.

Malignant narcissists are parasites. Their relationships are about attaching themselves to a host, feeding off the host and never letting go. You must protect yourself and get far away from the narcissist because if you allow a malignant narcissist to sink their evil tentacles into you, they will only dig in deeper and deeper until there is nothing left of you or your life.

My MN mother and MN sister exploit each other, they use each other, they cling to each other, feed off each other, and they take and take and take from one another without one ounce of concern as to whether their devouring nature is killing the other. I think this is one of the reasons why they are severely mentally disturbed. They are cannibalizing one another.

Damn! Do they deserve each another! In fact, it comes close to the best punishment I can think of for a malignant narcissist: to be fed on by another malignant narcissist.

A malignant narcissist doesn't give a crap about anyone but itself. If you can't grasp that simple reality then you will probably end up being controlled and abused by one as long as *it* has access to you. If you expend one ounce of energy sympathizing for the plight of the poor malignant narcissist because they didn't choose to be that way, or you excuse or justify its behavior, or assign the abuse excuse as the cause of its wretched ways, then you will continue to suffer under their tyranny. Believe me when I say, there is no help for these monsters. All signs point to malignant narcissism being a choice. I repeat. Malignant narcissists make a conscious decision to harm others. It's simple. They are what they are. If you can't accept the reality of malignant narcissism then you cannot successfully deal with these predators and they will have you eating out of their hands. And by successfully dealing with them, I mean: getting the hell away from them, and making damn sure they have NO ACCESS to you.

Another thing to remember about malignant narcissists is that you are dealing with a sadist that has the mentality of a three year old child. They are impulsive, irresponsible, and unreasonable and they feel entitled to do as they please – as long as they can get away with it. They have no regrets; they show no remorse; they don't get embarrassed, or feel guilt or shame. As a result, morality has no more influence on a malignant narcissist than it would a child at a pre-conscience stage of development. Scary stuff. This is what makes malignant narcissists dangerous and evil, and unfit for human interaction.

You are but a pretty doll in the nasty child's hand, and they will yank off your head without a second thought. You are but a putrid bug between the nasty child's fingers, and they will pluck off your legs just to watch you squirm. Sounds like a psychopath doesn't it? As far as I'm concerned, malignant narcissists and psychopaths are one and the same.

When narcissists slither along the continuum beyond deception into contemptible exploitation, despicable opportunism, delusional malice, and unmitigated vindictiveness then they have reached the stage of MALIGNANT and have sunk to the inhuman levels of the psychopath. At this stage, they are SADISTIC, and diabolically so. They act out their cruelest fantasies of a vindictive triumph, in effect saying, "I will frustrate, outwit, and defeat you no matter what it takes!"

And I have heard one too many stories of this psychopathic drive toward a vindictive triumph being played-out by a malignant narcissist mother (and, or father) against their adult child. And there's no stopping this little old granny because she's a MALIGNANT NARCISSIST.

Let's just forget about the little old granny called "mother" part for a second...

A malignant narcissist is a creature that ignores the normal limits of *human* behavior, and if they have nothing to lose they will stop at nothing to win the game of cat and mouse. And since they have no capacity to empathize with anyone, nothing restrains them from seriously harming others. Malignant narcissists don't need a motive or a reason to hurt others. They just destroy to continue to feel superior, and from their point of view, their malice is justified because of their pathological need to dominate.

We should always be judging *patterns* of behavior. It's a person's behavioural *pattern* that lets you know how they operate. Put aside the, yes but... she's my mom, my father, my brother, my sister, my daughter, my son, my wife, my grandmother etc. etc. Put all that aside and say, yes but... she's filled with ill-will, she's vindictive, and deceitful.... She's a MALIGNANT NARCISSIST, and she is dangerous, and I need to protect myself.

Only when you can fully accept and understand the level of malevolence malignant narcissists are capable of, will you be able to see them for what they are: EXTREMELY DANGEROUS.

Words like mother, father, sister, and brother won't even enter the equation and you will be able to defend and protect yourself from their irrational malice. Remember: a predator is a predator. If you don't want to be attacked, don't swim with the sharks.

COMMENTS:

Oh Yeah! Thanks for speaking truth to power (as the MN/Psychopath) is in terms of their relationship to us as kids and later adults.

I consider your blog more than a clarion call, an excellent source for information on MNs but a "Global Community Service/Public Announcement." Ignore it at your peril.

I cannot express how validating it is to hear other ACONs stories and to know that I'm not messed up, delusional, or whatever else my NFOO tries to pin on me.

It's time we acknowledged the evil in our lives in all its nastiness. And it's time for losing the "label" (mother/father/sister/brother etc.) and facing reality.

It's great we live in the age of the internet. If not for this, I would have never known that there are others who have suffered like me.

Thank you so much for informing others on the topic of malignant narcissism. I have lived in hell for many years not knowing exactly what to call this.

Being around people with NPD is like living in the Twighlight Zone. I catch myself sometimes saying in my Urkel voice "Did they really do that". They make it seems that being normal is the exception.

The evil smirk. I remember it well. My ex-husband was seen as kind and shy to the outside world, but not when the front door closed. When I left the marriage, I looked like a zombie. For a split second one day, I thought of ending my life. He made me feel that awful about myself. You're right, THEY ARE DANGEROUS!

If they spot any sign of distress in others their bloodlust kicks in.

The people with misplaced sympathy need to be taught a lesson. I wholeheartedly wish these people would get a taste of their own medicine, and then let's see how they handle things and see if it's nothing.

They'll side with whoever's against you (even if they don't know them) just to spite you.

Great post! I happen to know a little ol' granny-type who is a GRAND narc and she scares the shit out of me. These people are frightening wolves in sheep's clothing. Run from them and preserve your mental and physical well-being.

THE AFTERSHOCK OF NARCISSISTIC ABUSE

"If you're reading this because of problems with someone you know now, the chances are excellent that one or both of your parents was a narcissist. Narcissists are so much trouble that only people with special prior training (i.e., who were raised by narcissists) get seriously involved with them. Sometimes narcissists' children become narcissists, too, but this is by no means inevitable, provided stable love was given by someone, such as the non-narcissist parent or grandparents. Beyond that, a happy marriage will heal many old wounds for the narcissist's child. But, even though children of narcissists don't automatically become narcissists themselves and can survive with enough intact psychically to lead happy and productive lives away from their narcissistic parents, because we all love our parents whether they can love us back or not, children of narcissists are kind of bent -- "You can't get blood out of a stone," but children of narcissists keep trying, as if by bonding with new narcissists we could

somehow cure our narcissistic parents by finding the key to their heart.

Thus, we've been trained to keep loving people who can't love us back, and we will often tolerate or actively work to maintain connections with narcissistic individuals whom others, lacking our special training, find alienating and repellent from first contact, setting ourselves up to be hurt yet again in the same old way. Once narcissists know that you care for them, they'll suck you dry -- demand all your time, be more work than a newborn babe -- and they'll test your love by outrageous demands and power moves. In their world, love is a weakness and saying "I love you" is asking to be hurt, so be careful: they'll hurt you out of a sort of sacred duty. They can't or won't trust, so they will test your total devotion. If you won't submit to their tyranny, then you will be discarded as "no good," "a waste of time," "you don't really love me or you'd do whatever I ask."

----- **Joanna Ashmun** How to Recognize a Narcissist

I would not be writing this blog if my NFOO were the only narcissists to infect my life. Wouldn't that be nice? To be done with these pernicious creatures at the age of 18; clean-up the aftermath of their abuse and move forward with my life, narc free. No such luck! My narcissist family of origin was pretty much obliterated by the time I was 18, which means I have been out of that sick and twisted system longer than I was in it. But did I walk out of a world dominated by narcissists into a kinder, gentler one free of narcissists? Hell NO.

Transitioning from a NFOO into adulthood was like surviving a devastating car crash, and wandering away from the scene of the accident in severe shock and with a bad head injury. I entered adulthood traumatized, and I didn't even know it. Trauma is not a good foundation on which to build a life. Trauma is not a stable launching pad to make practical choices and wise decisions. I entered adulthood with my navigation and response systems compromised, and all my safety mechanisms corrupted. In short: I was brainwashed, with no boundaries and set to fight or flight mode. I had the narcissists to thank for erasing everything in me that would keep me safe in a dangerous world. I was groomed by wolves to be attractive to wolves.

Growing up in a "family" dominated by narcissists is akin to being raised in a cult. I wrote about this in the post *Narcissistic Abuse is Soul Murder* where I compared it to being imprisoned in a police state a la Big Brother. There is absolute control, invasion of privacy, brainwashing, punishment for original thought, isolation, silencing, secretiveness, group think, fraud, scapegoating and dictatorship to name a few.

Being raised in a NFOO is also like being combat soldiers on the front lines of war: facing the enemy without back-up, running as bullets fly and ducking for cover as grenades are tossed, and always living in a state of fear and apprehension as we nervously wait for the next bomb to drop. We could never relax. We were never safe from harm. We were hostages fighting to survive in a war that we didn't sign-up for. Yup, we ACONs were thrust out into the world brainwashed combat vets and POW survivors with post-war trauma. But no one would know this just by looking at us. Except of course, the enemy… other narcissists.

The most insidious aspect of narcissistic abuse is this: we were groomed by predators FOR predators. It's like the trafficking of human souls. Are all these evil fucks in it together? Is the cult of narcissistic abuse a form of organized crime? All I can say is; the narcs that trained me have blood on their hands. I was their human sacrifice to the world of predators and they are in collusion with every evil, sick fuck that ever harmed me. My narcissist parents shoved me out into the world with a map pointing me toward a life of traumatic events and abusive relationships. Some parent's give their children wings and a treasure map to guide them; mine clipped my wings and propelled me on a one way route to hell.

Having personal boundaries repeatedly trampled by N parents and siblings to the point where the lines of me and others no longer exists, is utterly cruel and selfish – it's soul theft and it's downright evil. The narcissist parent TRAINS their child to ignore the warning signs of danger so THEY can gain access and violate us without any interference.

When you make boundary trespassing "normal" you set the child up to be exploited. Because isn't that what boundaries are: an early warning detection system to keep out intruders?

Yup. Those N parents are as merciless as they come. In addition to the abuse at *their* hands, the N parent primes the child to be abused by the rest of the world and sets them up for a life of hazardous relationships. And because life among the NFOO is so dangerous, we essentially enter the world alone, as orphans with no support system. We are first rate narc bait without a safety line. We ACONs are simply irresistible to predators. Yum, yum. Let the feeding frenzy begin.

A few years after I had fled to the opposite end of the country to a city where I didn't know anyone, and with only $200 bucks in my pocket, I had a long distance chat with malignant narc mother. I told MNM about a *couple* of shitty experiences I had starting out in the big city, but there were *tons*. She became incredibly hostile and snapped, "Why do these things always happen to YOU?!" I remember saying, "I don't know. Bad luck? It's not my fault. Why can't you give me the benefit of the doubt?" She screamed back at me, "I would NEVER give YOU the benefit of the doubt!" It wasn't long after that, that I went no contact for good. I have not seen or spoke to the vicious, psycho, malignant monster in 26 years. Looking back at that conversation I think of things like, "Yeah 'mom' why do these things always happen to ME?" I was fucking set-up by YOU and the other narcs! That's why! Interestingly enough, malignant narcissist sister has never been exploited and abused as an adult. Want to know why? Because she was trained to be a PREDATOR.

And as far MN mother callously lacking any and all concern for my wellbeing - what the hell should I expect? She's a malignant narcissist. Malignant narcissists train you to bend-over for abuse, and then despise you for taking it. It truly is a Catch – 22.

Even before I discovered malignant narcissism and was *finally* able to slap a label on the "family" freak show, I was fully aware of N parent's extreme limitations. Friends that I made in the big city I fled to were always perplexed by my background. They would ask me, "Do your parents know where you are?" I would answer, "No." They would ask, "Do they wonder where you are?" I would answer, "No." They would ask, "Don't they care how you are?" I would answer, "No." They would ask, "Why?! Why?! Why?!" My stock response was, "They're not capable of caring." Funnily enough, I even had an N friend say to me, "In all the time I have known you, for the life of me, I can't figure out why your parents hate you." I replied, "Maybe it's not me, maybe it's them." And incidentally, I never told anyone my parents hate me. I guess they just equated their indifference with hate, which is not a stretch as indifference is the opposite of love.

So, as you can see, I was no fool. I was onto something. I went NO CONTACT for good with MN mother and MN sister in my early 20's. I knew at a fairly young age that my NFOO was dangerous and that I was better off without them. But despite my survival instincts, I still got involved with narcissists because of my special prior training.

Being raised in a home dominated by narcissists is not just a case of my family sucks so I'm outta here, and that's the end of the insanity. On no. Not a chance. I really wish it was that simple. For me, it was a case of my family sucks and no matter how far I run they continue to suck and suck and suck and suck. Narcissistic abuse is like a gigantic leech that latches on and continues to feed. No matter where you go, no matter what you do, the narcissist's voice lives inside of you (that should be a dysfunctional family greeting card).

Remember all those cults that sprung-up in the 1970's, and how those poncho wearing, pot-smoking, and sometimes just naive teenage hippies had to be "rescued" by their parents? But the parents didn't do the actual rescuing. The parents had to hire people that were specially trained at removing/kidnapping people from cults and de-programming them. I remember seeing documentaries on the subject. The "deprogrammers" would snatch the kid, shove them in a van, and then take them to a hotel room where there was no outside influence – NONE – and the deprogramming would commence.

And therein lies the reason why the adult children of narcissists are not free from abuse simply because they have escaped their family of origin - outside influences; other narcissists. How can you deprogram if members of the same cult keep slithering into your life? You can't! It is impossible to mitigate the effects of narcissistic abuse if your life continues to be infiltrated by narcissists.

I may have encountered "lesser narcissists" after my NFOO, but they were narcissists just the same. And even if some of these "relationships" were only short lived, there was still damage. It seemed I was always cleaning-up after these fuckers. And when I finally got rid of one infestation, there would be another. I swear these narcs are like cockroaches: you can't leave any tasty crumbs around for them to snack on. NOT A CRUMB.

The aftershock of narcissistic abuse has been more devastating to me than the original abuse. The "big one" hit in my NFOO, I survived it and walked away. What I didn't count on was the ripple effect: numerous smaller quakes repeatedly hitting me in the same spot at unpredictable and random intervals. Narcissists on the outside strike like terrorists. At least in an N home, there is some predictability, and if your parent isn't a stalker, there is the possibility of a clean exit strategy. But when N abuse becomes a part of your adult life - when you can't stop trying to get blood out of a stone - there seems to be no escape. It's never ending. You say to yourself "I guess most people are just like that." Or, "maybe something is wrong with me?" As Anna V said, the only thing wrong with us ACONs is that we tolerate narcissists. So please NEVER confuse being shell-shocked and brainwashed with a busted compass and a non-existent security and support system as being damaged or defective. Only narcissists want you to believe that, and it is only narcissists that are truly deserving of the description: damaged, disordered and defective. It is the mutant narcissist who is lacking in everything that makes us human.

So we ACONs are shell-shocked soldiers walking right into another battle. A battle that never ends until we figure-out the enemy. They say knowing your enemy is half the battle. This is true, especially when you discover it's not you, it's THEM - The Narcissists! And the only way to win the battle is to closely study your enemy and know your own weakness; the ones that your N parents cultivated in you during narc abuse training camp.

Only when you truly understand the enemy and know yourself will you be properly protected. That's what this book is about.

So as I wrap up this post, I notice a fellow soldier has found their way here by asking the Google oracle: *what does it truly mean to be narcissist free?*

To me, it means the war is my mind is finally over. It's the end of battling the narcissist's influence on my thoughts, feelings and behavior. I'm happy to report that part of the war is over for me. DONE. Narcissists no longer have any influence on me. Well... except for pissing me off. And I am well aware that narcissists will always exist, they are out there and they are numerous, and there's a part of me that humbly accepts that I will always be vulnerable. The only thing I can do, that any of us can do, is know the enemy and know thyself. And while you're at it, throw loads of love at yourself and NEVER love anyone that can't love you back.

COMMENTS:

Growing up within these NFOO Regimes guarantees we lack confidence in ourselves/perceptions and most certainly have endured consistent violations of every conceivable personal boundary. Trying to launch into the Adult World without the most basic template or model for healthy, appropriate relationships becomes IMO a set-up for failure simply because we don't have any reference point for such.

Based on life experience, I can say that everything in this post is true, even down to a point of wondering what was wrong with me. Sometimes I felt as if I had a stamp on back that said, "Calling all Ns! Come shaft me up the ass with no lube and I won't say a word!" The fact of the matter is that I continue to be a magnet for disordered people because I put up with more shit than a normal person would.

It took me 40 years and my brother's suicide to "SEE" that my mother was gratified by our pain.

This post resonated with me so much! Just a few days ago, I thought of how my Narcissistic Malignant Mother trained me to be prey to the world out there. She really did me a disfavor, and turned me into a defenseless adult. But I couldn't put my feelings into words, and you, Lisette, have come along and put in writing how I was feeling but couldn't express.

I cried a little (crying is very difficult for me).when I read the article, especially about the loneliness. In my youth I always felt very alone and have never understood that, until recently that is.

Yes, we are absolutely set up to be preyed upon by additional N Predators which has its genesis within NFOO Family dynamics: Any attempts to differentiate or exhibit autonomy within the strangling confines of an NFOO are met with frenzied resistance in view of their threat to the stable instability of these Family Systems aka, the NFOO Regime.

Thanks MN "parents" for shoving me out into the world a fucking target.

This is true without question. I know for a fact that the severe abuse and neglect I suffered as a child was simply a ploy to make sure I was constantly desperate and vulnerable. My MN parents fed off me for 21 years by depriving me of the things I needed to survive: love, safety and companionship. I was lonely, isolated, starved for attention, battered, brainwashed and suffered persistent and systematic violence. For so long I was stuck in the details, but now I know those things were nothing but a means to an end - to ensure I remained vulnerable and totally without defenses. It took me 21 years to get away, but I have never been back. Any visits/phone calls/emails just kept reminding me of why I needed to leave in the first place. Now I know NO CONTACT is the way to health and recovery. Thank you for giving a name for what was an extremely distressing and traumatising 21 years for me.

And The Award For Most Annoying Comment Goes To...

Last night I was watching the television show *Enlightened*. It stars Laura Dern as Amy Jellicoe, a 40 something woman who works for a pharmaceutical company, lives the corporate high-life, has a bit of a substance abuse problem, experiences a melt-down and ends up in a new agey type treatment centre in Hawaii. During her stay, she has a "spiritual awakening" and becomes determined to live an "enlightened" life. She returns to home and work and in her *desperate* quest for "enlightenment" she creates havoc, and annoys the living shit out of everyone in her vicinity.

The episode I saw last night was brilliant. It was directed by Jonathan Demme and guest starred Robin Wright as Sandy, a yoga instructor, and friend of Amy's from the treatment centre.

"It turns out Sandy has become something of a healer since her own breakdown, which was caused by a long time, high-stress job as a government speechwriter. Now Sandy has that lovely, subtly bronzed glow

159

of the truly at peace, or just comparatively at peace. But Amy isn't at all knocked down when Sandy swans in with advice on low-acid diets and a knack for getting reticent, repressed types like Amy's mom and Levi to open up to her, seeming so ahead in the recovery process, somehow better at it. But there are hints of strain, tremors from below, from the very start of the episode." (From nymag.com)

Although there are clues along the way, we find out at the end of the episode that Sandy is something of a fraud. Or. At the very least a deluded flake.

After watching *Enlightened* and the "Sandy" episode "*Let it Go*" it was time for bed. But before I turned off the lights, I checked my Blog for comments, and ironically found this little doozy. My first thought upon reading it was: Hmmm. This person has been sipping on the old Kool-Aid, and is insulting me and all ACONs. I decided not to post it as a comment, but blog post it instead, let it percolate with readers, and then perhaps dissect it line-by-line.

Or....

Let it go... (insert eye-roll here).

Annoying Anonymous said...

Lisette, thank you for all the work you've put into this blog. It both breaks my heart, yet it also grounds me to remember the distance I've travelled in my own desperate search for validation and visibility to myself as a result of my malignant narcissist mother and hatred of us, her children.

She infected one of my sisters - this sister has now become a carbon copy of her. But my word of warning is this, after your rage and justified need to explode - you must let go. Of them, of the hate of them and start to lead a self-loving life of LOVE. Let me tell you why - malignant narcissists are the children of... yes, malignant narcissists. My mother was cruelly abused by her own mother, it's a cycle. My sister is now my mother.

If we've been brought up in abuse we will have shades of it in our OWN characters. We have to face this and fight it. Not with hate but with love.

160

You talk about feeding them but you must remember they are fed by ANY attention, of any quality. In fact, they get as much of a 'kick' when you hate them as when you love them. Because you're holding hate in your heart (even if it is of her) is a wonderful sign of weakness to her because she knows that can self-damage.

Hate damages you and they know this, they are HAPPY to be hated. And they are as happy, though contemptuous, to be loved. It all spells your destruction. The only thing that reduces them is being ignored - whilst you lead a gentle, loving, happy life without thinking of them.

So though this blog does a wonderful service, and honestly, thank you again, at some point you must save yourself and leave it to rejoin a world of peace and fun, and love and joy where you are not hating anyone or getting vengeance on anyone but where you are (what they can never be), free.

Good luck sweetie and all other survivors. We can do it and 'do it' means loving life again, re-establishing a spiritual belief in 'Good' however you name it, and letting go COMPLETELY both externally and internally of evil, and that includes THEM and you let go by keeping your focus on good, writing about good, talking about good, loving a man/woman who is good, working on projects that help the world and saying to yourself, 'I matter, my happiness matters, this is my world too and it provides me with happiness.'

You reduce them, by recognizing that you are a good person who is happy and who does not mix in evil company. It is the way I 'killed' my family in my heart, they have no power now because I neither love nor hate them. Pretend you are in a science fiction film and your family who you once loved has been infected by the evil aliens, you pour over the 'evaporation' powder and they disappear in a circle of light. Do this. I evaporated them.

I changed all my numbers, changed address and disappeared from their lives. My focus is on all the fun and exciting and sweet things going on in my beautiful life which I created through determined focus.

never stop believing you are good and kind and hate cannot live in you like it lived in them, don't make a comfortable environment for hate in your body, mind or soul* If you are still attracting narcissists you must work hard on yourself to saturate your body, mind and soul with love and light.

Do affirmations constantly, focus only on good, become clear about where you need to monitor your own problematic behaviour etc. once you wake up and realize most of your friends and people in your life are balanced, ok people, and that you haven't felt that type of powerless rage you used to feel then forever then YAY!! you've arrived back in the normal world. Welcome back, you have earned it! xoxo.

Comments:

There's only one thing to say to people such as this commenter, and that's "Fuck off".

Bullshit. This whole comment amounts to "try to erase your feelings and only feel good!" - Thanks for nothing, asshole.

That sounds like it was written by an 8 legged sea creature.

I don't even know where to start with this one!

By the time I hit the words "you must let go" I was in an uproar.

"We're such ungrateful wretches for not recognizing what a HELPFUL approach she's got here - bathe yourself in light, it's just the cleanse you need!" Exactly! Why aren't we more grateful for the fact that he/she/it took the time to float down here to bless us mere mortals with so many helpful and oh-so cleansing pointers?

I have always despised the company of militant positive thinkers-- and I felt this revulsion for them long before I began to understand the reasons for my revulsion.

162

Please, grab yo pointy tin-foil hat and send those "Evaporating" rays my way.

Unsolicited advice is an act of aggression. It's a passive-aggressive way to blame the victim and judge them from a position of above.

It's about the condescending way she swooped in, and offered un-asked-for advice. It's the way she elected herself--it's in her tone, her patronizing word choices, and her imperatives--as the one with the secret, the key, the right way to think and feel about injustice.

It's seems that in a contest of two different realities, the reality with the most practiced denial wins! Which explains why victims themselves often give in, and join the ranks of those who would tell them to just shut up. When a victim violates his/her own reality with denial, at least there's an illusion of safety, strength, agency, choice, etc. The trouble comes when they go around prescribing and/or enforcing the same "cure" for others.

A big f@ck you to every single d!ckhead who told me "Come on leave this all behind you now" as the first reaction I was served after revealing that my mother is a psychopathic freak of nature that mentally played me for 30 straight years and meticulously programmed me into committing suicide for an entire life. And once I wake up and I am a shell of a person this is what I get... "just let it go". Well, JUST f@ck the hell off morons.

"Just let it go." God, I hate that. I will never stop hating that phrase. It's the verbal equivalent of ripping out stitches on a fresh wound and expecting it to heal faster and without a scar. I wonder if these fuckheads would expect broken bones to "HEAL NOW". I run like hell when I come across a "just let it go" person. What makes these people qualified to judge how we should respond to our own pain? Uttering those dismissive platitudes is proof positive they haven't a clue and should shut the fuck up. Anyone who lets those words fly out of their mouth needs to be humbled by a learning experience so severe they end up with no choice but to understand.

"Just let it go" = "Shut-up! Go away! You're making MEEE uncomfortable!"

Think about being brought home from birth by one of these people. That every single thing you learned and every adaptation you made to fit in the world for at least 18 years if not more was you bending your psyche around one of these narcissist freaks. We do not remember a time when they were not in our ears and heads telling us how to think and what to feel and who's the boss and why it is the way it is. Literally every single thing about us from the ground up was downloaded into our heads by one of these freaks.

We're damned no matter what. People think we are either pussies whining that our mommies and daddies didn't love us enough, or if your parents are crazy like make it into the news crazy, they look at us like we are sprouting a second head. So I don't go there. Not in real life.

Gawd. I love being around people that "get it."

Can we all be friends with benefits for a few years and work our way up???

Hey, this isn't Match.com

Breaking Free - Part 2

There are only two mistakes one can make along the road to truth;
not going all the way, and not starting. --- Buddha

I was raised in captivity by narcissists and because of my upbringing and
ACON status I have incredibly low standards when it comes to
interpersonal relationships. More accurately, I "had" incredibly low
standards and zero expectations when it came to the people in my life.

I am happy to report that all changed once I learned about narcissistic
abuse and received validation of my perceptions and experiences from
fellow adult children. The self-blame, shame, self-loathing and belief that
there was something inherently wrong with me evaporated almost
instantly once I realized the truth about my parents and sibling and all the
"others."

But before I get to my new perspective, I would like to share a little bit
about my old perspective and the filter of distortion from which I viewed
myself and the world around me.

The message that was delivered to me on an almost daily basis growing-up was: "You are worthless! You don't matter! WE DON'T CARE ABOUT YOU! YOU HAVE NO RIGHT TO LIVE!""

Being human, I longed to be loved and accepted by my "family." Unfortunately, you can't squeeze blood out of a stone, but that didn't stop me from trying. I did what I needed to do within that prison camp to not only survive, but to receive even just a smidgen of something other than contempt. I played the sycophant to all the narcissists' demanding Diva roles. I offered-up myself as a form of narcissistic supply tailored specifically to meet the needs of each narcissist.

For example, to my dad (the lesser narc) I adored, admired him, complimented him and carefully monitored his moods, gestures and every breath so I could predict in advance what kind of narc supply would be the most soothing to him. I remember being no older than 5 years old and rushing out the door when I heard his car pull-up the driveway. I ran to him like some faithful foot servant and begged to carry his case of beer into the house. I was 5 and there I was lugging a case of beer – a 12 pack of bottles! I guess he felt he was doing me some great favour by allowing me the pleasure to be his mini Sherpa. I remember one time I dropped the case of beer and SMASH, glass everywhere and his precious nectar went streaming down the walkway like a river. I was scared shitless, but truth be told, he wasn't mad. After all, he was the lesser narc and it gave him an excuse to take off again and buy more beer.

As a young girl, and even into my teens, I used to inspect my dad each night to make sure he was alive. He passed out nightly in a chair and being a child I thought he might be dead. Like a forensic examiner I would observe his corpse, poke it with a ruler and wait for him to breathe really loud or snore. Only when I witnessed some sign of life could I relax enough for bed. When I hit my teens, I knew my dad was dead drunk, but I still needed to hear him breathe before I could fall asleep. Old habits die hard. My dad checked-out of his life when I was quite young, and I would describe him as an enabler of my malignant narcissist mother and malignant narcissist sister and their tag team bullying and abuse of me. Being completely self-absorbed, numbed-out, not present, and turning a

166

blind eye to my suffering made his life easier. And being a narcissist, his needs always came first. His emotional needs took priority over his child's need to feel safe, loved and cared for.

The malignant narcissist mother demanded a different form of supply. She used me as a source to feed on - my misery, my pain, my fear, my embarrassment, my shame, my humiliation, my misfortune, my disappointment, loss and insecurities – that she caused! When she wasn't using me to slake her sadistic lust, she was callously indifferent to me. I recognized at a very young age that the woman was evil and I have not seen her in over 26 years. Unfortunately, this early detection and realization that any contact with her was detrimental did absolutely nothing to stop her emotional and psychological abuse from taking hold inside me. The predator had unrestricted access to me when I was a clean slate and she went in for the kill and caused a lot of damage that needed to be undone.

The greedy malignant narcissist older sister required an all you can stuff down your gullet banquet table of narcissistic supply. Including a combo platter of the worst cruelties she witnessed MN mother inflict on me and the myriad of exploitations N father extracted from me, along with a feed that was uniquely her own as the golden child. Unbeknownst to me, she harboured malicious envy toward me and used me as a measuring stick to gage how she felt about herself. She placed me as her competitor in a covert war where she had to win at all costs and get it all. And being a malignant narcissist/sociopath, at a very young age she was highly skilled at mind control and manipulation. What this meant was that she had both N parents in her back pocket and always had the upper hand. In other words, she always got her way.

What's more, the malignant narcissist sister grew-up believing that life is a zero-sum game and in order for her to win someone else has to lose – that meant me. In many ways she controlled the entire family system. Keep MN mother's Franken daughter happy then the MN mother isn't so nasty, when the MN mother isn't so nasty then N father isn't so angry.

My brother, being the youngest and the only boy knew what side his bread was buttered. He knew that it was to his advantage to stay on the good side of the mother/daughter demonic duo. Like my dad, he went along to get along and in doing so he saved his own skin. My brother was never sadistically abused by my mother. She doted on him or was callously indifferent to him.

I would describe MN mother's treatment of me as sadism peppered with callous indifference (neglect). I would describe N dad's treatment of me as callous indifference sprinkled with a streak of sadism. I would describe the MN sister's treatment of me as a combination of both parent's abuse mixed with extreme hostility, malicious envy and an irrational desire to either triumph over me or eliminate me altogether.

To add insult to the injury of my abusive upbringing, when I was a teenager my parents decided to get a divorce and once they signed the separation papers they both disappeared. The "dream house" that my dad had built and we lived in for only a couple of years was abandoned by both narc parents. Notice how I didn't say they abandoned their children? That's because they made it utterly clear that money and property and possessions were far more valuable than their own flesh and blood, so it's kind of shocking that they both walked away from a piece of property. I guess their contempt for their "family" outweighed their love of real estate.

The kids were left in the house and the parents were nowhere to be found.

My mom exited stage left, my dad stage right. I guess since they were divorcing the show was over. The narc parents brought their performance to an abrupt close, ended the "family" act and stormed off stage in a huff leaving the set and the props behind. The props – their children – came in handy when they used us as pawns in their almost 2 year war over the house.

So, just as I was getting ready to graduate from high school and launch into the world an adult and begin my future, the narcissist parents let me know in no uncertain terms – YOU MEAN NOTHING! WE DON'T CARE ABOUT YOU!

They are still pulling this shit in their old age with wills and power of attorney and inheritances and so on. Narcissist parents will never stop demonstrating their contempt for their children and they often plot and scheme to create situations that do the most lasting damage from beyond the grave. I can only image the drama they will create on their way out. The MN sister has taken it upon herself to be writer, producer and director of their final performance so no doubt it will be a horror show with one hell of a blood bath as the grand finale.

Given the fact that I was raised under the destructive influence of narcissists and morphed into narc supply in order to survive, it's probably easy to understand why I had incredibly low standards when it came to relationships, and why I attracted so many narcissists into my life.

No wonder I literally pulled-out my hair and suffered from bouts of depression and anxiety and sought refuge in isolation – I was surrounded by people who were feeding off me and my body was set to permanent fight or flight mode! Believe me; these narcissists do not have to be overtly abusive to suck the life out of you. Indifference is a slow, silent, soul crushing kill.

I believe I speak for most ACONs when I say narcissistic abuse doesn't just cut, it burrows in deep and lays egg. Then the eggs hatch. It's a constant battle, a lifelong battle to contain the outbreak and keep on functioning. But sooner or later you get tired of fighting just to stay one step ahead of the infestation that grows in your heart, your mind and your body and soul. And experience has shown me that you can't take narcissistic abuse and pack it away in a neat little box and just forget about it. The box turns into a jack-in-the-box and that crazy, deranged joker with a wire neck is going to spring-out at you when you least expect it. Sometimes the only way to avoid the traumatic shock of the "narc- in-the-box" is to live in complete denial of its existence. I will tell you right now, the illusion of safety in denial = captivity. Truth is the only exit route out of narcissistic abuse.

When I was in my early 20s, and even though I lived far away from the narcissists, I was still plagued by the devastating effects of their brainwashing and abuse. I knew on an intellectual level that they didn't care about me, but what I couldn't wrap my brain around was why they wanted to systematically destroy me. By the time I was in my mid-20s to early 30s, and even though I was no contact at that point, I had checked-out of my body and was living in a really deep fog. I was not present in my life at all. I used to go on long walks and would repeat over and over in my mind, "Why did they want to systematically destroy me? Why DO they want to systematically destroy me? What did I ever do to them?"

When I learned about narcissistic abuse, I discovered that other adult children of narcissists were giving voice to the exact thoughts I believed I alone suffered. I realized other ACONs had lived and survived this very real phenomenon of having parents and siblings and other so-called family members that sought to destroy them. I can't even put into the words the relief I felt when I recognized that I was not alone. The burden I carried fell away. My lens of distortion came into focus. I was lifted-up and carried out of the prison of oppression by those who found freedom in the truth.

The truth can honestly set you free. That is why when it comes to malignant narcissism it is so important to have a death grip on reality. You must let go of denial. You must grab the gift of truth when it's offered and hold-on tight. You need to understand the true spirit of the malignant narcissist and believe it to be true! It's total darkness and it's not natural. Narcissistic abuse is an abuse steeped in a desire to destroy another. That death grip on reality will keep you alive because it will stop you from ever going near someone who seeks to annihilate you.

Before I discovered narcissistic personality disorder and a world full of ACONs, I did everything out there to try and fix what the narcissists brainwashed me into believing was the problem – me!

I wasn't just programmed to believe that I wasn't good enough; I was programmed to believe that I wasn't enough, period. So I read every book out there on co-dependency and relationships and I saw shrinks, psychologists and counsellors, and I attended AL-ANON and ACOA thinking that my dad's drinking made me a problem. I even shelled-out over $2,000 to attend a week long group session for people with loved ones with addictions. What a joke! By the time I did that I had no loved ones. No family. When my parents divorced they obliterated the family. If they weren't going to have one, no one else was going to have one. By the time I was 18, I was completely on my own. All this searching for answers and misguided attempts at some kind of resolution of my abusive upbringing was exhausting, frustrating and disappointing.

I continued to go on with my life. I continued to stay away from the narcissists. I hit almost 20 years of no contact, but I still couldn't dodge the monkey on my back; that thing that made my world view so bleak, but that I couldn't quite put my finger on.

Eventually I googled the word narcissist. My life changed after that. Whatever depression I occasionally suffered from disappeared for good – GONE. I think it's because I was no longer ashamed to be me. You see, there I was trying to fix me – the problem – so the original narcissists and all those that followed would love me. But here's the kicker, the narcissists would never love me no matter who I was or what I did or how much supply I had to feed them. The truth of the matter was that when it came to creatures like the MN mother and MN sister, the "problem" was that I *existed*. They craved my total annihilation, and since I kept on living they worked like hell to rub me out in other ways. They erased any memory of me in an effort to obliterate my existence and they continue to control a system that is designed to marginalize me.

I admit it's not an easy concept to grasp that your parent(s) and/or sibling(s) – your "family" – could be evil. In fact it's downright spooky, but once I came to this realization and once I had that death grip on reality, it took me to a whole new level of understanding about malignant narcissists and how they operate to achieve their end goals.

In this part of the book, I go darker and dig deeper into the mindset of the malignant narcissist. Expressing what I have lived through and what I imagine to be true about malignant narcissists has at times been a little daunting. Only because some of the stunts they pull can be stranger than fiction and scarier than a Stephen King novel and there's a fear that I won't be believed or I will come off as some crank – I'm not crazy, I'm not paranoid, I'm experienced! Ultimately, writing on this dark subject has proven to be very cathartic because I have spoken my truth and received validation from other survivors – and you can too!

We adult children understand each other's struggles and nothing really surprises us. We are the ones that lived it because we had no choice. So we really don't need to convince each other. But sharing our experiences is liberating and sends us on the path to freedom!

There is no greater agony than bearing an untold story inside you --- Maya Angelou

So to recap: my whole internal and external point of view shifted when I learned the truth about malignant narcissism and gained clarity. I didn't have to do anything but read it, learn it, understand it, accept it, believe it, talk it and live it, and never forget it. Rinse and repeat. That's all you have to do. Read the book. Let it sink-in deep to the core of your being and then let your own process take over. *Breaking Free: A Way Out for Adult Children of Narcissists* will never let you forget it!

Looking back there were times in my life when I should have been on top of the world – I was in great health, had an awesome job, a killer penthouse condo, money in the bank, cool friends and a hot boyfriend. But I wasn't on top of the world because I was ashamed to be alive and I was still surrounded by exploitative narcissists. I don't want to sound like some loser because who wants to buy a book written by a loser, but right now I have nothing in the material sense and I have had one set back after the other, but I feel good about myself. I feel good about who I am.

You want to know why? Because the oppression I was under has lifted and I no longer bear the burden of shame. Shame is not a feeling; it's a state of being. It's oppression. And it's the prison of oppression that the narcissists want to lock you in for a life sentence.

Know this: They will try and do whatever it takes to keep you down, and sometimes they may even succeed, but if you understand what you are dealing with, when you truly understand the narcissist's designs on your life and live in truth and reality, they can only get to you on a surface level not that deep level within that really matters.

When you reconnect with your self – the person you really are inside and the person you are meant to be – and you scrap the pack of lies the narcissists brainwashed you into believing in order to disempower you – they cannot fuck with the YOU in you!

I currently have a pack of narcissists circling me and pointing their talons at me and labelling me the "problem." Yeah, it's a HUGE "problem" to the narcissists when you expose them and burn all their dirty little secrets and lies down to the ground. But if I didn't know about narcissistic personality disorder, I just might believe their outrageous projections. Hell, if I didn't know about NPD I would be a brainwashed shell of a person playing by their rules. Fuck that!

The truth about malignant narcissism is not for pussies. The truth is ugly and disturbing. The truth hurts. The truth is difficult to accept. What other platitude can I come up with? The truth DOES set you free.

Facing and accepting the truth, living in reality and having clarity are what you need to unlock the prison door and break free of narcissistic abuse.

Truth + Reality = Clarity

Clarity = Liberation

It's that simple.

You owe it to yourself to believe it's that simple.

You hold the key to your freedom.

See you on the outside!

Lisette

MALIGNANT NARCISSISTS ARE MORALLY INSANE

Shameless, callous, selfish, evil, murderous, insane, death - this is a real 'feel good' book. Maybe I should slip in a brownie recipe, or pictures of kittens to lighten the mood – NOT.

It is the intent of this book to shine the light of scrutiny on malignant narcissists: those who practice the black art of soul murder. It's a heavy subject. Malignant narcissists are numerous, and they are everywhere. There's no safety in denying that there is an invisible war for souls going on. Ignorance is bliss until a narcissist happens to you. We must get familiar with how they operate; slap them down on a cold metal slab; take a scalpel to them; pry them open and examine all their parts. I want to study their moves; discern their patterns and cut them off at the pass. Predictability means loss for them. Self -preservation is priority number one.

Narcissists are embarrassingly successful because of a universal human phobia and indifference to the existence of evil. I don't share that phobia. I recognize the dark side of human nature. I faced it, and looked it in the eye even before I could walk and talk. I am well aware of how dangerous it is to have a malignant narcissist(s) in one's sphere of influence – it's the stuff of thrillers. I have been at the receiving end of gaslighting so diabolical and post-abuse cover-up so Machiavellian it was stranger than fiction. And, there is no doubt in my mind that the malignant narcissist's paranoid fear of exposure makes them entirely capable of murder.

Am I angry? You bet I am. I cherish my anger; it's an energy that has kept me alive and motivated me to fight the good fight of a life filled with a constant threat to my very being. Though I've reached indifference - for the most part - with the malignant narcissists that have infected my life, I will always be passionately outraged not only at the narcissist's carefree existence as a 'species' but by the fact that we continually allow them to get away with their crimes, and often even collude with them. All hell must be laughing at us. When will the human race ever learn? The only form of accessible justice that I see – as a survivor of soul murder – is to use words like flaming arrows and burn all their secrets and lies down to the ground. The pen is mightier than the sword.

Narcissists are unsafe and it is not only stupid, but extremely dangerous to be in denial of that fact. Narcissists are *morally* insane not *legally* insane. Narcissists are by choice morally debauched, irresponsible, negligent, reckless and irrational. They deliberately choose to hurt others because they like it. They know that what they are doing is wrong, but they choose to do it anyway because it's a cheap and easy high – and a legal one to boot. They are not the victims of a 'disease' or an 'emotional handicap' who just can't help themselves. They are not at the mercy of their pathology or at the whim of their disorder; though they sure would have us believe it. There is no safety in feeling sorry for narcissists but that is *exactly* what they want.

In her book *The Sociopath Next Door*, Martha Stout, Ph.D. writes about a psychopath she interviewed. She asked him, "What is important to you in your life? What do you want more than anything else?" The man replied,

"Oh that's easy: What I like better than anything else is when people feel sorry for me. The thing I really want more than anything else out of life is people's pity." --- page 107

Thing rings absolutely true for me given what I experienced growing-up in a home with three full-blown narcissists. The underlying feeling that I had for my abusers, more than anything else, was pity. I felt sorry for them. I won't go in to the sordid details of each of their pitiful existences or how they capitalized on the 'pity play' and the sympathy they elicited from me. Sufficed to say it is the feeling of pity that disarmed me and blinded me to the fact that they were deliberately out to exploit me and destroy me.

Never EVER feel sorry for someone who intentionally inflicts harm. Being trained to feel sorry for a bunch of narcissists who abused me was one of the most dangerous aspects of narcissistic abuse. It set me up to not only accept bad behavior in all people but to sympathize and make excuses for them.

Healthy individuals do not want to be pitied – ever. Validated and understood? – Yes. But pitied? Hell no! Yet the devious narcissists want us to feel sorry for them all the time! Why? So we will assign a lower set of standards to them. They refuse to live by *sane* rules of common human decency because *they* are *morally insane* and their depravity clashes with normal human principles of right and wrong. Narcissists demand that we debase our value system in order to fit *their* agenda and that we give them free reign to slither around in this world without ever being held accountable. And guess what? We do it. We gratuitously enable their pathology.

How insane is that?

COMMENTS:

This post gave me an uneasy feeling about a close family member, one whom I still need to watch out for. The fact is we must always be on guard and take precautions of various kinds. Good post.

I am very grateful for your wonderfully insightful articles! I was raised by two alcoholic, physically and emotionally abusive narcissistic parents. They ruined all 5 of their children's lives, and still continue to do so into their elderly years. Our horrible childhoods were hard, but it made us made better parents for living through it!

If we can survive their destructive influence, and learn from their horrifyingly bad example then we can make it stop with us.

Thank you for this excellent insight because pity is exactly what always draws me back to the MN and it is very helpful to know that pity is unwarranted and just a ploy they use.

I can't believe that for my whole life I was gaslighted and called selfish and broken and was sadistically teased and manipulated AND I was made to carry around MN's sad childhood and feel sorry for her!

These MN "Parents" revel in throwing their own Projections all over their kids whom they've thrown under the bus throughout the adult child's life. And while they're reviling the AC, they're simultaneously inviting all the bystanders/minions to fete them at their "Pity Party:" After all, they must suck up all the available Attention, poor bay-bees, whether they're 7 or 70. A 7 yr. old seeking attention is a typical 7 yr. old. A 70 yr. old MN is engaging in this behavior with entirely different motivations and entirely without hope of ever out-growing this Stage of Development.

MN Perpetrators are pros at presenting themselves as "Victims" while the REAL victims are the kids they brought into this world for a bunch of (nefarious) reasons, none of which have anything remotely to do with truly wanting or loving this unique human being, their child. Once that child can't be played with like a doll, they'll spend the rest of their lives ripping that doll/child's head off, sticking it on a shelf or discarding it once it no longer "works" or they procured a "newer, shinier" more malleable toy.

The "turn the other cheek" and "forgiveness is best" mindsets are dangerous ones designed to keep avenues open for predatory attacks.

People have been brainwashed into thinking that we need to be sympathetic and nice to the narcs because they have a "disorder and need help." I have no sympathy for them.

It must be exhausting to work so hard at not being human.

I wouldn't put anything past these vile creatures, who reap death and destruction wherever they go.

I have no pity for them. Why? Because they know the difference between right and wrong, yet choose to do what feels good at that moment in time regardless of anything else. How do I know? Because I've seen my own mother behave different ways in front of different people. If she didn't know whatever she was doing was wrong, her behavior would be consistent regardless of who was around. She committed crimes, yet knew enough to cover them up. Did that bother her? Nope. That bitch was able to pass a polygraph test without batting an eyelash, only to come back and brag about it later.

Exposing The Malignant Narcissist

A malignant narcissist mother murders her child and runs free. This is what we're up against folks: a denial of the reality that a "mother" could kill her child simply to rid herself of the inconvenience. A denial of the reality that a malignant narcissist mother's greatest "triumph" would be to get away with murdering her child. A denial of the cold, calculating cunning of a malignant narcissist mother who feigned love for her daughter when there were witnesses, and murdered her on the sly. A DENIAL of the existence of EVIL.

The only thing stopping the malignant narcissist's extreme treachery is what she thinks she can get away with. Casey Anthony thought she could get away with murder. And she did. It was the "role" of "mother" that gave her the *power* to take her child's life, and it was the "cloak" of "motherhood" that allowed her to get away with her crime.

Annihilating others is essential to the malignant narcissist if they are to continue to feel superior. Public condemnation, affirmation and notoriety give them the attention they crave: being feared, despised or pitied affirms that they exist as "somebody." So what of the Blogs on the evil of malignant narcissists? Are they a form of public condemnation? Are they a form of public notoriety that allows the narcissist to exist as "somebody"? Are they a form of attention that the narcissist can exploit for their own gratification? What do narcissists think about Blogs on narcissism? Are they getting a power rush from being feared, despised, or in some cases pitied?

About a year after I made *final* contact with malignant narcissist sister – after 17 years of no contact – I discovered malignant narcissism by way of the internet. My brief run-in with malignant narcissist sister and the receipt of the second Ann Landers "Suicide Suggestion" from MN mother made it very clear that they were seriously disturbed and beyond redemption. Malignant narcissism squared with what I knew of their pathology. I finally had a label for their diabolical evil.

To say that I was obsessed with the information on malignant narcissism would be an understatement. I couldn't devour enough of the stuff. I relished the knowledge yet was incensed by it. I had to come to terms with the very real fact that most of my relationships were absolute lies. The people in my life, who I thought may have cared about me in some way, actually didn't care for me at all. It was *always* about them. I had been surrounded by narcissists. I had never been cared for, protected or genuinely loved.

I never once doubted that my family didn't care about me. I accepted that fact in my early twenties. What I had to come to terms with is that all the other people were just like my family. Not a hard concept to grasp, but a hard reality to accept because they didn't seem *as* bad. During this tumultuous period, I phoned up malignant narcissist mother – the first time in almost 20 years - and called her a malignant narcissist and hung-up. After enduring a lifetime of her systematic destruction, including the recent Ann Landers "Suicide Suggestion," I figured she was getting off easy by receiving one angry missive from me over the phone. I felt no guilt. No regrets. It never paid to treat a non-human humanely. Besides, I had already endured over a decade of her telephone terrorism. Minding my own business at the other end of the country, and completely out of the blue, I would pick-up the phone to hear her screaming at me. I never knew what she was raging about and I would say nothing and hang-up.

I spent most of my narcissism research on two very popular blogs. I read, and read, and read. One day I decided to make a very general comment, but did so anonymously. I continued to absorb the information and made the occasional anonymous comment. One time a comment appeared on one of the blogs and it gave me the creeps. It was clearly written by a narcissist and the tone made me think it was my sister. But I brushed if off as being paranoid. Nah! She wouldn't stalk me. Besides, it would take her forever to track me down. She couldn't be that deranged. Or, could she?

Months went by and I continued with my Blog obsession but a creepy feeling persisted. I couldn't put my finger on it, but I felt her presence. It turns out both malignant narcissist sister and MN mother cyberstalked and gaslighted me online for over a YEAR. I caught them because they are predators. As I became more personal in my comments, I made the grave mistake of revealing that I was both physically and psychologically vulnerable because I was being gaslighted by a malignant narcissist couple in my building and recovering from a traumatizing accident that resulted in surgery. It was precisely at that point that malignant narcissist sister and mother came out of the shadows and ferociously attacked and flamed me. They also made bizarre comments that were absurd exaggerations of abuse that I suffered at their hands. The comments before that point, which I later pinpointed as theirs, were incredibly subtle by comparison. It was a terrifying ordeal. I avoided Blogs on Narcissists for over two years, but not before I left some very obvious comments on the blogs directed at MN mother and sister and their sick little game.

At the time of the online attack, I was too fragile to defend myself with any force. I was also confused and disoriented because I had been gaslighted for over a year and was under extreme duress. Malignant narcissist sister and mother simply saw their prey as irresistibly vulnerable and their fangs came-out. They proved themselves to be exactly what I was writing about: they are outrageously cruel and vicious PREDATORS.

The yearlong cyberstalking that I endured at the hands of my malicious malignant narcissist mother and malignant narcissist sister placed me at risk of physical harm. I hold them in part responsible for my accident. I hold them fully responsible for emotionally traumatizing me and causing my psychological injury that resulted in a hospital stay and post-traumatic stress. As the shocking revelation of them hunting me online and violently attacking me when they knew I was under extreme duress, coupled with the trauma of my accident and the trauma of surgery, as well as the distress of being targeted by a geriatric malignant narcissist couple in my building (living onsite building managers) all led to psychological injury.

My sister *predictably* colluded with the malignant narcissist bullies in my building and the depraved MN couple were later charged with "harassment," "intimidation," and "violation of privacy" and ordered to pay me financial damages. MN sister and the female MN building manager are both COVETOUS malignant narcissists and violent predators that discovered a bond in their mutual desire to destroy and silence me. Birds of a feather.

So there was over a year long period in my life where I was stalked and gaslighted online by two malignant narcissists, and stalked and gaslighted in real life by two malignant narcissists. Oh boy, do I have stories. I haven't even begun to scratch the surface of the ordeal. The whole experience was stranger than fiction and scarier than any Stephen King novel. The post abuse cover-up by ALL the malignant narcissists was truly Machiavellian and worthy of a thriller. You couldn't make this stuff up. I sometimes am amazed that I survived the post-traumatic stress. But that's the thing about malignant narcissists; they target the strong ones that cast the bright light of truth on their dark deception.

When I was discharged from the hospital – completely traumatized – the malignant narcissist sister called me up screaming (just like mommy dearest). Her mask of sanity crashed to the ground as she unleashed her rage and fury on me. Right then, I knew she was *insanely* evil. She terrified me AGAIN.

It should be noted: I never confronted MN sister about her cyberstalking. I simply observed her behaviour as I did the MN couple and I documented everything (even in a state of trauma). The evidence I gathered proved my suspicions absolutely dead on. Plus, her resulting reaction to me being in the hospital for trauma (accident, surgery, stress) cinched the deal. She had no reaction to my pain and suffering and hospitalization, the only reaction she had was to me writing comments on blogs about *her* and *her* mother's malignant narcissism. She screamed, and I quote:

"HAVE YOU HIT ROCK BOTTOM LISETTE?! HAVE YOU HIT ROCK BOTTOM?! WHY DO YOU EXPECT ME TO ACT A CERTAIN WAY?! WHY CAN'T YOU JUST BE COMPLAISANT?!"

Now isn't it odd to scream that at someone who has been hospitalized for trauma resulting from an accident and injury? You see, I knew what she had done online, but the delusional bitch still thought she had pulled a fast one on me.

Malignant narcissist sister's concealed reaction to Blogs on narcissism and all the information she read on them about MNs as well as personal comments of other's experiences, including mine, was this:

"HAVE YOU HIT ROCK BOTTOM?!

Translation: Now that you've gotten a taste of my wrath and I've succeeded in terrifying you, emotionally brutalizing you, and traumatizing you psychologically are you going to stop writing on those Blogs!? Because if you ever write on those Blogs again, I will destroy you completely! There will be nothing left of you! You won't make it to the hospital!

In the narcissist's twisted mind, when the victim of their abuse claims their voice and speaks out, the victim has a problem. By writing on a Blog about narcissism we have "HIT ROCK BOTTOM!" There is something wrong with us. We are being uncooperative. We are being unreasonable. We are being unstable. We are challenging the narcissist's omnipotence so we must be destroyed. We must be silenced by any means possible. And when we collapse under the strain of their unrelenting sadism, to the point of hospitalization, we have "HIT ROCK BOTTOM!" I wonder if my 20 year recurring trauma nightmare where my jaw is locked shut and I can't shout for help is symbolic?

Malignant narcissist sister and mother would *never* see their cyberpathy as hitting rock bottom. Not at all. The narcissist would never see anything wrong with their sadistic online theatrics, spying, stalking, gaslighting, attacking, toying, tricking, traumatizing, degrading and humiliating their already hurting and vulnerable sister and daughter. Talk about rock bottom. The narcissist has none. They are not only shameless, they are mentally deranged. MN sister actually wrote a comment on the Blog where she said she didn't believe in revenge. Her hypocrisy knows no bounds.

As far as I'm concerned, psychologically terrorizing and emotionally traumatizing someone is no less violent than trying to murder them. By trying to destroy someone by gaslighting them for over a YEAR, and causing their psychological injury, you kill that person just as surely if you shot them dead. But it is far more cruel than shooting someone dead. It is evil. And it is no different than MN mother sending me that "Suicide Suggestion," or the time that MN sister tried to murder me as a kid. The only reason I survived is because the oncoming car that she trapped me in front of came to a screeching halt. She felt no remorse, no guilt. But she sure felt righteous indignation when her plan to kill was foiled. My parents never learned of the incident. They wouldn't have cared, and they would have dismissed it. My sister is a "Bad Seed" who thrived in a "family" environment dictated by Bad Seeds. MN sister and MN mother are psychologically violent, homicidal, soul-sucking malignant narcissists.

184

Despite knowing damn well about malignant narcissism, I will NEVER fathom what MN mother and MN sister did to me. I can't relate to their slimy mentality. I can't imagine being like their kind – AT ALL. But if you apply pure logic to the equation you can see what's going on. They felt a putrid bug like me was hurting *them*. By acting like I had a right to expect more than their unmitigated hatred, I was degrading *their* lofty image. How dare I speak-out about their abuse? How dare I question the behaviour of those so superior to little old me!? It was *my* behaviour that was called into question. It was my actions to be heard and validated that needed to be squashed. That's right – a pervert's reality.

"WHY DO YOU EXPECT ME TO ACT A CERTAIN WAY?!"

Translation: I am perfect. I am superior. I am entitled. I am right by virtue of *who* I am, not by my actions. I expect favourable treatment ALWAYS, for I am special. Why should *I* have to behave like all those other dumb saps?! Why should I have to be human?! I get to do whatever the hell I want, and don't you dare challenge my authority!

"WHY CAN'T YOU JUST BE COMPLAISANT?!"

Translation: I am in CONTROL and you must obey me and please me at all times! You seeking validation and support on Blogs about the crimes perpetrated by me and my kind do not please me! You have no right to speak! You have no right to feel! You have no right to see! You have no right to think! *I* am your voice, eyes, ears, and mind! There shall be no defiance of MY will! You are my puppet and failure to comply is considered an attack of my superiority. I will annihilate you for your disobedience!

Malignant narcissist sister had no connection to the information she read on narcissism or the comments I wrote. She is emotionally retarded with an arrested level of emotional development. She sees nothing wrong with her behaviour and no need to alter it. She cannot identify in any way to the pain and suffering of an insignificant bug like me. She simply was outraged that a bug like me dare complain. For it's her *right* to abuse me.

So when it comes to Blogs on narcissism, and the victims of narcissistic abuse, the narcissist has no connection whatsoever. They deny reality at every turn. They deny the facts. They deny the truth. They disbelieve the evidence. Narcissists use distortions and illusions to maintain their delusions of perfection. The malignant narcissist truly believes "You have NO right to live," let alone a right to self-preservation.

The only base "emotions" the Blogs incite in the malignant narcissist are anger, rage, fear and vengeance because they can't stand to give-up an inch of control. Their compulsive need to control everyone and everything you say, do, think and believe leads to quickly neutralizing anyone who doesn't follow their script as a supreme being.

What does the regular old narcissist think about the Blogs? My guess is, not much. They might be secretly amused. But they are more likely to dismiss them; viewing them as "lies" and "gossip" written by those they call "mentally ill" – the label they apply to their inferior victim, the scapegoat.

With their malignant sense of entitlement, MN sister and MN mother believed they were entitled to take the Blogs away from me – my support line. They believed they were entitled to take away my voice. They believed they were entitled to take away my RIGHT to *freedom of expression*. With their irrational grandiosity and arrogance they believed that they would succeed at their high-wire cyber machinations. They thought they were *that* clever, *that* cunning and *that* entitled. They thought wrong.

They overestimated themselves, and underestimated me. Their pathology blinded them to the reality of my strength and resolve. Their pathology blinded them to fact that I won't be silenced. Their delusions make them stupid. Their attempts to silence me failed miserably. I am not an object they can control by intimidation. It's *my* will to shout louder on a larger platform. It's *my* will to enter the arena of "battle" to engage their evil. And I'm sure they discovered my Blog long ago, as they are paranoids who live in a state of panicky fear of being unmasked.

The only way to undo some of the damage committed by narcissists is to expose them. They have been ruling untouched for far too long and it is high time we represent.

What is "exposing" the narcissist? It is telling the TRUTH. Truth always turns the tide against evil. Truth defeats and liberates from evil. Truth is not what fits the narcissist's agenda. Truth is the way things are. It is reality. It's what the bright light shows the situation to be, not what the darkness tries to pawn off.

The evil of malignant narcissism is swimming below the water lines of visible reality. The Blogs are about making that reality "visible". I don't give a crap what the narcissist's reactions are to Blogs on narcissism. The Blogs are NOT for them. There is no help for them. It's about *our* salvation. It's about shining *our* bright light of exposure on the narcissist's darkness so we can be liberated from their evil and others can be protected. And the Blogs are only a start, a small beginning in a world that desperately needs to live in truth and reality as witnessed by the annihilation of an innocent soul and the freedom of a "dark force" known as Casey Anthony, a malignant narcissist "mother."

Comments:

I can relate. Sharing your story not only helps you but it helps others. Like you, I devoured the information on the web about narcissists. Finally, this insidious abuse had a name. My filter for their twisted lies is finally coming into focus. You are right, they tried to DESTROY you. They are diabolical but not only did you survive but you lived to expose the truth about them.

My father is a silencer too. Not even remotely to that extent, though. He just routinely read my diary, was enraged when I wrote what he didn't like in it, and decoded my coded secret messages to my mother, then was angry because he didn't like what was said there.

What IS IT with MNs and stalking behavior? Why the perverted interest in OUR lives when we are no longer available to be a source of supply? Perhaps in walking away from the relationship the MN's paranoia and desire to "destroy" the victim really ramps-up or simply becomes more blatantly obvious....not that it really matters other than a sadistic function of continuing to terrorize the "one that got away."

I truly have received more from your observations, examples and well-articulated reasoning than I've ever found in a periodical or book. Stay safe, please keep writing and know you are helping far more people than you know. Thanks!

Speaking out is I believe what must be done also. It is as if you have lived inside of my shoes. Fear inhabits me still. Thank you for writing your story, I appreciate knowing that I am not alone in this nightmare.

Predators. That's what they are. It's awful enough the pain they inflict, but when you try to move on, THEY WON'T LET YOU.

You have such a good style of writing. It is like seeing all of my own thoughts carefully crafted on paper. In our minds this story is a

188

jumbled up mess of emotions, depravation and years and years of toxic head games and abuse. I am so sorry for what these types of people have done to your life, and anyone who has lived it understands it all too well. It is comforting to read your words.

As victims of these freaks, we are used to a life without comfort from their abuse, because they see to it that we have no support system to escape it.

If they don't destroy us, we might let out their vile secrets. It would never dawn on them, that if they want to be seen as decent human beings, they could do the work to earn it. They are too lazy, so they are of the mindset they can just steal it, and everything else they want in life from other people. The people they steal it from are witnesses to their crimes, by their own doings. It makes them hate us all the more. They thoroughly earn our hate and that is all they are worth from us, and not the pity they try so hard to get. What we all need to learn faster, to save as much of ourselves as possible, is that these creatures do not deserve anything back from us.

They all have the same MO. They are going to expose their victims for what they are not, so they will never be seen for what they themselves are.

Thank you for having the strength, brains and bravery to write something so absolutely TRUE in every single way possible about such evil.

Man major KUDOS to everyone who writes and expresses or shares anything about this stuff- it is SO hard to explain...I feel like, "WHERE DO I BEGIN!!!!!!"

Lisette, you wrote:

"As far as I'm concerned, psychologically terrorizing and emotionally traumatizing someone is no less violent than trying to murder them. By trying to destroy someone by gaslighting them for over a YEAR, and causing their psychological injury, you kill that

189

person just as surely if you shot them dead. But it is far more cruel than shooting someone dead. It is evil." THIS needs to be a t-shirt. No, a BILLBOARD...or a TV SHOW. THANK YOU. I know this is true! I am healing from this type of attempted murder.

Lisette, you are nothing less than TRUTHFULLY AWESOME. This type of person is a murderer, only they seem to get pleasure out of knowing you are alive and hopefully dwindling in to a mere speck. When they know the whistle is ready to blow, they get rid of you.

Just know there are people like myself out there who have seen it all and know you are exactly right in what you have shared. Only someone who has seen it up close and personal can even comprehend the truth in your words.

Lisette, I just want to say thank you so much for your blog. It's giving me strength during my five year NC, things have changed particularly malicious and aggressive these past few months, and I am trying to stay strong, this blog has helped.

This is an outstanding BLOG!!! This blog and others like it are VALUABLE!!!! Thank you. I am very thankful and grateful for the good, sane, loving people. Namaste.

Of all the things anyone can do, telling the truth may be the most radical act of all. It takes enormous courage. And the truth DOES set you free - from these terrible, evil captivities that we suffered at the hands and minds of monsters. Go Lisette, heart of ten lions.

Calling A Malignant Narcissist on Their Crap

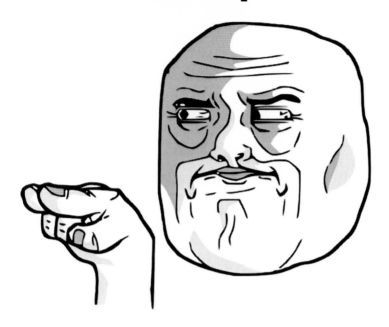

Malignant narcissism has been described as an extreme form of antisocial personality disorder that is manifest in a person who is pathologically grandiose, lacking in conscience and behavioural regulation, and with characteristic demonstrations of joyful cruelty and sadism.

Cruelty can be described as indifference to suffering, and even positive pleasure in inflicting it. If this habit is supported by a legal or social framework, then it receives the name of perversion.

Cruel ways of inflicting suffering may involve violence, but affirmative violence is not necessary for an act to be cruel. For example, if a person is drowning and begging for help, and another person is able to help, but merely watches with disinterest or perhaps mischievous amusement, that person is being cruel — rather than violent.

- Pathologically grandiose
- Demonstrations of joyful cruelty
- Mischievous amusement and positive pleasure at another's pain and suffering
- Callous indifference to another's need for help, care, attention etc.

Malignant narcissist is thy name, and they are all big time perverts. A person doesn't need to be drowning in water to be at the receiving end of the MN's cruelty. I see that example as a kind of a metaphor for basic mental, emotional, psychological and physical cruelty as well as indication of the malignant narcissist's callous indifference and disrespect of human life. The MN not only refuses to meet your needs, they *go out of their way* to deprive you of what you need. This game of control, vicious power-grabs and intentional infliction of malice gets them off. AND they get a sadistic feed witnessing the devastating effect the deprivation has on you. To put it in really creepy terms: watching us suffer is the narcissist's version of a snuff film. While you are drowning in the water, the MN will jump in and push your head down. Or, they'll look on with glee while you flay around and exhaust yourself trying to stay above the surface. However, once the malignant narcissist has had their orgasm, they will get bored and resentful of all the attention the fight for your life has sucked-out of poor little old them. So by the time you start to sink, they'll yawn and watch with disinterest. Remember, they have already gotten off on your pain. Actually, they've probably already abandoned you with smug satisfaction by the time you start to sink. Do you think these freaks make safe parents, siblings, friends, relatives or neighbours?

Hey, it's not enough that these sickos watch with mischievous amusement while you are under severe emotional distress, physical pain, and psychological trauma to the point where you are so disoriented that you can't help yourself. The malignant narcissist also gets frustrated and angry that you had the nerve to inconvenience them with your need for help and attention. So they walk out the door in a huff leaving you to fend for yourself. Your distress is entertaining for only so long. So you make it to emergency and end up in the hospital for a few days, and when you are out of the hospital the MN who abandoned you in your time of need, ever so bitter that you saved yourself and survived leaves you a cruel phone message where he mocks you and calls you a "wacko." And the malignant narcissist sister who caused the trauma that landed you in the hospital screams at you, "Have you hit rock bottom?!!"

That one is for you Clancy, you toxic sack of MN shit! And that one is for you sis, you malignant narcissist freak! And that one is for you Ted and Marilyn, you sick perverted old janitors. FYI: the only reason I don't use the MN's first and last name is not to protect the guilty, but to protect myself. I don't give a shit about the Malignant Narcissists. I really don't. I'm here to expose them for the criminals they are. If I didn't hate lawyers so much I would sue all their asses for mental cruelty and intentional infliction of emotional distress!

So you want to call a vile MN pervert on their crap? Well, let me re-cap things. Again, this came out of the mouth of malignant narcissist sister while she was screaming at me over the phone for having the nerve to succumb to abuse and trauma. In my own way, I begged her for mercy by saying, "Why can't you show me a little compassion?" The malignant narcissist freak reacted with indignation and her infamous response was and I quote:

"Why do you expect ME to act a certain way?! Why can't YOU just be complaisant?!!"

Malignant narcissists become even more vicious and cruel when you are vulnerable – so watch out! They are PATHLOGICALLY GRANDIOSE and that means: they are perfect in every way, they can do no wrong, they are above reproach, and so superior to us mere mortals. They are high, high above and we are way down below. As lowly peons, we exist to please the narcissist. We have no rights at all. Never mind the right to need help, attention, vital care or a drop of compassion. The narcissists view us as dirt beneath their feet and they will do whatever it takes to keep us down. They will also use every intimidation tactic available to stop us from questioning their despicable behaviour. For the grandiose malignant narcissist sadist, ever so lacking in conscience and behavioural regulations, is *entitled* to neglect you, deny you, dismiss you, ignore you, blame you, abandon you, humiliate you, slander you, judge you, criticize you, belittle you, denigrate you, control you, manipulate you, mentally bludgeon you, toy with you, harass you, attack you, stalk you, beat you, steal from you, and generally treat you like crap and destroy you. It's their right you see, because you are nothing but an object to be used for the narcissist's own gratification. And "objects" don't have the right to think, feel, need or even be. If you are in a relationshit with a narcissist, you really should know your place. And please don't complain. You really have no right to do so. Those at the bottom of the "family" hierarchy have no rights, and are expected to accept this without objection.

Malignant narcissists are NOT normal. They have never been normal, and they will never be normal. They are inhumane, period. So if you want to relate to them as a "normal" human being then good luck to you. The only value you have is how you can aggrandize the narcissist and more often than not that involves hurting you in some way: they crush you to vaunt themselves. So the vile MN crap machine doesn't want to hear about how they hurt you because hurting you in their sick minds is not only their right, but their intended goal, and they feel entitled to obtain their goal without receiving any flack. No one questions the behaviour of The Mighty Malignant Demi-God, no matter how heinous their crimes. For despite hard evidence to the contrary, the narcissist perceives themselves to be perfect and right by virtue of who they *think* they are. And remember: the narcissist's thinking is all lies. They have been tinkering with reality since inception so their minds are warped and twisted to the point of delusions. Don't try and reason with the insane.

Trying to reason with a narcissist and explain to them how they hurt you is as futile as trying to explain quantum physics to the cast of Jersey Shore. The best you'll get, and this is *the* best you'll get, is the narcissist trying to "fake" some semblance of understanding. It might look something like this: the narcissist's eyes will glaze over; they'll look at you with a dead stare, nod their big fat pointy heads and mutter such things as, "Duh. Umm. Okay. Yeah. I can see how you think that *seemed* this or that." And, if you listen real close there will be a "but" that justifies their crimes and prevents them from being held accountable. For the narcissist is *never* in the wrong. So do they actually get it? No! Not one bit. In fact, when the narcissist "fakes" understanding and "temporarily" adjusts their behaviour, often by over-the-top and smarmy displays of gratitude or flattery – BEWARE. At this point, they are simply afraid of being abandoned by their host, and all narcissists need a host to parasitize. The narcissist will do whatever it takes to keep their punching bag around. So you can expect some phony and very brief adjustments, but the narcissist will revert to default position in no time.

So please don't be a sucker for the Rat Game. The narcissist is delivering to you – the rat – a tasty treat. Treats may pop out with the first few pushes of the button, but eventually the treat will be replaced by an electric shock. And that's the narcissist's true nature. So don't bother pushing the button again and again and again in anticipation of a treat. Unless of course you are a masochist that enjoys pain.

The Rat Game is how the narcissist tries to keep their victims off-balance. You say to yourself, "But, they can be nice sometimes." No – they – can't! Narcissists may "act" normal sometimes when they are wearing their mask and when it's in *their* best interest to do so, but they are never genuinely nice, compassionate, caring or loving because they are missing the old empathy chip and a fully functioning conscience. Narcissists are not like you and me. They are factory assembled machines that all fell off the same conveyer belt. You've met one narcissist, you've met them all.

How many of us ACONs desperately clung to those few "normal" moments with an N parent(s)? Those fleeting normal moments were considered "The Good Times" in an N family. So like the rats that got the first tasty treat, children of narcissists hunger for another tasty treat and keep pushing and pushing that button in hope that they will deliver us a crumb like they did last week, or last month, or five years ago. THAT is narcissistic abuse. And that's the best you'll get with a narcissist: the occasional crumb. You deserve better.

As an ACON, I was brainwashed and trained by MN parents and MN sibling to believe that I had no rights. No rights at all. No right to defend myself. No right to fight back. I wasn't allowed to think or feel. In fact, thinking and feeling and trying to protect myself was *extremely* dangerous. You put up, and shut-up in an N family or suffer the consequences for your normal human behaviour, feelings, emotions and reactions. You are not allowed to BE in an N family, let alone protect and defend your

BEING. So you end up getting the shit kicked out of you emotionally, psychologically and physically and you carry the shame of the abuse through-out your life. But you never had a choice. You were doing what you needed to do to survive. You were taking the abuse.

Maybe when you were young you cried and screamed (you had a normal human reaction) when the narc parent(s) belted you. But the N parent raged, "You shut-up! Or, I'll let you have it again!" Maybe you got angry when they humiliated you, or you told them that they hurt your feelings. The malignant narcissist snapped, "Grow-up!" "You're too sensitive!" Or, they got that evil glint in their eyes, and that smirk crossed their face and they mocked you. You knew right there and then they loved your pain. So you learned the safest reaction to the abuse was no reaction. Don't give them the satisfaction.

And what if you did react in full-force by defending yourself and fighting back against the MN bullies by giving them a taste of their own medicine? What then? Well, rest assured you wouldn't hear the end of it. You see, the narcissist is entitled to behave like a pig and abuse you for a lifetime, but if you dare call them on their crap ONCE in that lifetime they will bitch and moan and complain, and whine and play the hard done by martyr over how mean you were to THEM that *one* time when you decided not to play by their sick rules and exercised your right to self-preservation. A relationshit with a narc is like this: they get to abuse you, and you get to take-it. Whether it's subtle N abuse or flat-out vicious MN cruelty, thems the rules.

Another thing that happens when the N target or MN family whipping pole/scapegoat rebels is they are labelled the one with all the problems, and the identified patient.

The N cult can't tolerate such disobedience so they re-group, have a conference, and pathologize and slander you to anyone who is stupid enough to listen. They go for the jugular by feigning creepy *concern*. I say "concern" is creepy because it's a derogatory term. It's another way of saying, "I'm flawless, wonderful and such a compassionate person but there's something wrong with you." That shit only comes out of the mouths of Ns who are knee deep in it and trying to mess with you or assassinate your character. "I really don't know why he/she is angry all the time." "He/she has problems." "I do my best, but she/he needs help." "Perhaps, he/she is mentally ill?" And the narcissist projection and liar machine rages on. "I'm very concerned." Yeah right, "concerned." The only thing the narcissist is "concerned" about is that you are not buying their bull-shit and are starting to talk. Exposure is a huge "concern" to the narcissist.

We ACONs are a smart lot and we could generally predict the devious post-abuse cover-up and defence mechanism of the Ns. So we opted to put-up and we shut-up. That's all we knew. And then we escaped! Yeah. We escaped alright, but we were still held prisoner of the N's training and brainwashing.

"God's concentration camp" is how some have described the life of children growing up with narcissist/psychopath parents.

So you leave the Narcissist Concentration Camp where you have been bullied, brainwashed and trained to play the Rat Game and put-up with the abuse, and other predators out there in the world lick their chops and see that they have a live one. Why do we ACONs attract other Ns? We don't. They are attracted to us because we are the only people who will put up with their bullshit.

Being trained to put up with narcissistic abuse goes something like this: if you call a narcissist on their crap they will have a raging tantrum, viciously attack you, guilt you, drown you out, block all communication, deny, evade, dismiss, minimize, blame-shift, project, feign victimhood, shun you and pathologize YOU. Remember, they are perfect and above reproach and they *always* get their way. That's what I learned in a MN family and that's what made me tasty N bait. I was too scared to call a narc on their crap, for if I dared to I would be threatened and intimidated into silence.

After I escaped the N family cult, other N wolves crept into my life. There was one in particular that was really mean and abusive. When I answered the phone and heard "Neil's" voice I would instantly get a stomach ache. So one day I told a normal person about this asshole and he said to me, "Why don't you say something to him as soon he becomes abusive?" I paused and said "I don't know. I guess I'm afraid to." He said, "Why? What do you think will happen?" After a long pause I said "He'll probably get mad." The normal guy replied, "So what if he gets mad. That's *his* problem!"

Ding! Ding! Ding! Light bulb moment. So while we think we are protecting ourselves and avoiding narc rage by not calling the narcissist on their crap, what we are really doing is protecting the tender feelings/ego of the malicious narcissist. We don't want to upset the poor, pathetic infantile little narcissist. THAT is precisely the crux of N abuse training. The narcissists make damn sure to keep their victims in a FOG of fear, obligation and guilt. We are programmed to take good care of the narcissist at all times because they are the only ones with rights and the only ones that matter.

So do you think it worked when I said something to Neil about his abusive treatment of me? Hells NO! He tried to intimidate me into silence with a raging narc attack. He yelled, "Oh come on, Lisette! Give me a fucking break! Get over it!" Then he stormed out and slammed the door behind him. That was the end of that Nship.

In the end, is it really worth it to call a narcissist on their crap? Do you really want to subject yourself to this kind of hell to make a point that the narcissist is too mentally, emotionally and morally retarded to get?

Moreover, is it really worth it to have this kind of nasty creature in your life at all? The only way to keep the peace with these mutants is to forfeit your self-respect and obey them, placate them, appease them and acquiesce to all their demands.

And this depraved mal-treatment by the narcissist goes so much further than the vicious attack they launch at you if you dare to stand-up to their abuse. They will have a massive hissy fit if you do anything that amounts to not treating them like they are god's gift. Here are some real life examples:

Clancy, the toxic sack of MN shit mentioned earlier in this post asked me to attend a wedding with him, and I said sure. The morning of the wedding I woke up with what felt like the flu. I was absolutely terrified to call Clancy and tell him that I was too sick to attend the wedding, but I did and I apologized profusely. Now did Clancy say, "That's ok. I'm sorry you're not feeling well. I hope you get better."?? Hells No! Clancy screamed at me, "Jesus Lisette! How could you do this to MEEE?! Come on!! You're not THAT sick! Just get dressed and I'll pick you up in a few hours!" I went on to explain that I was too ill to go anywhere. Clancy continued to rage, bark orders, bully and guilt me into compliance and then he said and I quote: "And to think I was going to be nice to you today." WTF?! How sick it that?! That's very telling, isn't it? The narcissist is not only admitting that he abuses me, he's telling me that everything he says and does is premeditated and done entirely for effect to get whatever it is he wants from me. In the case of Clancy, he was going to be nice to me at the wedding because he was going to be "performing" at the wedding with mask fully in place. Not only was he a wedding guest, but he was the photographer and he wanted to make a good impression to drum-up business. So he was going to be "nice" to me out in public and it wasn't even going to be real! And behind closed doors, how did this piece of shit behave? There is nothing genuine or natural about a narcissist, including the way they treat you. They are cold, calculating predatory machines.

Anyway, the conversation ended with me apologizing (for being sick) and Clancy slamming the phone down. The next day, I called him and left a message apologizing *again* and saying that I hope he had a good time at the wedding. I never heard back from Clancy. Not getting his way was simply too intolerable for his Highness so it was off with my head. He gave me the silent treatment. And this immature freak was in his 40's!!! The creep surfaced about a year later and left me a phone message that I ignored. I guess it took that long for King Shithead to recover from such a blow to his ego. Unfortunately, he surfaced again and again and because this was pre - NPD knowledge, I allowed low contact with the evil bastard, but minimum access is all it takes for a MN to harm you.

Oh, and if you get sick and cancel a date with a narcissist they will all react like Clancy. I tried to break a date once with Neil because of exhaustion from final exams, a part-time job and a massive head cold. Neil became furious and wasn't having me back out of the evening. He didn't give a damn if I was on my last breath, Neil simply wanted what he wanted so he bullied me, guilted me and coerced me into going out with him. It didn't matter that I was lousy company because I was about to keel over. In fact, my presence didn't matter at all. I was nothing but a human pacifier and the big fat N baby whined and wailed until he got his way.

There was another MN monster that slithered into my life. It was a new friendship so I hadn't known this MN very long, but I knew enough to tell that Michelle was bossy, demanding, and controlling just like MN sister — go figure. Anyway, one time she invited me over for dinner. She told me that she was making spaghetti. I said, "Thanks for the invite, but I'm busy that night." Then I laughed and told her that I had made a big batch of spaghetti the other day and had eaten it for the past 2 nights. I thought she was cool with me declining her invitation, but hell to the NO! A couple of days later I received a vicious narc attack from her by email. She tore a strip off me for saying that I had already eaten spaghetti! She told me not to call her unless I was calling to apologize for my behavior. Even though this was pre-NPD knowledge not only did I send her crazy, malicious, abusive email to other people that knew her, I called her up and left her a message telling her off and to never come near me. I scared the living shit out of her. And the MN predator slithered off with her tail between her legs. As far as her raging tantrum of an email went, I learned this was a common practice of malignant narcissist Michelle.

I seriously cannot make this stuff up. These are classic temper tantrums thrown by pathologically selfish, self-centred malignant narcissists demanding to get their way. And not only do you have no right to call a narcissist on their crap, break a date, or decline an invitation, under no circumstances are you allowed to ask for anything back that belongs to you. Here's one from the files on twisted MN sister.

The bitch considers herself Royalty and she is much too grandiose to lower herself and ask to borrow something. No. Her majesty merely tells you what she wants. She commands and demands. For example, one time she pointed at a belt I was wearing and barked, "I want to borrow that!" I just ignored her order, but I have made the mistake of bestowing the vile witch with kind offerings. Unfortunately, it took me a long time to understand that when you are gracious enough to "loan" something to a narcissist you are indeed "giving" to a narcissist. There is no loaning involved because the narcissist truly feels they are honouring you by letting you "give" to them.

Once I was kind enough to loan MN sister some of my most precious DVDs and books. Because she is a shut-in freak, I wasn't allowed to enter her home and hand them to her. No. I had to leave them on the stoop of her building. And when it was convenient for her majesty she would go outside and pick them up. Now I know MN sister is a weirdo so I've always felt sorry for her, and I followed her bizarre rules. Needless to say it worried me that my prized possessions were sitting on a sidewalk, and anyone could grab them, but I complied.

Malignant narcissist sister hung on to my DVDs and books for months and I was too scared to ask for them back. Just like I was too scared to break a date with Clancy. Anyway, during telephone conversations I would hint at getting my property back. I asked MN sister if she had enjoyed the DVDs. She would just side skirt the issue saying, "Yeah, yeah." And then change the subject. I would ask if she is done with the DVDs and she would say stuff like, "Yeah. Yeah. I guess I should give them back" and then quickly change the subject. She never once thanked me for loaning her this stuff. In fact, she actually continued to make demand for other films that I had mentioned. "Get me that film" was her direct order. I didn't comply. Over the years the bitch had taken, and stolen and claimed so many of my things as her own that I had ended-up writing off, and I had had enough. So come hell or high water, I was going to get those DVDs and books back.

A good five months after I lent the crazy psycho my DVDs she called me up. She was all chirpy on the phone, so I decided to take the opportunity to ask for my belongings back. I said, "I'm glad you called because I was going to call you to arrange a time to pick-up my DVDs." Now what does the chirpy MN do? She suddenly turns pathetic! She was aghast that I had the audacity to make a direct request for my DVDs so she screamed and I quote, "Is that the only reason you were going to call me?!! To ask for your DVDs back?!! Can't you see that my life is falling apart at the seams?!! I'm in dire straits and all you can think about is your DVDs??!!"

Yup. Suddenly the psycho bitch was in dire straits. She was pulling the old poor me pity-ploy to divert me from getting back what was rightfully mine. I wasn't buying it and said, "What does that have to do with me getting my DVDs back?" She screamed, "Well maybe Lloyd should take back the movies he gave you!!" You see, a friend of MN sister had downloaded a bunch of crap movies onto CDs and dropped them off to me as a thank you for doing him a favour. I didn't ask for them. I didn't even want them. They were given to me as a thank-you gift. And now suddenly when I asked for my property back, MN sister was demanding that I give back a shitty gift that was given to me by someone else! You see, malignant narcissists think they own everyone in their lives, and if they own you then they own all that you have. So if Lloyd gives me a gift then that's actually MN sister's property. Do you get the idea of how controlling and greedy and selfish and entitled and boundary busting and bat-shit-crazy malignant narcissists are?

Long story short, MN sister put on every mask in the book to try and get her way and NOT return the things I had graciously loaned her. In a single telephone conversation she played the pathetic victim, the business negotiator, the hard ass, the bitch, the bratty child and on and on. It truly was fascinating to see what lengths she would go to get her way and keep my property. I never backed down and she lost. That very day I went over to her place and picked-up my DVDs and books that she left outside for me in the rain. She's a fucked-up weird hoarder so no one gets inside her lair. And here's the kicker: this crazy bitch has made it her life work to go around conjuring-up diagnosis and pathologies of me. Once she held me hostage on the phone and when I politely tried over and over again to end the conversation to no avail, she got furious with me and said, "You sound irritated. You probably have a mood disorder. You could take medication for that." So even denying the mighty malignant narcissist all of your undivided attention means that there is something wrong with YOU.

To wrap things up; malignant narcissists are moral imbeciles and they are not safe on any level. They are sick and twisted and evil. They are parasites and predators and the only thing they are capable of is taking and taking and causing chaos and harm. It is an exercise in futility to try and make them see the error of their ways because they are too far gone and too damn disturbed to ever get it. The solution? Get rid of them. Don't let them near you and if another one crosses your path note the stench and scare it away. The malignant narcissist's delusions and lies and deranged way of being in the world is their crap to live with, NOT yours, so don't take it. Leave them to their putrid disordered lives.

They will never be capable of normal, so don't even go there.

Comments:

They are entitled and you are shit on the bottom of their foot wear. And don't forget that. They remind you of such at their "convenience." All together now: It's all about "MEEEEEE" and you're "too sensitive," too "demanding" (to be treated as a human being.) Any problem/issue belongs to YOU. Otherwise known as "Blaming the victim."

I'm so glad I found this site. It is one of the most comprehensive, tell-it-like-it is websites about narcs. You are very sensitive towards what the victims go through and you don't try to sugar-coat or make excuses for the narcs being the way they are. I've learned it's a waste of time to delve into the "whys." Now when I meet a potential narc, I run like hell.

With every narc I've known there were red flags that I saw loud and clear but chose to ignore because I thought, nah... they didn't do that on purpose... they didn't mean that... they would never do that. Ha! Oh-yes-they-did! I've been pissed at myself for being too trusting, and giving these cretins the benefit of the doubt. In other words, I've been mad at myself for being a decent human being.

These monsters require one of five things in order to suck you in and win you over. I have learned this from your wonderful web site. Don't ever let any of them happen: Proximity, intimacy, guilt, complacency (their fake kindness), or second-guessing yourself.

Once again, another post describing my entire family.

A Narcissist is nothing more than a Demon in human Form.

Narcs are creeps without a conscience. They fail to acknowledge and respect an individual's basic rights and personal space.

I don't believe in karma or in any magical forms of justice. Most evil people don't get what's coming to them.

I don't believe in Karma but I believe in the power of the chicken foot. One must approach the narcissist with your hand out and palm up. Let the chicken foot lay flat in the palm. After you have lulled him into a false sense of security plunge the foot claw end first into his eye.

AT THE CORE OF MALIGNANT NARCISSISM IS ENVY

ENVY IS THE ULCER OF THE SOUL

--- Socrates ---

In the black heart of the diseased soul of the Malignant Narcissist lies uncontrollable, all-consuming, dangerous and destructive ENVY. Envy is at the core of their malignancy and it's what prompts them to TARGET and PREY on others for DESTRUCTION.

Malignant Narcissists are different from Narcissists in that they are PREDATORS. Yes, other narcissists can be downright competitive, and jealous of other people for who they are, and/or what they have, but they do not target and stalk the objects of their envy. My hunch, based on observation is that narcissists instead target *narcissistic supply*. They may see some source of N supply that they feel entitled to and take-it. But it stops there. For example, they will hijack all available attention in the room. Another example would be stealing someone's trophy husband, wife, or job. They will move-in to obtain the *source* of supply so that it's theirs, but they do not have that vicious predatory drive to destroy the ex-wife of the husband they stole or the person whose job they ripped-off. They seem to be so grandiose and so callously indifferent to another's existence that it would be beneath them to expend an ounce of energy focusing on anything but their own selfish wants and needs. They just want the narcissistic supply, period. Because it puffs-up their image.

However, more than toxic anger, more than unmitigated hatred, it is MALICIOUS ENVY that is at the root of malignant narcissism, and the driving force behind the MN's predation. It is what motivates them to stalk and destroy the object(s) of their envy.

If you have been targeted by a malignant narcissist and have never done anything to that MN and never would (they might not even be on your radar), it is because they envy you. I don't care if the MN is your parent, sibling, cousin, neighbour, co-worker, so-called "friend" or cyber pal, support group member, fellow church goer or what. They have honed in on you - first and foremost - because you have unwittingly inflamed their malicious envy... just for being you, and or, having what you have.

Malignant narcissists do not target those they feel superior to, they target those they feel inferior to and envious of. Take the story of David in the film *Shine* who was targeted for destruction by his malignant narcissist father. David's father didn't prey-on any of his other children, he chose David. Why? Because David was a kind and gentle soul AND a gifted musician with the opportunity to follow his passion. David possessed the talent and virtues that gave him a chance at life that his father never had. As a result, David's MN father seethed with envy over his son's potential life opportunities and wanted to destroy them and David in the process.

Have you ever heard a malignant narcissist parent say when you are simply living your own life, "You get to do whatever the hell you want! Who the hell do you think you are?! What gives YOU the right?!" You mean the right to exist, mother dearest? I heard this shit repeatedly growing-up under the rule of a MN parent that was hell-bent on annihilating me, my potential and my future.

206

Remember; malignant narcissists do not have *normal human feelings*. They may *appear* to be like us, but inside they are very different. So, if you are loving, kind, gentle, sensitive, courageous, gifted, funny, smart, passionate, joyful etc. In other words, if you are a normal human being who is simply enjoying life then you are a threat to them, and an object of their malicious envy. The MN parent doesn't target a child for destruction who is like them; they go after the child who is NOT like them; the normal one who they envy just for being human. YOU ARE NOT AN EXTENSION OF ME SO YOU HAVE NO RIGHT TO LIVE! Malignant narcissists want to kill your passion and destroy what gives you joy because they are empty inside. Passion, joy for life, goals, accomplishments, achievements and other virtues are cultivated from within. They are a result of having a SOUL (HUMANITY). They are not born of sullying, destroying, and plundering from another.

What may pass for a "soul" in a malignant narcissist is just one big bubbling ulcer - they are rotten to the core. Malicious envy is a volcanic wave of toxic energy and a potent source of discomfort for the malignant narcissist. And it's an energy that only consumes its host. So, the MN must diffuse of her poison all over the object of her irrational envy (also known as dirtying-up the victim). Sliming and maligning the victim rids the malignant narcissist of the nagging well-spring of pain associated with envy.

It's War!

But the other side – the target of the MN's envy – often doesn't know they are under attack, until it's too late. Looting and spoiling another's bounty quickly acts as a pain killer for the malignant narcissist. It sooths the discomfort caused by the MN's self-loathing, and gives her a good power rush. It's the malignant narcissist's drug of choice. We've all been at the receiving end of some vicious snipe aimed to bring us down when we are enjoying the fruits of our labour. The nasty snipe is always followed by an evil smirk creeping across the MN's contorted face. That evil smirk is evidence that they just got a good dose of their narcotic, and their painful ULCER/ENVY has been temporarily soothed. They can go from vicious envy attack mode to a smooth, smug, drug calm all in a matter of seconds. These freaks are shape shifters.

Malignant narcissists steal from others by dirtying up what others possess. The fun lies not only in taking, but in emotionally beating down the target and ruining his/her reputation, and or life. Successful character assassination and being the cause of dissension in families and other factions, as well as destroying what others have worked hard to create – in their crazy green eyed envy – is victory! For the MN, it's not about having it for themselves, it's about annihilating it so no one else can have it. They don't want the meaningful things in life. They wouldn't know what do with them, other than destroy them.

Malignant narcissists can be copycats, friend snatchers, spouse stealers, family puppet masters and career saboteurs, but the friend, husband, relative, job, same car newer model, in fact, all the stolen booty means nothing to them. They're just happy that you can no longer have it, or enjoy it as much. For example, how can you enjoy a rewarding and cherished career when all of your colleague's minds have been poisoned and they are whispering behind your back? It's destroying their prey's mental and emotional well-being as well as turning them into some kind of a pariah that really floats their boat. They get off on causing strife all around and kicking back and watching the conflict they created from a position high above as everyone's judge. War games make the malignant narcissist feel SO superior to all her little chess pieces.

A pathological sense of entitlement and pathological greed also spring from the cesspool of the malignant narcissist's envy. They want it all and they actually believe they deserve it. Stealing it, squandering it, tainting it, and destroying it feed their delusions of power and control over the Universe and everyone and everything in it. Needless to say; the MN's malicious envy and need to have it all leads to rampant boundary violations. All their malignant traits feed and fuel one another and keep that pathological steam-roller running down anyone that incites their envy.

It seems it's just Mother Nature that female MNs have the whole nosy, sneaky, emotional, psychological, petty, catty, rumour and scandal mongering stuff down. Beware the MN woman's wrath of envy. They are emotional and psychological predators, and they are extremely violent! Yet, amidst this violence they are also subtle and smooth operators and go about the game more *covertly* than MN men. As a result, they are more difficult to detect as stalkers. They are devious and crafty and good at what they do because they have been practicing since birth. No surprise MN sister majored in psychology at University – they love that stuff. It refines their skills at mind-control and manipulation: their *weapons* of choice. Maliciously envy IS the malignant narcissist's true nature and they slither through life consoling that envy with every weapon in their arsenal.

There are things about narcissists that have earth shattering ramifications, chiefly:

- *their need to "have it all"*
- *the nature of their interactions with others*

Both these things about narcissists fly beneath people's radar but they are extremely serious matters. That's because these things bear fruit in two serious threats to others:

- *predation*
- *manipulation/mind control*

Let's say you feel the need to have all the dollars in the world. Then, no matter how many you get, you compete with others for every single one. That's avaricious, unbridled greed and it makes you an adversary of everyone else in the world.

What's more, if you see a dollar in someone else's hand, you will want to take it away, just because he has it. That's the desire to plunder others. In other words, you will view the possessor of that dollar as a predator views preys.

Therein lies the malignant in malignant narcissism. Narcissists are predators. Being predators puts malignant narcissists in a special class with psychopaths - that class of people who do not wish you well, no matter how friendly their façade.

"What Makes Narcissists Tick" pages 40 -41.

It makes no difference how much bounty is bequeathed to the malignant narcissist. They can be spoiled, pampered, protected, privileged, supported, loved and admired etc. But since they view everyone as an adversary, enough is *never* enough. So it would seem, the actual dollars – no matter what form they come in – are of no consequence. I'm convinced it's the game of keep away and the covert destructive influence over their target's life – mental and physical health, finances, relationships, career and reputation – that gives the malignant narcissist the real thrill. Now that's sheer evil.

MN women in particular are good at not arousing suspicion in their targets and witnesses. They don't appear jealous and vindictive because that would look like motive. And should their target(s) become vocal about their abuse then others would side with them. So instead, MNs *appear* meek and mild while cloaking their malice behind a guise of *false concern*. Meanwhile, behind closed doors, they are bullying, provoking, gaslighting and maligning the target of their irrational envy through flying monkeys and unsuspecting third parties. MNs can be *overtly* sweet as pie to their target when there are witnesses present. So heed the transparent pleasantries of someone who makes you uneasy. They're just keeping you – the target – off balance so you will doubt your own reality when they pull the rug out from under you: Nah. They didn't do that. Nah. They wouldn't do that. Nah. They didn't mean that. OH - YES - THEY - DID!

To suspect, and try and explain to others that you have been targeted by a malignant narcissist IS to be gaslighted.

Overt grandiosity seems to be a hallmark of narcissism, but it is the *hidden* grandiosity that is the biggest red flag of malignant narcissism. The most dangerous MNs are the ones who appear the most kindly and humble to the outside world.

Final thoughts: gaslighting is the weapon of choice for most malignant narcissists. Emotional and psychological violence is clean violence and is difficult to detect. The effects of it are devastating. It can lead to such unnamed fear and confusion and severe emotional distress that if you don't quickly pin-point it and name it, you could become a danger to yourself. So, if someone makes you uneasy (even if you don't know why) and you get that *feeling* that something's not quite right – document, document, document. It is exactly at the point when you think someone "might" be messing with you, that you should start recording everything. Forget about: this could be a coincidence... I'm just imagining things etc. – write it all down (dates, times, *their every move*).

Having thoughts of doubt is precisely why you should be noting this stuff - no matter how innocuous events may appear at the time, or how "paranoid" you may feel. Trust your intuition because it is *never* wrong. One day you will be presented with hard evidence that cannot be ignored. Then you will look back at your notes and see patterns in the malignant narcissist's behavior, and it will all add-up. These highly disturbed and deluded predators view us as "unsuspecting" prey. They rely on our virtuous human projections to get away with it: denial that anyone could be that sinister, that depraved, and that evil-minded. Never give a malignant narcissist the benefit of the doubt.

Turn the tables on the creepy narcs. Watch and monitor *their* every move. Discern twisted patterns. It is a *pattern* of behaviour that determines stalking, harassment and intimidation (no matter how subtle and strange). Patterns give us the clue that this is not some weird, one-shot occurrence, but a deliberate attempt to derail us and our lives. You cannot report one incident to the police, but you can report two. The authorities need to discern patterns in the perp's behaviour in order to name it harassment, and prove the perpetrator is acting willfully to cause you harm, whether it be physical, psychological or emotional intimidation.

I brought down two dangerous gaslighting, malignant narcissist perverts in part by their vacuuming patterns in the building where I lived. At first while I was jotting this stuff down, I thought, "Nah." Turns out, my suspicions were right on the money. The vacuuming was just one clue, among mounds of evidence of all their bat-shit crazy, predatory, mind-messing malignant behaviour that proved they had targeted me and were intentionally inflicting emotional distress. And the authorities outside the malignant narcissists' pathological space agreed. Looking back, it was satisfying to take-down these evil fuckers that masqueraded as "good Christian love thy neighbour" types and make them pay-up for their Charles Manson style covert psychological violence.

Let your intuition be your guide, and take action to be your own authority on the predators in our midst.

COMMENTS:

Great post. As always, it's like the War Games quote: "A strange game. The only winning move is not to play."

Haven't you heard? With therapy a malignant narcissist can make progress. I guess progress for cannibals is getting them to eat with a fork. I am for launching them on a slow boat with a fast leak.

Destroying the receptacle never works. It's the core of a person that survives, no matter what shape the battle has left them. The narcs lose hands-down. We're still standing and the truth lives on!

It's the strangest thing to finally come to the conclusion that a person who should be geared to feel happiness for you... despises you. For no good reason. That's the only way to explain their contempt of us. Pure envy.

You have to wonder what happens to these people as they approach their own death and you have to wonder if they have any idea, any insight, of how others feel about them.

I simply, even now, do not understand the effort required to be like that, the 'never let up' evilness and how the hell they aren't walking around looking over their shoulder because if I had behaved like this to someone I would fully expect them to take me out.

I almost fell out of my chair when NM accused someone else of having NPD, so I am not shocked that a narcissist can read this blog, and then still not "get it". All they do is project their weaknesses onto others.

Envy is definitely the ulcer of the soul. It leads to irrational behavior and if like mine, your Ns are powerful, influential people who can control the people and events taking place in the world then you need to be very strong spirited to accept the fact that you cannot do anything about them crossing all limits of decency, civility and propriety and ruining your life for nothing.

This post is therapeutic for me having recently distanced myself from my N friend/neighbor after having been her primary source of supply for 6 years. She put on the charm at first (of course) and had befriended me at a low point in my life. As things began to turn around for me the N showed her true colors. She became pathologically envious of everything she felt I had...material possessions, friends, jobs... ANYTHING! If she couldn't outdo me, she would make up a lie or insult me. She tried to sabotage my friendships, and make sure that all of our neighbors and people in our social circle liked her better. If I confided in her, she would exploit my confidence. In the end, I felt so controlled, bullied, abused, and angry. I used to ask "why" all the time. When I came upon NPD I didn't ask why anymore!

THE SKINSUIT MALIGNANT NARCISSIST

A Skinsuit Malignant Narcissist is a female MN whose all-consuming envy and pathological greed is so out of control that she is driven to not only take from you, and destroy you and what you have, she must BECOME you in the process. She wants your life, she wants to BE you. And she won't stop until she is in your skin and you are vapour.

The "Skinsuit" is in reference to the fictional character Buffalo Bill, from the film *Silence of The Lambs*. In the film, Buffalo Bill is a serial killer who murders overweight women and skins them so he can make a "woman suit" for himself. In the case of Buffalo Bill, he has gender confusion issues and not only does he want to wear women's skin; he wants to become a woman.

Film theorists Barbara Creed wrote: "To experience rebirth as a woman, Buffalo Bill must wear the skin of women not just to experience the physical transformation but also to acquire the *Power of transformation* associated with the woman's ability to give birth. Buffalo Bill wears the skin of his totem animal to assume its power."

In terms of Skinsuit Malignant Narcissists, all we have to do is replace gender confusion with IDENTITY confusion. Female MNs have severe identity issues, particularly if they are enmeshed with a MN mother and still under her influence. The MN mother drains the daughter of a self so she can fill her with her own self and/or use the daughter as a dumping ground for all her toxic waste. This creates one poisonous and deranged creature that is not only disconnected from her "self," but disconnected from reality. It also sets the stage for the MN daughter to learn the ways of identity theft.

Skinsuit MNs have undeveloped selves and this is what makes them so immature. There is nothing essential about them; they have no genuine feelings, no deeply held opinions, no idiosyncrasies, no individual style, no personal vision and no passion for anything. There is no there, there. They are empty inside and they know it. As a result, they see no intrinsic value in themselves – only image. Like all Narcissists, Skinsuit MNs are chameleons who go through life creating personas and projecting images and synthesized emotional states one after the other. And all their various personas never add up to a whole person. Who the Skinsuit MN *really* is, is difficult to identify because they have no real self. Without an identity, the Skinsuit MN is in constant pursuit of one; one that will give the MN the most POWER in any given situation. These are women who get their cues on how to dress, act and behave from TV, magazines, films, those they envy AND their crazy MN mothers.

Whereas Buffalo Bill "wore the skin" of his totem animal – women – to assume their power, Skinsuit MNs "wear the identity" of the object of their obsessional envy – YOU – to assume the power they believe you possess. We ARE only objects of the Skinsuit MN's delusional thinking, objects that the MN is so furious at she wants to destroy.

I received a letter from a reader named "Dawn" who was targeted by Skinsuit MN "Linda." Now Linda didn't kidnap Dawn and stick her in a pit in her basement and send down lotion on a string in a basket, far from

215

it. Dawn was targeted by Skinsuit Linda when she was volunteering at her daughter's private school. Here is Dawn's story:

"Thank you! You have no idea what your blog has meant to me. I thought there was something wrong with me to attract such ill behavior from others. It all started about three years ago, we put our daughter in a new private school, as soon as I met the room mom my stomach turned. I decided to listen to my gut feeling and tried to stay as far as possible from (I'll call her) Linda.

Unfortunately, private schools require a lot of volunteer. Once I started volunteering Linda wanted to be around me to see what I was doing. As my work became known and appreciated, I noticed she wanted to take credit for it (for example, as a room mom, Linda wanted others to believe that she had me do the work), so I tried even harder to stay away from her.

Her behavior became so odd, that I thought I was imagining things. She started to dress like me. She would stare at what I was wearing, and the following day was wearing the same thing or very similar. I was creeped out! Then I caught her staring at my daughter with that weird stare. The next day her daughter is wearing a similar outfit to my daughter's. At that point I knew something was very wrong. Then, Linda would watch whom I was talking with, and the next day she would be talking to them. That would not have been a problem except that after she was done talking to them, they would not talk to me again.

What was even creepier was that she started acting like me, and using the same phrases I used! I was shocked. I couldn't believe that a grown woman was acting like that. Eventually I became ostracized by the other moms; that would not have been a problem until my daughter became ostracized by her classmates. It broke my heart to explain to my daughter why she was not being invited to birthday parties and play dates. I decided to talk to a psychologist friend of mine and she told me to move my child from the school, she said "Linda" would not stop until she destroyed me and mine. I have never felt so much anger and anguish in my entire life.

I did get even though, I made sure not to do anything I knew she needed to look good as a room mom. What is funny is once she saw that I had withdrawn, she became desperate to get me (my work) back; she actually asked my daughter to tell me she missed me! It is no coincidence that Linda said that right before the school auction (where my work went for a lot of money) where she needed me the most to look really good as the room mom. Linda did other crazy things, but I think you get the gist of it.

I thought I somehow did something to get such ill treatment, but after reading your blog, I know it was not me! I am disgusted with these monsters, and can truly say I hate them!"

True to form, it all started with a Smear Campaign against Dawn. But we know it "started" for Linda long before that with internal greed and envy, not over Dawn, because Ms. Skinsuit Linda didn't even know Dawn. Then Linda comes across Dawn, and Dawn represents everything that her jealous rage and covetousness. Dawn unwittingly makes Linda furious just by existing. So the MN Skinsuit must do her utmost to ruin the source of her frustration while pretending to be her friend.

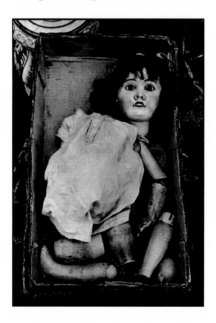

I've had my own experiences with Skinsuit malignant narcissists to varying degrees. The worst case was many years ago when I was in my early 20s. It was a friend I made at work "Robin" whose malicious obsession with me progressed gradually over time. I won't go into all the gory details but sufficed to say when the film *Single White Female* was released, I felt I could have written it. I still have the occasional nightmare about that crazy Skinsuit MN bitch and yes, like MN sister, she was fused with her MN mother and still living at home.

Like Dawn's Skinsuit MN Linda, "Robin" started to emulate everything about me. She started dressing like me and taking on my mannerisms and lingo and she even started walking like me. I have a specific gait and I'm slightly pigeon toed. It's something that was more pronounced when I was younger and I was always a little self-conscious of my walk. Anyway, one day I caught Skinsuit MN Robin walking like me, slightly pigeon toed and that totally creeped me out. Who would ever purposely want to walk pigeon toed? A Skinsuit MN who wants to embody you, that's who.

Skinsuit Robin began to increasingly invade my privacy. She had the same answering machine as me and she knew that the code it came with was on the bottom of the machine, so one day when she was at my apartment, and my back was turned, she got my code and started retrieving my messages. Of course, the dumb bitch once retrieved my messages when I was home so I knew it had to be her, and changed my code. This betrayal came out of nowhere, as far as I knew we were friends. Little did I know that beneath the veneer of fun and friendship this MN was seething with hatred toward me and wanted to obliterate me. I was shocked by her behavior but chose to keep quiet about the telephone message invasion and remain watchful.

Skinsuit MN Robin had a petulant, immature presence and friends who met her found her incredibly off-putting. At a party I threw she brazenly bad-mouthed me to a trusted friend. Vera came to me and said, "Lisette, Robin is SO jealous of you and I think she's dangerous. She's the kind of girl who would hide in the bushes and jump out and throw acid on you." I took this warning seriously and completely distanced myself from Skinsuit Robin. She was a twisted, lonely, insatiably needy young woman who was coddled by her MN mother and was looking to find fulfillment by literally trying to become her more mature and successful friend – me. Like all Skinsuit MNs, Robin didn't like me distancing myself and began harassing and stalking me by phone doing things like flushing the toilet and leaving that noise on my answering machine; calling and hanging-up at all hours of the day and night, and ordering pizzas to my address. I never reacted to her telephone terrorism and went complete no contact but this only ramped-up her behavior.

I was forced to get an unlisted number, but in about 2 years time she found me and started harassing me again by phone. I was dumbfounded, I couldn't figure out how the hell she got my unlisted number. Then I remembered that I had applied for Employment Insurance and had to give my telephone number in my application. So I called-up the EI office and asked if she worked there. After much smooth talking, I got the woman to finally admit that Skinsuit Robin indeed worked at the Employment Insurance office, and I got the name of her supervisor. Long story short, even though what she did was illegal – she was constantly on the hunt for me and exploited a confidential government database for her sick purposes – the Government idiots did jack shit about it. They didn't really believe me, and questioned everything I said. She ended up mailing an apology to me on an EI envelope that was shoved into another envelope. She outright lied to her employer telling them that she needed to reach me because I owed her money, and that's what it said on the bizarre, mess of non-apology she sent me: "Sorry I bothered you but I wanted to get back the money you owed me." Huh? Calling and hanging up and leaving deranged messages or being completely silent on the other end when I answered the phone was about money? Yeah. Her sinister behavior was about money alright, money I had that she envied.

It makes sense that I didn't have the good sense to avoid these Skinsuit MNs from the outset, and that I ended-up in the same Skinsuit MN dynamic that I had with MN sister. Like Skinsuit Robin, Skinsuit sister is mentally damaged, immature, off-putting and weird, insatiably needy and still dependent on mommy. I am and have always been the object of Skinsuit MN sister's pathological envy. When I saw her 26 years ago at

Christmas she had my books on her shelf, my clothes in her closet and my dishes in her cupboards. She also had my photo albums, personal keepsakes and high school yearbooks that she refused to give back. How twisted is that?! She clings to yearbooks of a high school she never attended. I can picture her wearing my clothing and rocking back and forth in a trance; reading my signed high school yearbooks and pretending to be me.

In addition to claiming my property as her own, MN sister chronically snooped in my life. She used to joke that she lives "vicariously" through me. Lucky for me, I lived 1000s of miles away and went NC early. I have seen her twice in 26 years. The first time was during a visit at Christmas holidays 26 years ago. During this visit I reconnected with an ex-boyfriend who I had a long term relationship with. "James" came over to MNM's house for dinner and we spent New Year's together. MN sister had nothing going on for New Year's so she went to a party with me and James and a bunch of my friends. James was one of the few guys I've dated who wasn't a narc. And because he wasn't a narc, MN sister was interested in him. She needs total control and would never date one of her own. So after I flew back home, she organized a big party as a ruse to see James. I have a feeling MN mother - who always acted like a pathetic flirt around James - had something to do with it. So MN sister invited James to this "party" that apparently MNM went all out to cook for, and he declined. He told MN sister that he had to clean the gutters of his house that night. Of all the guys that MN sister could target, she zeroed in on my first long term boyfriend. That was a personal intrusion that felt almost incestuous to me. Luckily she failed. And I'm convinced that if I did not go NO CONTACT when I did, MN mother would have skinned me alive and suited-up MN sister in my life.

The second time I saw Skinsuit MN sister was 10 years ago. I had not seen her in 17 years and she showed-up at a film industry party that she knew I was attending. Dawn mentioned the "weird stare" in her story about Skinsuit Linda. Well, let me tell you, when I saw Skinsuit MN sister after 17 years of no contact, I got that WEIRD STARE. It was beyond creepy. The only way I can describe it is lecherous. She eyed me up and down like a hungry wolf with its tongue hanging-out and saliva dripping from its chops. Wow MN sister what big teeth you have. It was like that; like she wanted to devour me; consume me. The way Skinsuit MN sister scanned me after 17 years of no access to me was like a lustful predator examining its prey. I'm surprised she didn't start to sniff me. I felt totally objectified. It was a very dehumanizing and unnerving encounter and I have not seen her since.

I believe all female Malignant Narcissists are pathologically spiteful and envious and they are all predators, but not all of them want a single full-body Skinsuit. Some of them prefer the patchwork kind. These MNs like to target a variety of prey and sew pieces of other women's lives together in order to cast a wider net in terms of attention gathering.

These MNs are much more difficult to detect as Skinsuit MNs because their obsessive envy isn't focused on just one woman; their envy is directed at ALL women. Take for example Myra, a narcissist I knew for 20 years. Every boyfriend Myra ever had was stolen from another woman. I believe she enjoyed the man more if she had lured him away from his girlfriend or wife. One time I was over at her apartment and I noticed a dried-up bouquet of black roses in her sink. I asked her about them, and she told me that her boyfriend's ex had sent them to her. She seemed quite smug about it. She clearly enjoyed infuriating other women. And I'm sure the girlfriend wasn't his "ex" when Myra dug her claws into him.

Myra had a 5 year affair with a married man and one day I asked her how it all started. She gleefully explained how she met him at a party, and right there and then she decided that she would seduce him and steal him away from his wife and children. Like all MNs she was cold and calculating. And get this; the married man was the husband of her friend's sister. So there were multiple betrayals in that deal.

Myra was also a friend stealer, and that's how she targeted me: she moved in on me for friendship through her friend Vera, and then she moved in on a couple of my friends when I moved away and did whatever she could to make sure I would not reconnect with them again. She also slept with a boyfriend of mine after he and I had temporarily broken-up.

Myra was a painter, but I wouldn't call her an artist because she doesn't possess an ounce of creativity. She's technically a good painter but doesn't have an original thought in her head. Our mutual friend Vera on the other hand was a brilliant artist filled with spontaneous creativity and Myra seethed with envy over Vera's natural talent. Vera set up a little make shift art gallery and even though Myra was Vera's so-called "friend" she never went to visit Vera at her gallery – she was literally paralyzed with envy. So what did Myra do? She sent in her nasty old MN Monkey Mother to do some sniffing around at Vera's art gallery. The next thing you know, Myra has a big art exhibition of a flower series that was a complete rip-off of Vera's work. And she also stole Vera's idea of taking old cigar boxes and painting and decorating them. But Myra was much too superior to sell the cigar boxes like Vera did, instead she gave hers out as gifts at a party she threw in honour of herself. No area of your life was safe with this Patchwork Skinsuit bitch. She was on the take all the time from everyone. Fortunately, she was too busy sewing together bits and pieces of various people's lives to put any serious effort into completely destroying one person.

Skinsuit MNs who target one person are perverse. They are not only obsessive but possessive of the object of their malicious envy. They are plain scary, and in addition to their eerie penetrating stare is the way they bombard the object of their envy with intense flattery in an idol worship kind of way. They are either nauseatingly effusive to their target or they criticize, belittle and denigrate them. There is no middle ground with these freaks, and that speaks of their messed-up heads, and how *everything* about them is unbalanced and off kilter.

When you take a malignant narcissist who is lacking in conscience and empathy AND identity, and you toss in raging envy, rampant greed, pathological entitlement, sadism, hatred, and aggression and an insatiable need for power and control then you are going to have a creature that is quite capable of literally and metaphorically skinning people alive. Do you think someone who is built that way is going to be even remotely connected to reality? Malignant narcissists are mentally deranged. Their perceptions are completely skewed, their thought process is distorted and their primary experience is made up of delusions.

Those they envy are internalized as objects of the Skinsuit MN's fury. How sick is that? To be so furious at the object of your delusional thinking and irrational envy that you want to destroy it. To feel so empty inside that you must steal the identity of another just to feel the power of being a whole person.

Again, how sick is that?

COMMENTS:

Wow! You just described my sister! She has always been so jealous and envious of me. I am so glad I found your blog. You have helped me to understand my family and why I have wisely want nothing to do with them.

Yet another post to describe what I'm living as we speak. Wow! There's so much I'd like to say about this post.

This article gave me the willies, because my sister copies my mother to the point me and my brother have called her my mother's "mini-me".

That "Stare"- I know that, I've experienced it and it's beyond creepy. It always felt to me as if I was being visually "eaten alive" by the MN Predator. This goes way beyond imitation or copying your look or your talents/interests etc. to the very core of your being. Every *last* detail they can suss-out about you they devour, seeking out friends, neighbours, employers etc. It's just scary. All though they're all Predators, these are the ones I personally consider the most dangerous to your health: These are the "Bunny Boilers" of the world, the ones who truly wish you dead so they can fulfill their crazy delusion of actually being you without the "inconvenience" of a real "you" still breathing and walking this planet.

Thank you for this article. This fits perfect for my life right now. I just recently had to go NC with a MN woman that I had been "friends" with for a few years.

"Living in fight or flight mode is exhausting" You got this right!!! I could never figure out what was up with my lack of energy and poor physical health for YEARS!

Of course they have more energy -- they're stealing everybody else's 24/7. Imagine if they were bank robbers who never had to worry about getting caught. They'd have way more money than you too.

It's NOT that these narcs are inherently and naturally hyper-energized creatures. The more hyper-energized they seem only means they have prey nearby and accessible to and controlled by them. Dracula sucks blood. They relentlessly suck on their victims' soul energies. Dracula/the Narcs want to reduce their victims to either death, or a hopeless state of dependency and exploitation, (what they intended to do to us) or to a carbon copy of themselves (the golden child).

Yeah, there is definitely a difference between healthy admiration of another person in terms of that person's personality traits and what that person has accomplished, and then hostile feelings like envy and contempt.

This is so creepily true. They mould their skins and become...you, or a twisted-sister version thereof.

I feel as though I have been damming up a river of emotion, of my very life for so many decades. I totally understand if anyone does not feel like reading all that I have to say but I am so thankful for the chance to finally let it all out.

Love this post, Lisette! Experienced this phenomenon with a roommate in college.

Amazing blog! This post in particular describes my mother in law to a tee.

The Narc's' takeover of others' selves, is a form of theft, like literary plagiarism.

Lisette, I don't think I would be labouring the point by saying that this article validates the experiences of my entire life. The hours I have spent pondering how unnatural my mother and, subsequently, sister are, just annoys me when I look back at it.

STILL shocked by both their behaviour and the stories of others. I can't see how they could debase themselves or appear any more insane and then they go and best that. If it wasn't serious it would be funny.

MALIGNANT NARCISSISTS FEED OFF YOUR PAIN

From my experience, all narcissists feed off our pain and suffering. They ALL get a little rush from seeing us hurt. But the high they experience in reaction to our pain seems to be determined by where they sit on the continuum. For example, a low level narc might first react to your misfortune with indifference but then a shift may occur in their mood. The narcissist may appear a little more upbeat and have a subtle spring in their step after hearing of your troubles. These low-level narcs are pretty good at hiding their aggressive impulses. I guess because their spite isn't that strong, at least not as strong as the malignant narcissist who can't seem to contain their glee when we suffer. We've all seen that maniacal smirk.

Another type of narc may use your misfortune as an opportunity to get angry at you, insult you and somehow vaunt themselves. For example, you leave an expensive pair of sunglasses on the dashboard of your car and your car gets broken into and your sunglasses are stolen. The narcissist will say to you, "Well that was stupid! You shouldn't have left your sunglasses in the car. My car has *never* been vandalized." The narcissist is

226

telling you that you are stupid and they are smart and it's your fault that you were a victim of a crime. It's interactions where the narcissist gets to remind you that you are the cause of your victimization and you are inferior and they are superior that really float their boat. Finding a way to get a power rush from your misfortune is just one of the many ways these narcs feed.

Then there are those narcissists who find sheer amusement in your mental, emotional and physical suffering. These narc buffoons will laugh their heads off at the sight of you slipping and falling. It doesn't matter that you are in a great pain and have thrown out your back; the narc is feeding on the hilarity of your accident. And because it is such a good feed they don't want it to end so they will replay your painful fall over and over in their mind. Some narcs may get a mild feed and smirk after you fall, mainly because they aren't happy that you fell in the first place. Don't get me wrong, they are glad you are hurting but they are pissed-off that your wipe-out stopped you from giving them all your undivided attention as they blathered on about the most important and interesting person in the world – them. But the buffoon narcs, and I've known a few, will revel in your mental, emotional and physical down fall. These narcs refuse to acknowledge anything about you, but they know every last detail of the most embarrassing moment of your life. And they will tell that story over and over again so you can relive it and they can continue to feed.

I used to wonder why the people in my life always seemed to derive some form of gratification from my misfortune. Not only were they devoid of sympathy and support, understanding or a kind word; they always seemed to make me feel worse. Having been brainwashed by narcissists, here's what I came up with: I thought that I must have done something at some point to upset the narcissist and they were secretly resenting me for it. So when they saw me get hurt, they viewed it as some form of existential payback for the wrong I unknowingly committed against them.

Looking back on my narcissist induced thinking patterns makes me cringe. Based on that thread of logic, the narcissists were feeding off my pain because "I" had done something wrong. Yup, it was my entire fault. I was responsible for the narcissist's callous behavior. This type of N programming was so ingrained in my thinking that even after years of no contact, I still believed on some level that I was the cause of the narcissist's vile personality and heartless treatment of me. Fuck! The rationalizing, the justifying, and the excuses I invented for outright cruel behavior is truly mind-boggling. But that's the thing: my mind was boggled.

The narcissistic abuse I experienced in my NFOO completely tangled my normal, healthy thought process. I guess it's only natural that the truth was twisted and turned in my head. The narcs brainwashed me into believing that there was something inherently wrong with me, and that was a lot easier to accept than the disturbing reality that these "people" my "family" did not wish me well. They sacrificed my mental and emotional health to protect the dirty little secret of who and what they are. And it's taken years to untangle the mess they left in my head. But no more rationalizing the narcissist's warped behavior. They want to us to feel bad because it makes them feel good, period.

Narcissists are extremely sneaky and they will probe you in order seek out your soft spots. The bruised areas are always the sweetest part of the fruit. And once the narcissist discovers your weaknesses you can expect them to poke, jab and dig their fingers in to them. Never show vulnerability to a narcissist because they will not only feed off your pain, they will find a way to increase it. But it is the predatory Malignant Narcissist who will go out of their way to CAUSE your bruising because the MN gets the biggest power high from your lows. The MN loves to exploit your weaknesses, and they hate to see you strong. They are gluttons for your pain and they want you to be incapacitated so you'll be easier to feed off.

I'll say it one more time with *feeling.* The Malignant narcissist doesn't care about you; they never have and they never will. The only thing the MN "cares" about in regards to you is how they can HURT you. That's right; mommy didn't love you, she "loved" to hurt you. Your pain brings momma joy. Of course "joy" to a malignant narcissist is just some form of sadism. But sadistic pleasure is pleasure nonetheless and momma is going to pursue a lifelong campaign of destruction against you so she can continue to indulge in the only thing that truly makes her happy – your misery.

Think of it this way: A malignant narcissist is an addict; they are addicted to the drug rush they get from seeing you in pain. Your downer is their upper. Your pain is their pain killer. I once told someone, who I now believe to be a borderline MN, something horrific MN sister did to me. After hearing the awful thing that my sister did that landed me in the hospital, this MN replied, "Well, maybe SHE feels better now." Whaaat?! What an ass backward reaction! I knew right there and then that she identified more with vile, shamefully abusive MN sister than she ever did with me. That MN hag not only fed-off the retelling of my painful experience, she dug her fangs into me and drew more blood.

If the malignant narcissist can be the *cause* of your pain or additional pain, the drug rush is even more intense. So if you remain in a MN's life, you are sort of like a drug pusher. You are enabling the MN's addiction: your own destruction. Picture this: you go over to your sweet little old granny's house and shoot some heroin into her arm. The drug course through her veins and the effects start to kick-in. Granny flops back into a blissful trance; her eyes roll back in her head and drool slides down the corner of her mouth. She's in a state of nirvana all thanks to you. But guess who suffers the destructive side-effects of granny's drug abuse? That's right, YOU. "Abuse" says it all.

You are the drug that malignant narcissists love to abuse. And like all addicts, the more they indulge the more they need to sustain a high. That's why MNs *always* ramp-up their abuse with time and opportunity. With that in mind, why the hell would you ever allow an MN access to you? It doesn't matter if it's your "mother" or "father" or some other assorted relative; they are all the same. In fact, the closer your relation to the MN, the higher the expectation that you will "supply" them. And don't think for a second that they won't try and get a hit off your children. You don't leave addicts alone in your home because you know they will steal something to support their habit. The same thing applies when leaving MNs alone with your children. They support their habit by extracting from the next generation.

There's a reason why we have all found each other online: we have all experienced abuse at the hands of people who are motivated by nothing but pure malice. That is difficult to explain, especially when it is taken for granted – by society – that the special someone "loves" us and "did the best they could" and we should be willing to "forgive" them for all their mistakes. But she's your mother, why would she do such a thing? We don't know why. Their behavior defies rational explanation. What's even more difficult to explain are the MNs who are outrageously sinister but operate in immaculately covert fashion so the things they do could be interpreted as benign.

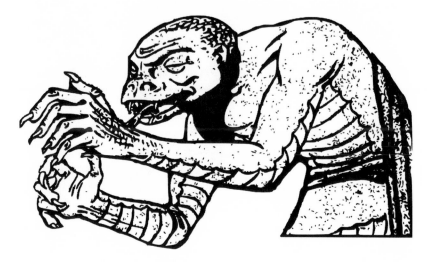

What we have had to endure in our lives is incredibly unnatural. We've had to accept the grim reality that our parent(s) and or relative(s) are evil. That they react to the smell of our blood by lusting for more because the taste of our blood gives them a hit of the pain killing drug they so desperately crave. When it comes right down to it, the only people who will ever truly understand are the ones who need no explanation.

Here's what Tundra Woman had to say regarding her MN mother "Psychobitch."

That damn bitch wanted to destroy my joy in my little home, embarrass the hell out of me in front of my friends, and literally "dirty me up." And I was still dumb enough to believe her. The reality was, she would out-right LIE, make something, anything up from thin air and a life-time of experience to that point taught me she absolutely would do exactly this. But ya know all that lacking in confidence in our perceptions etc.? I mean, your "mother" doesn't lie, right? She "wants what's best for you," right? HAHAHAAAAAA!

If the truth was/is a challenge for us to accept, think how deniable it is to people who have never lived it. Especially when the malignant narcissist is so damn devious and good at hiding who and what it really is.

The malignant narcissist is not only good at hiding who they are, they are experts at "getting away with it." They are always dreaming-up elaborate ways to avoid the consequences of their actions. They do things so gratuitously mean that people find it impossible to believe that anyone could ever be that nasty, particularly a little old lady. People find it implausible that a young, healthy adult could not defend themselves against a little old lady. But they don't GET that the little old lady is a malignant narcissist and she has perfected the art of the smear campaign. The little old lady knows how to discredit the victim in advance should they start talking. Yes, the "little old lady" is your mother or any other MN cloaked in disguise.

Tundra Woman had this to say in another comment:

They DO know just exactly what they've done and they DO know it was at least morally repugnant: They CHOSE to actively predate on others. And from the pathetic to elaborate "cover-ups" which can be anything from them flat out denying what they just said/did 20 sec. ago to Hitchcockian mechanizations, who the hell would go to all this BS if they didn't KNOW exactly what they did? Damn, consciousness of guilt does NOT speak to actually HAVING a "guilty conscience." The stalking, the cover-ups are just epically revealing IMO to their crazy "reality:" They do NOT "feel guilty." They feel "Busted," "Caught" not to mention fuckin' furious.

Getting away with their evil deeds is a vindictive triumph to the malignant narcissist and a tasty part of their feeding experience. They know what they are doing is wrong and not getting caught gives them one hell of an adrenaline rush. Their feeding frenzy is *intensified* by destroying the victim's credibility, and placing them in a double-bind situation where the malignant narcissist comes out smelling like a rose and the victim is framed as the guilty party. As far as the feeding metaphor goes: After the MN has abused the living shit out of you, they pound and pound you down until you are so tender your meat melts in their mouth. Seeing you disintegrate is a delicacy to a malignant narcissist, and one of the most unbelievable highs they could ever experience. Or they put you on a low boil all your life and slowly simmer you down until you are reduced to nothing. When you think about it, they really do a lot of food prep on us.

Life is nothing but an invisible war of control that the Machiavellian MN is determined to win. They never back down, they never give-up, and they never seem to lose their sadistic drive to triumph over others any way they can. They are the predators of the N clan. They predate on others with the intent to cause harm. And they don't need a reason to do it. Malignant narcissists are motivated purely by MALICE. They are the cat and you are the mouse and life is a game of fucking with you until they decide to eat you. And they love the game playing, they never want it to end because that's where they get to do the real feeding – tormenting you and watching you squirm.

But who would ever believe a "mother" would be a killer of the very life she gave? Who would believe that a mother would smell her daughter's blood and go in for the kill? Who would believe that a mother would taste her daughter's blood and crave more? Who could ever comprehend that the malignant narcissist is a mental and emotional cannibal?

The mouse that got away, that's who.

COMMENTS:

I just want to thank you for all your work. You do a fantastic job unveiling what lurks hidden in plain sight. I didn't even understand the concept of a narcissist until about a year ago. I was being eaten alive by these zombies, and I knew something was wrong with THEM, not me. I hopped on a computer and a few clicks later the light began to shine in. What a process it is to come to terms with. If it wasn't for blogs like this, I might have thought I was the crazy one.

No-one would enrage them more than you, Lisette, because of the stark non-collusive ways you unmask them, the way your descriptions capture the malignant essence of their behaviour and characters.

Lisette, I am learning so much from your blog. Thank you for taking the time to educate and bring victims together. Your writing helped me to figure out that I have a narc MIL.

Yes, they feed off your pain. It makes them feel GREAT.

To anyone who is still trapped as a source of supply I want to scream: STOP THEIR FEEDING OFF YOU!!! Don't get stuck in figuring it out, trying to get even, trying to explain, trying harder, waiting for justice, or just hoping that one day they will wake up and decide to act like normal decent human beings. Don't get stuck in what did I ever do to deserve this, or if I was a better person this wouldn't happen to me, or any other the self-serving shit they want to keep you stuck in. Do whatever it takes to secure your safety, however impossible that might seem.

Where does all their irrational hatred come from? That is the question. Lack of empathy and lack of conscience is one thing, but that all-consuming, unrelenting drive to go out of their way to destroy, is another. What the fuck drives these monsters is beyond all imagination. It's as if they feel the need to hunt and stalk and destroy in order to survive. They are nothing but predators.

I think you have saved my life...It's like you cracked open my soul and all the pain and unacknowledged abuses just poured out onto the screen.

Yup, it's all about control...through pain, confusion, mind games, etc... It's astonishing to think that a mother could do this to her own child

Great article it really nails it and the part about how no one believes you doubling the pain, is very very accurate. I have faced facts that my mother is evil even on a spiritual level.

Thanks for telling us we made the right choice to cut these Ns out of our lives. It feels good to be validated for something most of society still condemns us for.

Trying to "understand" narcs while you are still in their target range is like trying to learn to swim when you are drowning.

Here: I'm handing you a cyber chain-saw: It's set to rock-'n-roll. Just wave it around in front of you and I can assure you, considering the population of MNs you should be able to make a wide and very productive swath through what appears to be a significant portion of the "human" race.

Any instance of any Narc saying to any of us anything that starts with "You're too..." is a manipulation. Even when Narcs do tell the truth, it is only done in the service of another of their lies.

I learned some valuable things from your blog. I was getting ready to go talk to my sister about the pain and agony I've endured from my mother, but then I realized that what you said is true: she will be giddy with glee and seize the opportunity to feed off me.

HOW TO CAUSE NARCISSISTIC INJURY WITHOUT REALLY TRYING

Causing "narcissistic injury" is a walk in the park; you don't have to do a damn thing. What's difficult is NOT causing narcissistic injury.

First off, I don't care for wishy-washy psychiatric phrases like "narcissistic injury." They are extremely misleading and seem to suggest that the poor narcissist is "feeling" hurt or wounded and is suffering as a result. Give me a break. When you cause narcissistic injury you simply threaten the narcissist's delusions of uniqueness and superiority and THAT pisses them off, period. All narcissistic injuries lead to rage. Therefore, "narcissistic injury" and "rage" aren't just linked; they are one and the same. Sure, the narcissist's reaction to a perceived threat may sometimes look like snootiness, cold detachment, apathy, mild irritation or indifference but it isn't, it is rage.

The title of this post is a little tongue-in-cheek because it doesn't take any effort whatsoever to cause "narcissistic injury." Hell, sometimes all it takes to enrage a narcissist is to breathe the same air as them. The narcissist's image is one of perfection: they view themselves as exclusive, faultless, flawless, irreproachable, magnificent bastards and if we lowly plebs ever forget it then look out, there will be hell to pay! Because with every narcissistic "injury" there is a reflexive urge toward violence. And guess who is at the receiving end of that violence? That's right, we the people. WE are the ones that suffer "injuries" when the narcissist's infantile little ego gets bruised.

It goes something like this: We somehow inadvertently threaten the narcissist's grandiosity. In reaction to that threat, the narcissist experiences rage. The natural by-product of rage is violence. Depending on the narcissist, the violence can range from anything to name calling, shouting, a dirty look, walking away in a huff, the silent treatment, slamming a door, blasting the stereo, smashing a plate, breaking a chair, vandalizing your property, vandalizing your image, stalking, harassment, murder, and the ultimate… suicide. The narcissist's violence is a knee jerk reaction to a threat of their narcissism. It is immediate and it is inevitable. It can be mitigated and controlled, but the impulse is *always* there. Narcissists are always seething with anger and ready to explode. BOOM!

The way I see it, the narcissist's rage/violence serves a few purposes. First, it acts as a fortress to protect their image: They scare the living shit out of us and therefore deter us from ever speaking the truth about them and their behavior. We simply don't speak-up for fear of retribution. We keep our mouths shut to keep the peace. We walk on egg-shells around narcissists because we know that they are loose cannons ready to blow if we say or do the wrong thing. If you had N parents then you lived with the tension of always waiting for the other shoe to drop.

We cause the narcissist "injury" when we don't play by their script. All the worlds a stage and we are merely players to the narcissist's starring role. Our job as lowly bit players/extras/filler in the narcissist's spectacular big budget drama is to enable and support their narcissism, *not* threaten it. But because these Ns don't take the time to hand-out our lines for the day, and the scenes we'll be in and the roles we're supposed to play, we end-up flubbing our parts and running the risk of being a target of N rage. And it's *very* easy to flub our part. Make an innocent observation that contravenes with the narcissist's self-image of perfection; dare to contradict the narcissist; subject the narcissist to an attitude that challenges their sense of entitlement; treat the narcissist as an equal and call their superiority into question; offer a damning yet accurate assessment of the narcissist's behavior; make a statement of fact that impinges on the narcissist's confabulated reality and watch the shit hit the fan!

Instead of calling CUT! TAKE 2! the narcissist has a raging temper tantrum. They control their fantasy of themselves by controlling us with fear. And if we're not buying their "act" then their performances aren't convincing enough and THAT freaks them out. If you had N parents/siblings then you've been silenced in those relationship all your life and you may even still be afraid of them. I survived in my NFOO by playing the groupie to the N's demanding Diva role.

Another purpose the narcissist's rage/violence serves is to keep them front and centre stage in the lead role. They are not only the star of their own movie; they are the star of your movie/his movie/her movie/everyone's movie. If they are lifting cars, tipping dumpsters, shooting evil glares, causing drama, spewing bile and creating chaos then roll camera because the spot light is on them, and that's when the narcissist is ready for their close-up. If they can control a whole room of people with their mood, THAT is fucking star power!

Also, narcs always feel better after a good rage session. They're like big babies with gas that have a good burp and let it all out. Oh so satisfying. And they not only expect us to feel better too after they rage, but to act like their ugly, psycho performance never happened. But do we feel better after the narcissist's rage fest? Hellz no! First, the narcissist lightens their toxic load by dumping their anger onto us and into us, so we carry that around for them. Then, because we are not allowed to "feel" anything, we are forced to repress our own natural rage at the abuse they inflict. So there we are, carrying around the narc's poisonous rage and suppressing our own righteous anger. If that's not a recipe for illness/addiction/self-sabotage/effed-up relationships etc. etc., I don't know what is.

My malignant narcissist mother would always scream at me, "You're so damn moody!" MN sister would always whine, "You always seem so angry. I don't know why you're always so mad at me all the time?" Of course, most of this was projection, but the reality was: Why the hell wouldn't I be moody? I was a dumping ground for the toxic waste of three miserable full-blown narcs. Was I supposed to be singing and dancing and whistling and smiling and doing back-flips of joy through the living room when I had no choice but to accept abuse and repress my every last feeling?! Put it this way: if I wasn't quiet, withdrawn and apprehensive then there would be something seriously wrong with me... I would be a dumbed-down, lifeless, hollowed-out zombie and that would mean there's nothing left of me, I no longer feel anything and the narcs had won. And get this, because I didn't become what the narc's wanted me to be - a compliant zombie - MN mother and MN sister who are certifiable and batshit crazy, are telling people that I have a "mood disorder," "emotional problems," "mental-health issues." Yup, that's what happens when you decide to protect yourself from abuse. The narcs label YOU the sick one. HA! The irony of the injustice is mind-boggling.

Also, because I have gone NO CONTACT – the mother of all N injury – the two evil witches can no longer unleash their rage on me in person. So the next best thing to do with their violence is to vandalize my image through lies, slander and gossip. Narcissistic abuse is the kind of abuse that keeps on giving long after you're gone, and the reason is simple: Malignant narcissists must *always* remain linked to their prey in some way. They are fused to you whether you like it or not.

This leads me to another function of the narcissist's violence: It serves to perpetuate the relationship between the malignant narcissist and their victim. Their smear campaigns and abusive, crazy, deranged, dangerous, illegal, and bizarre behavior are done in an effort to maintain a relationship with you. The fact that it is a BAD relationship - a TERRORIST situation - is beside the point. The point is the MN is still linked to you through arguing, screaming matches, restraining orders, police reports, court proceedings and lawyers. And if the MN can't have a physical presence in their victim's life, then they create a way to live on in their victim's mind. The MN mother says to herself, "Well, she might have a life of her own, but I will make her forever afraid of me!" Therefore ensuring that her victim, target, daughter won't be able to live without thinking about her… and the movie plays on with MN mother in the lead. Or, the MN carries-out some spectacular display of evil right before their final curtain: For example, arranging for your inheritance to go to your mortal enemy. That way, the MN continues to live-on in the minds of others through conflict and strife. For the MN, there is no final curtain call, graceful bow, or exit stage left. Their horror show rages on long after they are dead and buried.

Here are some examples of narcissistic injury, starting with the big ones:

Exist independently of the N parent/Get married/Go no contact: That is the motherload of narcissistic injury. When the MN parent is confronted with the reality that they are not the main character in their child's movie; that you have your own movie and they aren't even in it, THIS is the worst calamity that can befall a malignant narcissist parent. They suddenly find themselves reduced to a bit part or completely cut-out, and are now doomed to be just like all the other 6 billion extras in the world. THIS makes the MN Diva mad as hell! How dare they be assigned to some lowly supporting role or end-up on the cutting room floor! They are a Star and don't you ever forget it. This is probably why so many Ns pull crazy stunts at their children's wedding: They want to make the event ALL ABOUT THEM, and maintain their starring role.

The following comment left by ANON, perfectly illustrates narcissistic injury/rage when the N discovers that their supply exists independent of them:

"I remember my mother having a hissy fit because one of her husbands was flirting with another woman. This crazy bitch had a full blown temper tantrum, screaming, cussing, and picking up the back end of a car, with the grand finale being that she tossed a couple of large green dumpsters over like they were nothing (big, heavy, full of trash - the kind you roll on wheels because nobody can pick them up)...I was scared as hell, but knew not to say a word or I'd receive whatever was left of her rage. I stayed quiet until we got home, went to my room and ended up drawing a cartoon of a cross between her and the incredible hulk tossing dumpsters in the air - the fear melted into giggles."

In this instance, the malignant narcissist sees her husband flirting with another woman and is confronted with the reality that she is not the main character in his movie. The movie is his, and it keeps on playing even when she's not around. And the by-product of that terrifying realization for this MN is to morph into The Hulk and go on a rampage until her fury is spent. And her fury wasn't even directed at the husband, it was unleashed on innocent cars and dumpster. Can you imagine what the MN would have done to the husband? This is the kind of narcissistic injury that causes a MN to poison their spouse's meal with cyanide. It's a good thing ANON knew NOT to react to her raging lunatic of a MN mother.

A raging MN doesn't have to act like a roaring, over-sized green beast, busting out of the seams of their clothing, trashing objects and running amok. Sometimes all the MN monster needs to rely on is good old verbal violence, a withering glare or gaslighting.

Here's what happened to another Anonymous after looking "disappointed" after receiving an unfitting gift from N parents: "When I looked disappointed - a torrent of shoulds/gaslighting/verbal abuse. "You're never grateful for anything you selfish little bitch nothing ever pleases you I don't know why I bother you're never satisfied etc." delivered with the most hateful glare and harsh strident tone imaginable. It was really very terrifying, like being confronted by Medusa."

Even a simple "look" of disappointment, frustration, sadness, anger, or joy can cause the testy narcissist injury/rage. Once, I got belted across the face at the dinner table for a look I wasn't even aware I gave MN mother. The violence came out of thin air, and shocked me so much that I wet my pants. And I never uttered a word. I just sat at the table and continued eating my meal; face stinging. It was N father who hit me, and he didn't give a crap what "look" I gave MN mother, he hated her, he just needed to release some pent-up rage and I was the family whipping post.

Whether it was Medusa, The Hulk, The Hand or The Smirk; the effect was all the same to the children of narcissists: The N parent's rage was terrifying. Even after I fled to the opposite end of the country, and was officially an adult, I was still terrified of NFOO's rage. I remember a boyfriend who I did a lot of travelling with suggesting that I send post-cards to MN mother and MN sister. I kept on saying no. He kept on insisting. He was family oriented and wanted me to have a wonderful relationship with them. He just didn't get it. Anyway, he kept on insisting I send post cards, and I kept on saying no. Finally he asked, "Why not?!" I answered, "Because they'll get mad!" This was absolutely true. For me to live my own life, a full life, a happy life caused MN mother and MN sister narcissistic injury.

Hell, you can "injure" a narcissist simply by ending a telephone conversation with them. One morning – many years ago, before I fled to the opposite end of the country – MN sister called me up all chirpy. I was still sleeping, and a little hung-over. I was working three jobs, lived in a shit basement suite with a noisy family above me, and I had been out the night before until all hours and had to work that day and into the night. I needed my sleep. So she's blathering on and on, and I guess I wasn't acting overly enthused about whatever she was yapping about, or giving her the royal treatment that she feels entitled to so she sensed this and we cut the conversation short. Fine by me, I needed to take advantage of whatever sleep I could get. So I fell back asleep and was dozing comfortably when about 20 minutes later the phone rang and woke me up. I answer the phone, "Hello?" What do I hear at the other end but MN mother raging at the top of her lungs, "Where the hell is that lawn chair?! Who the hell do you think you are for taking that lawn furniture?! You goddamn get to do whatever the hell you want!"

What happened was this: MN sister, who was living with MN mother, got upset because I wasn't doing back-flips of joy during our conversation. In other words, I didn't enable and support MN sister's narcissism and give her the preferential treatment she feels entitled to. This caused the psychotic little bitch injury, so she whined to MN mother about how rude I was. Now because MN mother and MN sister are fused, this also caused MN mother injury and she lashed-out and raged at me about some piece of shit lawn chair that I took to use in my apartment years prior. When it comes to MNs It's NEVER about a crap lawn chair or a ratty old beach towel, it's about their delusions of being superior beings and their expectations of always being treated as such.

Long story short, just by existing I caused MN mother's limb - MN sister - injury. I was removed from activities that I loved and excelled in because my success made MN sister "feel bad." I was taken out of figure skating after doing well in a province wide competition because according to MN mother, "Your figure skating makes your sister feel bad, and you don't really like it anyway." I remember MN mother giving me instructions to tell my coach I was quitting because my family couldn't afford it. Yeah right. Money was never an issue.

Earlier in the post I explained that the narcissist's rage is inevitable and is immediate but it can be mitigated and controlled. Here's an example of delayed release narcissistic rage:

I was visiting N father for a few days, and went out and picked-up a bunch of Danishes to have with our morning coffee that week. It was the afternoon when I got back, and I asked N father if he would like to have

Danish. He said sure, so I put a selection out on a plate and left them on the kitchen counter for him to choose from. A while later I went back to the kitchen and found N father reading the paper with an empty plate of Danishes in front of him. With about as much interest as I would put into noticing rain, I innocently remarked, "Oh, you ate them all." N father snapped back, "They were small!" It was true, they were small, but he ate 6 of them. Anyway, there were still 6 left so I could at least enjoy one with my coffee the next morning.

Even with NPD knowledge I was thinking, shit! I shouldn't have said that, now he's going to be in a bad mood for the rest of the day. I don't recall him being in a noticeably bad mood, or maybe I just avoided him. Anyway, the next morning I awoke eager for my morning ritual of a coffee and something sweet, in this case Danish. I was about to go down the stairs when I heard N father crumpling a paper bag and the sound of the crumpled bag slamming against a wall. Before I even descended the stairs and entered the kitchen, I knew what he had done. Sure enough, I found the bag of Danishes crushed and crumpled at the opposite end of the kitchen from where I had left them. I grabbed the bag of squished and mangled Danishes and plunked it into the garbage. I never said a word to N father about this seriously messed-up act. Why? Because I wanted to avoid WW3.

Crushed Danishes were narcissistic rage. So what was the narcissistic injury? Delivering what N father perceived to be disturbing data about him. In N father's eyes, my remark about eating all the Danishes wasn't addressing his actions; it was addressing who he is as a person. And N father believes himself to be perfect and he can never be seen as anything but perfect, and a perfect person doesn't make a pig of themselves. I never took him for a pig because he isn't a pig. He isn't a hog and he has no issues with weight. And it's not as if I said, "Hey Tubby, you scarfed ALL those Danishes down?! Would you like me to fill-up you're trough while I'm standing here?" There was narcissistic injury and there was rage and my innocent observation must have kept him up that night plotting his revenge. But why the Danishes?! Anything but the Danishes!

Causing "narcissistic injury" is a walk in the park; you don't have to do a damn thing. What's difficult is NOT causing narcissistic injury. My life among the narcissists has been an exercise in not tripping the wire that causes the N to detonate. And living in a narc minefield is no way to live. If however, you would like to cause a MN lifelong injury and all-consuming rage and maybe a little fear; here's what you do: Sometime before, during or after you go NO CONTACT make sure the narcissist knows that you've got their number and you've NEVER bought their act AND you're mad as hell. Then disappear. You will forever be a thorn in the malignant narcissist's side if they know you're out there with the truth of who and what they are, and YOU are loose a cannon that is not afraid to blow.

COMMENTS:

Thank you for putting the truth out there. This is knowledge that will save people's lives.

This information is spot-on, and explains so much, such as why someone in the NFOO always *had* to act out at any gathering. It just wasn't a get-together unless someone was exploding in rage, screaming, and knocking over restaurant tables (seriously) over imagined slights.

You are so right about not having to try to cause a narcissistic injury - you'll inadvertently do it just by sharing common air with them (their air should be too special to be shared with us mere mortals you know). If you have a brain and an opinion, you'll injure their fragile little egos on a daily basis. And if you want to see the mother of all meltdowns, just allow a little reality to seep into their distorted fantasy world.

Gun control... How about MOTHER CONTROL? That would get rid of half of all the violent crime out there. We're not wrestling with the 2nd amendment. We're wrestling with and taking aim against the violent people who raised us.

Wonderful article here. It's such a joy to piss off the ones you are still in contact with just by rewriting your lines and role. THEY CAN'T HANDLE IT!

This is a question we Acons eventually ask ourselves. How did we survive? I have to think really hard about my survival skills. They must have begun at birth, and then some spark of life must have carried me through. My existence was one of running and hiding, deciphering codes of abusive behavior, watching my siblings being abused and neglected. Being invisible and most of all having no feelings.

I have issues with the name mother and father. They are not even honourable enough to be called "mother(mom)" and "father(dad)." Guess I need to think of something that suits them.

One has to wonder if it's actually possible to starve them to death; if it's possible that their health would deteriorate from lack of supply. I'm convinced their mental health goes with no supply, but I wonder if their physical health is also affected.

Excellent article thank you so much. I was told my entire life by my MN mother that I was a sensitive bitch. I always had an "attitude".

Okay, freely admit this is cruel and unusual punishment, but I have a proposition. Malignant Narcissists seem to go through life taking sadistic pleasure from verbally hurting and abusing others. So... have a proposition that would force MNs to stop this type of behavior for good...

They DO know just exactly what they've done and they DO know it was at least morally repugnant: They CHOSE to actively predate on others. And from the pathetic to elaborate "cover-ups" which can be anything from them flat out denying what they just said/did 20 sec. ago to Hitchcockian mechanizations, who the hell would go to all this BS if they didn't KNOW exactly what they did? Damn, consciousness of guilt does NOT speak to actually HAVING a "guilty conscience."

This post explained my childhood. I played my part in the script perfectly for 3 decades. I found myself having PTSD, anxiety, passing my behaviors to my kids, exposing them to Narcs. Then thankfully i woke up. I had to laugh reading about the dumpster throwing, HA HA! That's a story I can relate to. It really hits home remembering my parents raging and having to sit through it with plates, chairs and food flying and it going on for hours. Then the next day when I woke up dreading my day with the Narcs, having to pretend NOTHING ever happened. And that was a mild experience in the full spectrum of time in the first 18 years of my life. It never ended. My parents had me controlled and numbed to "narc injury".

NARCISSISTS ARE ATTENTION WHORES

ALL Narcissists are big babies. And like babies, they cannot comprehend being anything but the centre of the Universe – Wah! Look at me! Narcissists never outgrew the expectation they had as children: that all available attention should be freely lavished on them. And they approach EVERY relationship with that same infantile expectation. If you married a narcissist then you married a 3 year old – my condolences. If you're in an Nship then you're babysitting. If you were parented by a narc then you were treated as a rival. Narcissists are selfish children trapped in the body of an adult. And they are not just immature; they are spoiled brats who are *always* jockeying for all available attention.

And what does always jockeying for attention make them? That's right – PREDATORY.

Here's one of my favorite quotes from Kathy Krajco. If you get this then you will understand the true spirit of the narcissist.

A Narcissist's need to "have it all" invests him or her with a spirit hostile to the needs and wellbeing of others.

If you feel a compelling need to have all the dollars in the world, no matter how many you get, you will compete with others for every single one; and if you see a dollar in someone else's hand, you will want to take it away. Just because he has it. That makes you an ADVERSARY of everyone else in the world. It makes you view the possessor of the dollar as a PREDATOR views prey.

---- Kathy Krajco "What Makes Narcissists Tick" page 40

Now just replace "dollar" with "attention."

When it comes to attention, ALL narcissists are predatory; they ALL go out of their way to con, trick, manipulate, coax, pressure, deceive, manoeuver, fight and compete for their most desired source of supply. They really are shameless whores in that regard: they will spread their proverbial legs just to get a drop of the stuff. To the narcissist, attention is nothing but a form of currency. You know how some people can be bought with money? Well, narcissists can be bought with attention. The unscrupulous among us "bank" on that fact and heap mounds of attention on the narcissist in exchange for actual cash payments and property.

MN sister preys on aging N father by bombarding him with an excess of attention in the form of over-the-top concern for his health and safety, and complete fascination with his diet, bowel movements and every itch or tick in his body. This scheming MN presents herself to the old N as being utterly captivated by everything he says or does and he rewards her handsomely with money, possessions and property. MN sister knows, if she gives N father the right kind of attention in the right dose; he is putty in her hands and she can control, manipulate and exploit him. In terms of attention for HER, the payoff is getting N father to listen only to her, believe only her, trust only her, and be dependent on her for care, information, and advice etc. MN sister is a crafty bitch who knows exploiting two aging N parent's is a win win situation. She reaps two of her favorite things out of the deal: ALL of her parents' undivided attention, and ALL their assets. Narcissists never pay attention to anyone unless they get a return. MN sister's feigned devotion of N father – who she resents – is nothing but a business transaction for the greedy bitch. She reinforces his narcissism and gets to exploit him in return.

So to recap: Narcissists have the mentality of a selfish child playing keep away, and they predate on others and whore themselves in order to gain ATTENTION. And if they're getting all of it, you're getting none of it. They are all alike in this regard: they all have the same end goal and they achieve it by playing for the right reaction from their environment. But since they each inhabit different environments, they each have their own personal strategy - one adapted best to suit the particular attention they crave in a specific milieu.

For example, the attention a MN mother may demand at home is Queen of The Castle, and she may garner that kind of attention by making her husband and children react to her with fear. But this same MN may crave pity and sympathy from her cronies, so she will extract that kind of attention by playing the martyr and the poor, over-worked house wife with a sick child. And maybe this same MN likes to be respected and admired by members of her volunteer group, so she will pull-off contrived acts of do-goodery to score awe and appreciation. In other words, narcissists tailor their attention whoring style to reflect the type of attention they crave in a particular role, rank and position among a particular group, setting, situation or battlefield.

If the narcissist craves a certain kind of attention and is deluded enough to pursue it in an inappropriate setting, then the attention she receives can be downright awkward and embarrassing.

I have vivid memories of a Friday night in high school when my class mate "Dean" had a party in his basement. There were about 15 of us hanging-out and listening to music when who sashays down the stairs wearing a sheer nightie; ice cubes clinking in her highball glass, but his mother. Dean looked absolutely mortified and gently tried to coax his mother back upstairs. Tipsy and slurring her words; she angrily pulled away from him and wondered aimlessly into the crowd. I was horrified for Dean. In fact, everyone was, the room went dead silent. Then a couple of

Dean's good-looking pals addressed his mother by her first name "June" and persuaded her to go have a drink with them upstairs. June was maneuvered back upstairs and eventually Dean and his friends came back down to join the party. Dean looked absolutely crushed. His mother had hijacked all the attention at HIS party, and left him for dead. It was a tragic scene. And it always is when you get an attention whoring narcissist looking for their drug in the wrong part of town.

Something I've observed about these once "hot stuff" narcs, is that they are all stuck in some kind of a time warp. For example, if they drew the most attention for their physical appearance back in College they stay stuck in that look for the rest of their life: same hair style, make-up, way of dressing etc., and they end up looking old fashioned.

N father back in his prime resembled Mad Men's Don Draper, but I think he got the most attention in the 70's when he was seen as a Burt Reynolds type. I remember a summer by the lake, he was sitting in one those Adirondack chairs; giggling teenage girls flanked on either side. "Oooh... I love your moustache," they cooed. MN mother walked by and shot him the most withering of glares. He was in heaven, she was enraged, and I was embarrassed. Since then, the man has clung to his out-dated moustache.

I recall a grotesquely narcissistic ex-Nfriend "Kevin" who was single and on the prowl for a new girlfriend. He was 42 at the time, so I suggested a mutual friend who was 39. He became incredibly hostile and snapped, "She's TOO OLD!"

Many male and females narcissists garner attention by being sultry and seductive and using their sex appeal to increase their ability to get noticed. Looking good, literally and figuratively is extremely important to them, but attention whoring is never more obvious than when they are being openly physical: they strike poses, display "attitude," flip their hair and strut their stuff. These are the narcissists who behave as if a camera is always on them, but the reality is, no one is even looking their way.

Narcissists want others to desire and admire them, and physical qualities are an important part of their attention seeking. However, not all narcissists are physically attractive - and if they're lucid enough to realize that – they may substitute with other enhancing traits such as intelligence, cleverness, money, success, fame and prestige.

If however, the narcissist does not receive the attention they need, they shift into an over-drive of shameless self-promotion to impress others. They advertise themselves relentlessly, brag about their accomplishments, name drop, hype their achievements; making themselves sound incredibly wonderful, and making whatever they do seem better than whatever anyone else does – and better than it actually is. Everything they do is for show, to get people to notice them and admire them.

Because of my background in the entertainment industry, I have known many shameless, self-promoting narcissists. I have worked with them, had Nships with them, and dated them. They are all braggarts showing off their culture, their education, their status, their careers, their intelligence, their creativity, their – whatever they think will garner attention. Their only subject of conversation is themselves, their first, last, and only love. And the documented evidence of their shameless self-promotion is splashed across the internet – Ugh!

Recently, I did a little Google search of a few of these entertainment narcs and I came across a virtual cornucopia of "Look at MEEEE!" I discovered that "Kevin" who is a director, cameraman, photographer, musician – Artiste – and the biggest attention whore on the face of the earth started a rock gospel choir and named it: "Kevin's Angels." Talk about a god complex. Yup, that's right; he places himself front and centre stage while his "Angels" the gospel singers, sing in the background. And get this, he doesn't even sing. He plays the drums. So here's this attention whoring narc playing the drums at the front of the stage while a large group of young, attractive women sing at least 10 feet behind him. And if that's not enough to make you puke, I came across the video of his wedding ceremony on YouTube. Yes, Kevin got married at the ripe age of 50 to a much younger woman. His wedding ceremony was a paid event, attended by all his "fans," and he and his wife exchanged vows while doing an interpretative dance number to The Who's – See Me, Feel Me… Gag me!

You can't make this stuff up. I swear, in their desperate attempt to get all the available attention, all the time, these narcs make complete fools of themselves.

A cheap, selfish, arrogant, pretentious, grandiose narcissist ex-boyfriend "Graham" who is a documentary filmmaker and a magazine editor does a lot of appearance at tradeshows to promote the motorcycle magazine he works for. I read that at a recent tradeshow he attended, he pledged to give out a free T shirt to the first person to rush the stage yelling his name! He's a magazine editor who expects rock star calibre attention. However, in contrast to that showy number, he put on an academy award winning performance of modesty and humility when he bashfully accepted an award for a social documentary he produced. He was always such a fucking phony. Different role, different audience, different Graham. Sad thing is, people swallow his act and he is slathered in attention, just like Kevin.

Narcs don't have friends, they have fans. And people either idolize them, or hate their fucking guts – there is no in between because they aren't normal people. The have an unnatural need and predatory drive to obtain excessive amounts of attention. These arrogant, cocky, attention whoring narcs are so impressed with themselves and they act as if we are, or should be enthralled by everything they say and do - as if we should be honoured to know them. They all scream, "Look at me!!" And they never appear more alive than when others are noticing them. I tell you, garden variety or malignant, ALL narcissists truly light up when they are the centre of attention. It is their favorite N supply, and the fastest acting drug. During my field studies in the narc jungle, I have witnessed miserable, crusty old narcissists morph into delightful, childlike creatures as soon as they were fussed and fawned over.

As I said in the beginning of the post, narcissists have their own personal style to get attention. Not all of them have attractive traits, special talents, or are even capable of garnering positive attention. Many are just plain ordinary and some are just repelling, especially the malignant narcissists. Nevertheless, ALL narcissists seek attention and they will employ strategies to get it at all cost.

MN sister had some physical health issues growing-up that allowed her to absolutely thrive in a twisted N family dynamic. Her "special needs" and her position as MN Golden Child garnered her never-ending attention and gave her carte blanche to control, manipulate and exploit every family member and every aspect of the N family system. She could get away with doing things like shoving my face into a plate of food, but if I so much as tapped her, she would scream "MY HIP!! MY HIP!!"

Bitch is still screaming, "MY HIP!! MY HIP!!" Being the "sick" one in a NFOO really worked for her and she took that and ran with it. Now she is a full-fledged hypochondriac who is riddled with imaginary illnesses and gets hoards of attention – her favorite kind being pity – by playing the poor, sad, house bound patient who is afflicted with an endless array of health problems. HA! She loves being sick, or pretending to be sick – it's her life. She spends all day researching illnesses; fancies herself a medical expert and plays the concerned "doctor" to aging N father.

I find that a lot of these narcissists take whatever role got them the most attention in their FOO and use that as an adult. For example, I had one N friend who was the youngest in her family; the baby. She got attention by being the "cute" one. This annoying N played "the cute one" well into her 30's and probably beyond. She was the type of juvenile N who, among a group of friends hanging out and talking, would bounce up and start giggling and playing with the hostess's dog. Of course, a hyper narcissist and a hyper dog is sure fire way to divert everyone's attention away from the conversation and onto her.

Then there are the narcissists who demand we pay attention to them by being loud, obnoxious, noisy boors. These types of attention seeking narcs are the neighbours from hell. They barge into apartment buildings whistling, singing, and yacking on their phone; they slam doors, walk like elephants and always crank their stereos or televisions. They disturb everyone around them, and if anyone dare complains then they stomp harder and blast their music louder. The noise-making, attention whoring narc is your typical immature asshole with a pathological sense of entitlement that believes he is the centre of the universe, and should always be noticed. Brutes like this were probably the type of bratty child who tossed bowls of spaghetti across the kitchen and banged pots and pans to get mommy to notice him.

Of course, the devious malignant narcissist *always* uses trickery and treachery to get noticed. MNs are sneaky and two-faced; placing themselves as the spider in the family web and the only reliable source of information and the only person others should confide in. These despicable, attention whoring malignants triangulate regularly and play one person off the other; always betraying the trust that others have given them. MN sister is a master of this. The few times I spoke to her in the last 26 years she always spread dirt about N father, brother, and MN mother and anyone else she could drag into her subterfuge. She gets a sadistic thrill and a power rush from playing the puppet master to anyone that comes in contact with her. And she fucking loves the attention of being seen as the all-knowing powerful OZ.

Malignant narcissists do not hesitate to ruin reputations, stir-up trouble, double-cross friends and family, and betray the trust that others have given them. They do not keep secrets, they spread false rumours and they are never more alive than when they are in the middle of a Smear Campaign. Their vicious stunts and vendettas FORCE people to pay attention to them. Sometimes it's negative attention: "You crazy bitch! How could you do such a thing?! I'm going to sue you! I'm going to fire you! I'm going to kill you!"

But more often than not, the revolting malignant narcissist garners positive attention in the form of sympathy, understanding and support as well as assistance from her minions and flying monkeys to carry out her crimes. Yes, the nasty MN hag is adept a playing the victim/the martyr/the injured party/ the concerned citizen who is just grossly misunderstood by the people she's annihilating. Not only does the evil MN predator get to feed off her prey's suffering, she gets to feed off the attention she receives for excellence in staging, casting and production as well as accolades for her Oscar winning portrayal as woeful victim.

No matter what their style and strategy, all narcissists are weird. That's because they all have a weird need – the need for ALL AVAILABLE

ATTENTION. They do truly bizarre things to AVOID paying others any attention and they behave strangely to draw-in or hijack attention. And whatever attention they can't attract or steal, they BLOCK. So look out!! Because when someone is getting the attention the narcissist feels entitled to, they become extremely jealous and incredibly hostile and will not hesitate to throw dramatic fits and childish temper tantrums to divert the attention away from others.

My N father is a self-absorbed, emotionally absent, neglectful, indifferent, grandiose big baby and a total attention whore. He never gave his children a drop of regard. In fact, I honestly believe the man hates kids because he has to compete with them for attention. I remember him getting really sarcastic about the only child at a family get together. He huffed, "That kid gets so much damn attention! It's as if they think she can walk on water!" Walk on water? Project much narc?! This god in his own mind resented ever having to notice his children, and now that we are adults, well, nothing has changed. His rules still apply: "Don't you dare talk about yourself or I'll make you sorry you did!"

Because of narcissistic abuse and trauma, I grind my teeth. And because I've been grinding my teeth for decades, my teeth have shifted and become crooked. A few years ago, I mentioned to N father I was thinking about getting braces. He sniped, "Nobody cares!" Then he changed the subject. Another time, many years ago, I started to speak in regard to my brother. "I don't think Brad...." N father cut me right off and snapped, "It doesn't matter what you think! It doesn't matter what you feel!"

You see in an N home with narcissist parents, not only are you not allowed attention, but you are not allowed to think or feel or be. You don't matter. These rules never change. Narcissists are greedy attention whoring babies and that means they get all of it and you get none of it.

My N parents did not attend my University graduation? No, of course not. And when I had the nerve to show N father a photo of me accepting my diploma, he burst out laughing. You see, the photo was sent to me by a photographer who would be sending me copies, and on the border of the photo he had written: "How many would you like to *recieve*?" Get it? He spelled "receive" wrong and that's how N father blocked giving me any attention. He couldn't bear to offer as measly "congratulations." He just pointed at "receive" and howled, "Haha – recieve!" N father is way too superior to give me even a modicum of positive regard.

When I travelled all over Europe for the first time, I sent N father postcards from all the places I visited. When he found out I had done some European travel, he promptly booked a European trip of his own. In the 10 years that I lived at the opposite end of the country not once did he visit me. At least not until he booked his European vacation. He hates flying so he drove across Canada and stayed with me for 5 days before he took a train to New York to catch the Queen Mary over to England. So while he was visiting, I decided to show him a few photos from my European trip (big mistake). I was quickly whipping through them: "Here's the Sistine Chapel. Here's the Roman Coliseum. Here's the Leaning Tower of Pisa." I noticed him getting visibly irritated so I just kept my mouth shut and flashed the photos in front of him. When I showed him one of me standing in front of The Palace of Versailles, N father looked at the photo, pointed at me and in a scornful, childish tone sniped, "Who's THAT?!"

I remember being so shocked and thinking what a fucking weirdo. I responded to his nastiness by saying, "I have no idea who that is." What did N father do? You guessed it – he smirked! He looked fucking crazy; totally drugged out with demon eyes. I gathered-up the photos and put them away. This fucking psycho couldn't handle giving his daughter 15 minutes of attention to look at photos of her trip to Europe, yet she's supposed to be absolutely enthralled when he drones on about his trip to the bathroom.

About 10 years later, and following a few remarkably horrible years – I was in a bad accident, had to have plastic surgery, ended up hospitalized for psychological trauma, and was stalked by my building managers – I took another trip to Europe, this time to explore my roots. I never told N father in advance about my trip, I just sent him a couple of postcards. When I returned home, I spoke to him on the phone and he said to me, "You know Lisette, when I found out you were in Europe... I was really jealous."

N father wasn't happy that his daughter - who had been hospitalized several times in the last 6 months and was forced out of her home by psychos finally got an opportunity to enjoy herself and have some fun. No. He was jealous. And he didn't ask me anything about my trip. Also, the MN sister was so fucking furious when she learned her psychological violence didn't paralyse me and so jealous to hear I went traveling that she hit my dad up for a large lump of cash to make herself feel better. Like all narcissists, life is a competition for her to get it ALL and she uses me as a measuring stick to gage how good she feels about herself. And the only way narcissist are able to feel better about themselves is through fraud and extortion - that's how they shake everyone down for every last drop of attention in all its manifestations.

Ladies and Gentleman! I present to you... The Greedy! The Envious! The Entitled! The Attention Whores!!

Comments:

Well, of course, I could say volumes on this one, we all could.

Yes volumes here too. I will never forget the blank stare my NM would get when I tried to tell her something about myself. Deaf ears and blank stare. Then she would say uh-huh and start talking about herself.

Yep, that is how it was with N parents. GC has to be the centre of attention and gets pissed even when a child gets in their way.

I'm having a good time giving them the blank stare back and watching them squirm with the non-attention thrown back at them. As smart as some of these vermin are they literally do not know how to say "and how are YOU?"

Another great article, thank you Lisette! You describe these wackos so accurately. Isn't it interesting how similar they all are? Doesn't matter if it's in different cultures or countries --I guess selfish evil people are the same in every language.

Lisette, I feel comforted that there are people out there like myself. Being an ACON and the way society can be makes me feel like I'm the unusual one because I'm the minority in my thinking, not the majority.

You're correct. It's a no-win situation with these fuckheads. The only way you win is not to play. Of course they will hate you for that too.

Mon Dieu, They'll poach on their AC's kids, spouses/SO's (to the point of temporarily changing sexual orientation if that's what it takes) because they can't abide not being the focus of all the attention as well as chaos and resulting destruction.

This post so hits home with me. It seems in my life every special event has been taken over by one MN or another. I'm so glad I've gone NC with them all.

It is so nice to have somewhere I can go where people have had similar experiences and I can share without people telling you "It couldn't be that bad. She's your mother/sister/mother-in-law etc. You just need to forgive her/him." I'm sick of hearing that crap. They are what they are and no amount of forgiving them will change the monsters they are. They are pathetic!

These people don't deserve the same AIR that most of us breathe... but they have theirs AND take ours... and worse, get away with it! I need much more info about empowering myself against MNs!

I am glad I no longer feel responsible for my mother's emotional happiness which I had done and carried this burden for 50 years. Now I know not one second has my mother ever cared about me it was all about her and what she wanted and needed from me.

THE MALIGNANT NARCISSIST'S FLYING MONKEYS

Malignant Narcissists feel superior when they are using and abusing others for their immediate gratification. And if MNs are not feeling superior, they become incredibly hostile, particularly toward anyone who has frustrated their narcissistic demands. Never forget that Malignant Narcissists feel ENTITLED to get whatever the hell they want from others, and it's that sense of entitlement that whets their appetite for revenge against those who do not submit to their tyranny. The MN will stop at nothing to gain control and obtain supply. They will use manipulation, coercion and deception to get their way, and when that doesn't work, the only thing left for the Malignant Narcissist to do is – SEND IN THE MONKEYS!

Wicked Witch of the West to the Chief Flying Monkey: "Take your army to the Haunted Forest and bring me that girl and her dog!"

The Malignant Narcissist will send in her Monkeys to capture you and bring you back to her lair so she can control and exploit you, or the MN will send in her Monkeys to hunt you down and destroy you. From my experience with MNs, they view their target as holding the ruby slippers (narc supply) or holding a bucket of water (the truth/exposure).

More than a year after I told MN sister to fuck-off for good, she was arrogant enough to believe that I still held those ruby slippers, and the bitch tried every trick in the MN handbook to get them. She doesn't leave her house so she plied her trade over the phone. The first telephone message I received from her was completely out of the blue. She was incredibly smarmy and pretended to be my confidant: "Lisette, I'm just calling to say hi…. if you ever need to talk I'm here …." Huh?! Talk about what?! I told you to fuck off… for good! It didn't work. I ignored her. Next, she tried HOOVERING: She tried to manipulate me in to either contacting her, or indirectly feeding information to her through my only NFOO relationship – N Dad. She left another slimy telephone message: "Lisette, Dad is having health problems. You should contact him. He would really like that. You don't have to contact me if you don't want to, but it would be good if you contact him… Oh, the fragility of life." Oh, the fragility of life?! What a phony bitch. She was lying and I knew it so I didn't take the bait. So what did the evil MN bitch do next? That's right, she sent in her sleazebag Monkey. MN sister's Monkey, who has never called me in the 25 years they have been together, out of the blue, leaves me a message asking some lame question about a video. It was so obvious that he was merely carrying out her orders. I ignored his message.

Do you want to know why MN sister suddenly wanted to contact me? At the time she was stalking me on an ACON blog where I was leaving Anonymous comments about her and MN mother. She was covertly trying to slip into my life and into my head because I knew the TRUTH and was EXPOSING her and MN mother's evil ass. She was on a fishing expedition to dig-up dirt and info she could use against me and gaslight me with. So what was MN sister's next move? Nothing. What was my next move? About a month later, I contacted N Dad. I sent him a post card from Ireland telling him what a great time I was having. Malignant narcissist sister finally figured out that I'm not holding the ruby slippers; I'm packing a fucking fire hose and she quickly dropped the friendly pretence and ramped-up her behaviour to outright destroy me.

Dealing with a stealth Malignant Narcissist sibling who's on a lifelong Smear Campaign to annihilate you is like being in a chess match – it's all strategy. But first you need to figure out who you're playing with. Who are The Witch's Monkeys?

During my studies in the MN jungle, I have observed a variety of Flying Monkey species. First off, I come from a family with 3 full-blown Narcs, and I've noticed each Narc's ability to shape-shift into a Monkey in order to carry-out the commands of their fellow Narc co-conspirator. MN mother, MN sister and N father are all liars/narcissists. They are all in collusion. They are all drinking the same Kool-Aid and they all do each other's bidding. And they always will; even if they hate each other.

Currently N father is an instrument of MN sister's harassment of me: He chooses to believe her lies about me because she supports his narcissistic delusions. Indeed, she share's his delusions and contempt for reality – the reality that I am willing to hold-up to the bright light of exposure. As a result, N father is dishonest toward me, withholds information from me, and spreads her false information about me. MN sister doesn't leave the house because she's a freak, shut-in, hoarder yet she has two obedient Flying Monkeys doing her bidding. She uses N father as a conduit for her Smear Campaign against me, and she uses her personal Monkey "Lloyd" to make herself look good to N Dad while at the same time using him as a tool to exploit N Dad for money and property.

For example, MN sister calls up N Dad and pressures him to replace all of his perfectly good flat screen TVs and all his cordless telephones. She sends in her Flying Monkey Lloyd to "help" N father shop for new brand new TVs and telephones. The equally parasitic Monkey Lloyd flies back to her Majesty's lair with 3 "old" flat screen TVs, one brand new TV that she sweet talked daddy into buying her while he was shopping with her monkey, plus 6 "old" cordless telephones. The greedy bitch snatched-up 4 TVs and 6 phones from my dad without ever leaving her lair.

So I'm over at N father's house and notice he has 3 new TVs. He replaced 2 and bought an extra one for the guest room. Naturally, I assume MN sister's Monkey got his grubby paws on the 2 TVs that were replaced. I assume this because MN sister's Monkey has swooped-in to "assist" N Dad for other "purchases" and he has never left empty handed.

N Dad tells me that the first TV he bought for the guest room was too small so Lloyd the Monkey returned it and got a bigger one. I discover 4 empty TV boxes in N Dad's basement yet N Dad only has 3 new TVs. I ask N Dad why there are 4 empty TV boxes and he only has 3 TVs. N father tells me, "Lloyd must have returned the TV without the box." I don't believe him. So he screams at me, "I gave it to your sister!! Okay?! Why do you care about this?! YOU MAKE ME LIE!!"

Just like a good little obedient Monkey, N Dad covers for the selfish, scheming MN sister Witch.

So you got that? MN sister is able to – without leaving her lair – score 3 flat screen TVs (one brand new) and 6 cordless phones AND make me the scapegoat for all of her thievery. Again, she gets electronics galore, and I get shouted at and held responsible for N Dad Monkey's duplicity. And N Dad is lying to cover-up MN sister's blatant greed and pathological sense of entitlement that he and MN mother have assiduously enabled. MN sister is very wealthy. Her mortgage free condo is stuffed to the rafters with furniture and other possessions. And she has plenty of money in the bank. Yet, she is still able to get Daddy to buy her brand new TVs and get mommy to liquidate her assets like jewellery so she can get the cash. Meanwhile, because of trauma, I've been living in fight or flight mode my entire life and because of trauma inflicted by MN sister and some other MNs a few years ago, I've lost everything. I barely have any furniture. I could have really used one of those TVs. And just prior to MN sister scoring 3 TVs, I did all the leg work to help N Dad sell his stair climber and happily made him $250. And he took that money and bought MN sister a TV!

But it's not really about the TVs. I don't give a shit about TVs. I only offer this example because getting all 3 TVs, without one being offered to me, is the perfect metaphor to illustrate MN sister's corruption, and how she has been working her entire life to manipulate MN Monkey parents into believing that she deserves it ALL, and that I am nothing and deserve nothing. The evil bitch is nothing more than a career thief and she's in fat city.

If you come from a family with more than one Narcissist there will be Monkeys. If there are family members who still abide by N cult rules, there will be Monkeys. As long as there is mutually parasitic relationships, there will be Monkeys.

So that's my NFOO Monkey business. MN mother and MN sister use each other as Monkeys and MN sister uses N father as a Monkey. N father has no personal Monkeys, but he has always been afraid of the evil MN sister/mother duo so he will always do their bidding for them. He's a wimp and a coward who is complicit in their abuse of me. My brother – who I don't believe is a narcissist – accepts MN mother and MN sisters distorted reality so he is an unwitting Monkey. And even though he does not actively participate in Monkey business, because he is under MN influence, he is dangerous to me.

From what I've observed in the MN wild, it's mainly female MNs who retain Monkeys. Some powerful male MNs may recruit female sycophants as Monkeys, but I haven't seen it. The reason why Monkeys are usually accessories to female MNs is because men in general don't possess the Monkey recruiting skills that female MNs have. Female Malignant Narcissists are much more adept at poisoning peoples' minds, creating doubts and suspicions, and distorting peoples' perceptions of others while playing the victim or concerned rescuer of their target. Everyone wants to believe that the little old lady cares about her daughter and is only looking out for her. Female MNs are more devious, more cunning and more psychological. They are expert at reading emotional cues and zeroing in vulnerabilities to exploit. Whereas men are brash, have a tendency toward physical violence and usually are not as astute at reading others.

So who are these lowlifes who are oh so willing to do the MN's bidding? In the case of MN sister's personal Flying Monkey "Lloyd" he is just as slimy and predatory as she is. They share the same goal: Like MN sister, Lloyd is a parasite who is also on the take. In other words, it's beneficial for him to exploit N father and make sure Witchy Pooh gets it ALL because that means more for Lloyd who is an ineffectual loser who can't hold down a job and lives in something resembling a storage locker. He's also a wimp and a coward like N father, and the obedient underling to a

MN woman who holds all the power. No self-respecting man of integrity would have anything to do with a Malignant Narcissist woman so let's take a look at the scumbags who would.

I've had two home owning experiences in my life, in two different cities, and both times a MN woman was the President of the Condo Council and had a Flying Monkey thug at her side. Both MNs fit the same profile: They were unmarried, middle-aged woman with no children that were power hungry control freaks. They were both employed in high profile positions, and were both involved in numerous charities and volunteer organizations. And get this, both these "pillars" of the community embezzled money from the condo funds through the help of a male Flying Monkey property manager. And I'm talking dumb, small-time hoods that no doubt had police records and did jail time. And guess who was on to them both and trying to get other homeowners to see what was going on? That's right, me. And guess who was bullied and harassed and slandered by the MN's Flying Monkeys? That's right, me. And guess who took the fall for each evil MN bitch's criminal activity? That's right – her thug Monkey!

I tell you this to demonstrate that at the core of every Malignant Narcissist – sweet little old granny, high profile business lady, sickly little shut-in, or multi-tasking soccer mom – is the mind of a criminal. The MN bitch recruits the unsavoury and the unscrupulous and the dense to do her bidding.

One aspect of psychopathic bullies is that they home in on Wannabe types - non-psychopathic lesser bullies - and then empower these individuals to gain the positions of power and authority they crave. Once installed, the Wannabe's lack of competence makes them dependent on the chief psychopath, which means they become unwitting but willing compliant puppets. They also lack the intellect to understand the nature and manner of their compliant subservience. Bullyonline

These Wannabe Monkeys believe that by association with the MN they too are powerful, but these dumb fucks have no clue that they are nothing but puppets on a string. As Malignant Narcissists see it, exploitation of some sort is necessary to continue to project a superior self-image. So while the MN is getting off at having her Monkeys stalk and harass her target, she is also getting off on exploiting, manipulating and controlling her Monkeys. The MN hag knows that most people have a price or a need, and she is more than happy to bribe her Monkeys with whatever will buy their loyalty. Toying with her Monkeys fill the void that the original target left.

In addition to MN mother and MN sister's Campaign of Destruction against me, I was the victim of a Smear Campaign and vengeful Mobbing executed by a Malignant Narcissist and her MN husband who managed the apartment building where I lived. In each instance, the vile MNs knew that I was about to expose their despicable asses so they sent in their Monkeys!

The Monkeys that attacked me in the building where I lived scared me so much that I got the hell out of there. What happened was, I was about to expose the MN building managers as incompetents and bullies to the building owner, so they moved fast to try and have me evicted, and canvassed tenants to write-up false reports about me. I received the pack of lies by registered mail and was out of the building in less than 24 hours. My sense of safety was completely shattered. I could not spend one more night in an environment filled with a mob of callous people that would viciously lie about someone they had never even met. In addition to the stack of lies about me, there were a bunch of glowing references for the repugnant MN hag and MN warlock building managers. I was absolutely disgusted with humanity that day.

I know some of the lowlifes that participated in this Flying Monkey mobbing were the MNs fellow bullies and minions, but I had no idea what compelled the others to lie and bend so easily to the will of a couple of really unpleasant and off-putting Malignant Narcissists. That was until it struck me that most people ARE fucking monkeys and sheep - see no evil, hear no evil, and speak no evil, bah! bah! bah! The Malignant Narcissist building managers were power hungry control freaks and BULLIES, and most Tenants viewed them as authority figures and were therefore obedient. They never dared to question the MN's motives to slander a fellow tenant, or second guess the abuse of their authority. They just blindly complied with their orders. It brings to mind the Milgram Experiment on obedience to authority.

Malignant Narcissists hate freethinkers and truth tellers and they will do whatever it takes to silence you – send in the Monkeys! These Flying Monkeys are N accomplices; they are lowlifes and scoundrels, exploiters and opportunists, mindless sheep, spineless cowards, stupid, needy and naïve. But most of all, they are dangerous and they can never be trusted. I don't care what the Monkey's intentions are, or how they were manipulated into doing the Malignant Narcissist's bidding. The fact remains; the Monkey is *choosing* to act as co-abuser. The Monkey is *choosing* to accept the MN's lies and share her distorted reality. The Monkey is *choosing* to side with an evil Malignant Narcissist.

Doesn't that make Flying Monkeys evil by proxy?

COMMENTS:

The pay-offs to monkeys are considerable. They share in the bloating of the ego by disempowering the targets and stealing their power. They ego-trip on that, and it's a positive for them. They often steal the target's potential inheritance as a member of the family; they benefit from getting 'positive comparison compliments' from the Narc, (in comparison to the denigration of the target). They get to share in the goodies all along. They get off on watching the target's pain and confusion, which gratifies them and shores up their feeling of being superior. They manipulate, steal and lie to hijack promotions, property, power, the target's reputation.

I have had many experiences with the flying monkeys. Once you figure out what the MN Witch is up to you can almost smell them swooping in. They seem to pop up more often around, birthdays, holidays and major life events.

I have no positive regard for any FM's at all: In my mind, they're all co-abusers whether they "intend" to be or not. I'm not impressed with "intentions" or cloaking oneself as the "Mediator."

Letting in the FMs is like opening yet another door to the MN and what you want is to close as many as possible.

This subject, MNs and their flying monkeys, is perfectly timed with recent info I'm contending with right now. I'm soaking this info up like a sponge and it's soothing what would have been uncontrollable rage, shame and despair; which, instead, has become sad wisdom and insight into more family members than I ever thought I'd have such horrific issues with. Every line contains a gem that helps me understand what's going on. Thank you, Lisette; you're like a guardian angel dispensing healing knowledge to us ACONs; and the comments on this page are speaking directly to my current situation which makes me very grateful to all of you who are willing to share your stories and feelings.

How To Play A Narcissist in Robot Mode

I titled this post "How To Play A Narcissist" because based on the most popular key search words listed in my blog stats, that's what people want to know – how to fuck with a narcissist, how to mess with a narcissist, piss off a narcissist, squash a narcissist, get back at a narcissist, destroy a narcissist, drive a narcissist insane, and beat a narcissist at his own game.

The general public isn't searching for information on how to "relate" with a narcissist because narcissists don't relate – narcissists play games. Every interaction with a narcissist is about mind control and manipulation. In every interaction, the narcissist is calculating formulas to come out on top. Figuring this out - that a "normal" human interaction/relationship with a narcissist is impossible because you are merely a chess piece in the game a narcissist is *always* playing and must *always* play *to* win - is the first step. The second step is playing the game by NOT playing the game. THAT'S how you mess with a narcissist, that's how you "PLAY" a narcissist. At least it's one way, and it will be the focus of this post.

A narcissist once said to me, "Lisette, I'm finding you very difficult to read." With a blank expression, I looked him square in the eyes and shrugged. He turned away from me, and shook his head in confusion. One the outside, I may have looked like an unemotional automaton, but on the inside I was air punching and giving the N a devious smirk. Not being able to "read" me was EXACTLY what I was aiming for. This particular N got his jollies keeping women off-balance by making them feel inadequate and insecure. I knew his game well. It had been "played" on me a million times. Now I knew better. Before his eyes, I morphed into "Robot Mode" and threw him off his game. Growing-up in a family with three full-blown narcissists, where I was not allowed to feel anything or express anything – even on my face – enabled me to perfect the art of Robot Mode. I can't tell you the number of times MN mother and father sniped: "Wipe that look off your face, or I'll wipe it off for you!"

But the Robot Mode I'm talking about now is not the same hiding place I retreated to as a child or a young adult. It's not a mode of mental or emotional withdrawal, in fact, it's just the opposite. It's about conducting yourself like a sharply honed machine that takes in data from the narcissist, quickly assimilates it and responds accordingly. It's about staying very present around a narcissist, and focusing on the narcissist's behaviour, not how the narcissist makes you feel. Sure, the narcissist may very well succeed at making you feel insecure, angry, guilty or ashamed but in the presence of a narcissist, you cannot focus on your feelings because then you will emote. Feel it, you're only human, but don't reveal it... to a narcissist.

Actors are trained to "emote" for the camera so they can convey to the movie audience what they are thinking and feeling. But because film screens are so huge, actors must learn the art of subtlety so they don't look like they are over-acting. They show the audience what's going on inside of them with understated clues. For example, a squint, an arched eyebrow, a hand gesture, a scratch, a change in posture etc. – these are all "tells."

In the game of poker – and remember narcissists are *always* playing games – a "tell" is any physical reaction, change in behaviour, demeanour or habit that gives clues about your hand. A player gains an advantage if they observe and understand the meaning of another's tell, particularly if the tell is unconscious.

Narcissists continually play this clandestine game of me versus you, and they never stop scanning their (unsuspecting) opponent for verbal and non-verbal cues that they can exploit to gain the upper hand. Playing people is what they do. They play to win and they don't like to be challenged. Never let a narcissist know what's in your hand.

How do you challenge a narcissist in this game? Like I said, by giving them nothing – zero, zip, nada. Play your cards close to your vest, put on your poker face, and don't give away any "tells." The narcissist's game is mental. It's all about controlling and manipulating your THOUGHTS. Your emotions and behaviours are connected to your feelings and your feelings are connected to your thoughts, so the narcissist pays very close attention to people's reactions and to everything they say and do. They are manipulation machines that constantly regulate your reactions so they can plant thoughts into your head that you think are yours. But these thoughts are not yours; they are nasty seeds of doubts planted by the narcissist game player who wants to control your mind. Yup, thoughts planted in your head by someone else is plain and simple mind-control. It's the basis of narcissistic abuse.

Narcissists are essentially technicians who search for a precise technique that they can turn into a formula for success. They are programmed to do what works. The narc machine knows to get "Y" kind of reaction, do an "X" kind of behaviour or to get "Y" kind of reaction say an "X" kind of thing. Narcissists know that certain types of behavior elicit a particular type of response. They acquire these stock behaviours as children and then they become habits. These nasty habits soon become second nature, and eventually ARE the narcissist's true nature. Narcissists all seem to be hard-wired the same way. Maybe that's the reason they all seem to follow the same set of instructions – what many ACONs have referred to as the "Narc Handbook."

You need to distance yourself psychologically and emotionally from narcissists. To beat a narcissist machine, you must think and behave like a machine. In Robot Mode you do not respond to emotional and psychological stimuli. Robots are detached. They don't emote. Robots don't react. A Robot's hard drive (your mind and emotions) cannot be tampered with. Remember; despite the narcissist's unfeeling nature, they are very aware that your emotions fuel how you see and experience your reality, and your perceptions ultimately drive your behaviour. When our emotions are out-of-control, our perceptions become obscured and this can drive us to self-destructive acts. Bingo! The scheming narcissists wants you to self-destruct, and an emotionally uncontrolled target with combat fatigue is ripe for a hijacking.

The Narcissist's lack of affect is particularly valuable to them. They can respond to situations without being constrained by principles, morality or feelings. They can callously use people without the slightest thought for their welfare, and at the same time smile to their face while "playing" them, which usually involves exploitation of some sort, and plotting and scheming behind their back. So, as you can see, a lack of affect works well for the narcissist, and a lack of affect can also work for you. Particularly when the narcissist machine is trying to get the desired reaction from you. In other words, "information" (verbal or non-verbal, conscious or unconscious cues) they can use to EXPLOIT you.

So, the narcissist learns formulas to achieve the desired effect: to get a certain kind of reaction from you. The old saying "they do what works" is very true. All that matters to the N is how they appear in the mirror of your face. Nothing else is any consideration. Not morality, consequence, or the good of the other person. Narcissists only look at others to see how others are reacting to them. The narcissist is not connected to themselves in any real way. They are connected to an image that is reflected back to them. The face doesn't matter – you don't matter – only the expression on the face does. The narcissist is someone who goes through life fixated on images, which amounts to the "right" kind of looks on other people's faces. And you aren't even responsible for the expression on your face or the "right" look. The narcissist is! By sheer manipulation, the narcissist has manufactured in you, his/her desired mirror image.

Essentially, narcissists have figured out a formula to get you to unwittingly collude in their game of delusions and lies. They are shady tricksters who adjust their image and manipulate you in order to meet the demands of their narcissism. So what kind of impression does their narcissism demand? What is the most potent reflection in their mirror? POWER. That's what the narcissist lusts after – POWER. Nothing makes a narc feel grander. Nothing gives a narcissist a bigger high than POWER. Even if that power is reflected in the frightened eyes of a vulnerable child. Pretty sick – huh?

Power can look like many different things in each of the narcissist's mirrors. One that comes to mind is confusion. The evil narcissist gets something akin to a drug rush seeing confusion reflected back. Confusion means that the narcissist has gained access to your mind, and mind-control is the name of the game when it comes to narcissistic abuse.

At the beginning of the post I mentioned that I confused a narcissist because he found me hard to "read." Narcissists use sneaky, subtle ways to aggrandize themselves, and get you to reflect back to them their desired mirror image. This particular narc was playing me so that I would bounce back a look that would make him feel psychologically dominant. But I would not engage/react and this confused him. Psychological domination is the most glorious form of power for the malignant narcissist. In fact, any negative reaction the narcissist elicits in you makes him feel powerful. For the narcissist, it's all about destroying his opponent bit by bit, piece by piece. Engaging in the narcissist's game is like offering up your juiciest vein and letting the narcissist stick a needle in it, and feed his poison to you intravenously. Drip, drop, drip, drop. Slowly but surely the narcissist destroys his victim.

Now real power for a narcissist is seeing people miserable and heart-broken and begging for mercy. I'm not saying morph into an expressionless Robot and stand there and take abuse and not fight back. I'm suggesting you give the narcissist nothing, no reaction, and get the hell away from them. Narcissists are black and white, Jekyll and Hyde and sometimes that's how you have to react to them. In other words, all or nothing. If it's safe to do so, give it right back to them, get away, or give them nothing at all. It's your call. Every situation is unique.

Feeling good? Feeling fine? Feeling happy? Well, that's out of line. Unless the narcissist is the cause of your happiness, they don't want to see it in your face when they look at you. Narcs hate you for being happy, so they will do whatever it takes to make you unhappy.

Narcissists see no value in people other than what they can get from them as supply. There is an inner emptiness, a massive dark void beneath their slick machine-like operating system, and as a result, they are cold and calculating and everything they say and do is systematically premeditated for effect – to get the desired look, reaction or behaviour from you. I would rather give my toaster oven a big hug over a narc. If I want comforting, I will turn to my toaster. So give your toaster oven a big hug because that piece of metal has more feeling for you than a narcissist ever will. And it will also broil cheese on toast for you. Now that's comforting.

Morphing into Robot Mode around a narcissist is not about numbness, and disassociating. It's about applying cold calculating machinations on someone who is trying to get into your head and mess with it. It's about "appearing" to be an unfeeling machine toward the narcissist, just like the

274

narcissist is toward you. Robot Mode is essentially disengaging from the narcissist's game. It's about being self-controlled and alert because a lack of emotional control will *always* make you vulnerable to a narcissist.

Now those who have had the life sucked out of them by a narcissist really are hollowed-out zombies. They are the people that's souls have been murdered but their body is still alive. They are dead inside. They are the people who we regard as having the lights on, but no one's home. I say dupe the narcissist into believing they have erased your brain. Your lights may appear "out" but someone is most definitely home; placing booby traps, setting alarm systems, and standing by the door in the dark with a baseball bat ready to bash-in the head of the narc intruder.

Narcs have a way of controlling and manipulating people's emotions without even trying. Not letting a narc "read" you is like refusing to let them know where you live, or where you hide your house keys or what your home security code is. Don't give it up to a narcissist. Invalidate them. Have you ever gotten a reptilian stare back and zero response from a narc while you're having a face-to-face conversation with one, and after you've told them something that was important to you? I have. That dead air is a way for them to invalidate you. That weird silence is a way for them to communicate that a response to you is not worth their breath. They outright ignore you like you aren't even there. And the N machine doesn't even flinch while he does this. I say we invalidate and ignore the narcissist right back. When they look at the mirror of your face to gaze upon their reflection, reflect nothing back. Let the narcissist see nothing, let the narcissist feel like he does not exist. So how do we do this? Robot Mode.

Robot Mode is about reflecting NOTHING back to the narcissist. It's about taking away the narcissist's mirror.

So, here's how I am when I am visiting planet narcissism – without witnesses - in the presence of the only narcissist I have a relationship: I am a Robot. Yup, that's right. No noticeable joy and happiness, no sadness, no anger, nothing much in between. No emotions, period. No reactions, no reflections. I don't want to give the narcissist any ammo. I refuse to engage. I keep a low profile and don't draw attention to myself. Sadly, this is exactly what the narcissist wants: for others to be mindless automatons, a non-person who won't make them feel bad or usurp their attention. The thing is; I give the narcissist nothing. I've grown completely indifferent to them. No attention, no regard, no reason to attack. Hell, I'm a Robot; just like the narcissist and I'm not capable of a normal human interaction on planet narcissism and I'm devoid of all supply.

Be your own Robot Commando. Obey YOUR every command, NOT the narcissist's. Be in charge of YOU.

Comments:

I consider their lack of affect another form of gas lighting. If they do exhibit emotions it never pairs up with the emotions we expect from normal people in the situation is at hand.

I also like the effect of either smiling and laughing when they say something mean, or saying 'that's interesting that you would think that'.

You're right - they are looking for the reaction they have trained you to have. Hurt, surprise, defensiveness - they will search your face for it.

I think that if I were to encounter a narcissist now, I would definitely be able to get into Robot Mode and have a few quick lines to throw them off track.

I had searched endlessly on how to handle Ns and am I ever so glad that you posted this! I swear, a sense of peace and serenity came over me after reading your blog post, because I told myself, now I'm one step ahead of these soul murderers. Now I have tools on how to deal with them. Finally, I've been given the answers I was searching for! I'm off to hug my toaster now, lol!

I resorted to showing no emotion before I went NC. It was from being worn down to a nub. I could tell it infuriated my mother and what I was really shooting for was for her to just leave me the fuck alone.

OMG -- this was so helpful. I was on the right path, but I needed this to show me I did better than before with her. Please keep writing the blog. I need the lessons!

You not only validated what I thought, but you fleshed it out even further. I laughed and laughed about the toaster oven, because it is so TRUE! THANK YOU!

*I just practiced my Robot skills for the first time at Christmas this year ^_^*

Lisette: I've been reading everything you've done old and new, and this post is still my favorite. The M-narcissist IS making conscious choices, and fighting back means we have to have a game plan, and be smarter than hell.

They will totally attack you at your lowest state. It is so exhausting having to constantly protect yourself in any and every way you can possibly imagine (even though their thinking is so warped and inhumane, you couldn't possibly prepare for their abuse), you can't help but feel tired and it is so difficult to not let them see the self-doubt they've created, the lowered self-esteem and lack of confidence that is so difficult to hide, but it's true. You allow the slightest sliver of anything "weak" to show, then you might as well have just handed them the sword of which to stab you with.

MALIGNANT NARCISSISTS ARE HOMICIDAL

My very first post on House of Mirrors blog was *Malignant Narcissist: Death Personified*. I will never waver from this belief: that everything that characterizes the malignant narcissist is about killing life. I recognize that at the heart of my malignant narcissist mother, malignant narcissist sister and any other malignant narcissist lives a murderous criminal. One who is fully conscious that their impulses are morally repugnant, but choose to act on them anyway.

The malignant narcissist is well aware that a moral code of right and wrong exists – they just don't believe it applies to them. They place themselves above the laws of universal morality, thereby justifying their crimes and making them exempt from judgement. Haven't you heard? Malignant Narcissists are superior beings, and as superiors beings they don't follow any rules; they write their own and the inevitable result is corruption. The malignant narcissist's "amoral" code is based on sucking in every single human resource toward them and blocking it all from you. The malignant narcissist's morality is based on positioning themselves as gods that deserve it all, and placing you beneath them as a big fat zero who deserves nothing.

Nice, huh? What do you expect from a mentally deranged creature with a retarded conscience and lack of empathy? In their lying eyes they are better than you, they are above you, and only their laws apply; laws that protect them; laws that excuse them; laws that give them all the rights and you none. Indeed, the malignant narcissist makes up the laws of morality on the fly so they always end up on top as the gods they are, and you always end up beneath them as the worthless nothing they believe you to be. And if you dare question the one-sided standards of a MN god you will face their vengeful wrath. Or, they'll just say "No I didn't" or "Get over it" – calling *your* behaviour into question because you refused to obey the law of acting like it never happened. Or, they'll just make something up – the malignant narcissist conjures up morality and reality as they go.

The malignant narcissist flat out denies there is an objective morality that stands outside them and judges them. The malignant narcissist denies that *anything* outside of them holds any value; not principles, truth, reality, justice and certainly not you. The zero valuation of others and their contempt for morality and reality is what makes malignant narcissists capable of the basest crimes against humanity; it's what makes them extremely dangerous. It's what you need to believe to be true so you will never have anything to do with them again.

I fully acknowledge the murderer that lives in the heart of my mother and sister. They may lack the power of a tyrant, or the motivation of a serial killer but the root of malignant narcissism contaminates them just the same. They are no less evil than noteworthy evil people. My MN mother and MN sister may not be capable of hurting humanity on a large scale, but they exercise the murderer within by slaking their lusts in the family dictatorship. In the family dictatorship, the malignant narcissist lacks accountability and has no fear of the law. Indeed, in the family dictatorship, the MN writes the law.

For example, my malignant narcissist sister could easily get away with murder within the confines of the MN family system, and she did get away with attempted murder – she tried to kill me as a kid by strangling me to the point of near unconsciousness and trapping me in front of an oncoming car. The only reason I lived is because the car came to a screeching halt. However, if MN sister tried to pull that same stunt with some random kid in public school there would be hell to pay. She would be held accountable, disciplined by the systems and likely expelled and labelled a psycho. In other words, MN sister could commit murder without consequence in a morally insane environment like a MN family, but she was restrained from homicidal activity in public school because of societal norms, punishment and the law.

Malignant narcissists don't give a shit about the law, the rules, limits or you. The only thing that has the power to restrain their violence is the constraints of their circumstances, their FEAR of exposure, their fear of the law, and their fear of what people might think. The malignant narcissist is afraid of getting busted. So how does the malignant narcissist go about satiating her murderous impulses without getting caught?

Some of them use their psychological slaves to carry-out murder. Think: the femme fatale who convinces her lover to shoot her husband. That type of MN has two kills on the go: one is her psychological slave that she is slowly killing by eroding his identity and sanity and then stealing his freedom and his life by making him guilty of a prison sentence. The other, is the dead husband. That's two dead men and not a hair out of place.

Though many malignant narcissists are capable of orchestrating a homicide, most just stick to covert psychological murder. Covert psychological murder leaves no evidence and no one has ever been convicted of it. In fact, covert psychological murder is the fall back murder for those MNs who are not as strong as their target or lack physical access to their target. It's also the murder of choice for those MNs like my mother who have never developed a taste for blood and are very concerned about outward appearances.

But here's the thing about covert psychological murder: NOTHING is stopping the malignant narcissist from killing someone psychologically. Nothing. Physical violence is tangible – you can see it. A homicidal maniac is out there in the open for all to see leaving blood, bruises and broken bones, and if there are witnesses present they can pull the killer off the victim. With a covert psychological murderer the victim often has no proof they are being attacked. In fact, the victim often isn't aware that it is happening. Some of the most severe psychological violence happens in plain sight and that's what makes it so insidious.

Gaslighting, mind games, brainwashing, manipulation, torment, domination, subjugation, ostracizing, isolating, lies, slander and gossip are just some weapons of psychological murder. They don't call it character "assassination" for nothing. And driving someone crazy or to self-destructive acts or suicide is about as close to killing the person as if you shot them dead. Covert psychological murder is the invisible intravenous feed of poison that kills a person's spirit. I believe that our souls are our consciousness, and wiping out a person's individual consciousness and turning them into a zombie that is unable to think, feel, or be is the same thing as death.

And that is how it all begins: the malignant narcissist attempts to convince someone who is conscious of their secrets, lies and corruption that they are crazy and proceeds to annihilate them in order to keep them quiet. The more the victims resists, the more severe the mental abuse becomes.

One of my earliest memories of MN mother is her getting off on psychologically torturing me by locking me in a room with a rat. The "rat story" can be found in "Narcissists are Paranoid" article. I was aware of her unbelievably deviant and shallow nature at an early age and as a result she has been hell-bent on trying to covertly psychologically murder me ever since.

Diminishing a person's self-confidence, self-concept, self-esteem and very sense of self is a slow form of murder. When you manipulate and brainwash someone into believing they are worthless, you kill that person's spirit. When you annihilate the very qualities that amount to a human BEING, you murder that person's soul and erase their liveliness. My malignant narcissist mother's lust for killing was not limited to soul murder; she actually wanted me to commit suicide. And she attempted to drive me to suicide by using the "power of suggestion" to plant the thought in my mind. If the power of suggestion is a success then the person who you planted the thought in, actually believes that the idea is their own. I was a teenager the first time MN mother tried to use the power of suggestion on me to commit suicide. About 25 years later, and after 17 years of no contact with her, she used MN sister to plant the same suicide thought in my head via email. You can read about that in *You Have No Right to Live!*

Malignant narcissist mother has groomed MN sister in the black art of psychological murder and I must confess she is more dangerous than her master because she is smarter and more blood thirsty. She is a sadist who is entirely capable of physically killing me, poisoning me, running me down in her car, pushing me off a cliff, manipulating her flying monkey into shooting me – you name it. And the MN parents will cover-up her crimes no questions asked. But she's a shut-in who doesn't leave her house and I won't go near the crazy bitch, so her options are limited. All she can do now is assassinate my character and steal my inheritance... and that she does.

MN sister does however continue to murder N father psychologically. She uses her own hysteria to create fear and worry in his mind for his health and safety which makes him dependent on her for guidance, and she guides him to give her power, control and all his assets. The last time I spoke with her, about 9 years ago, she giggled and said "It's so easy to use the power of suggestion on dad."

Then there's the MN bitch's Flying Monkey "Lloyd" who is her psychological slave. She barks order, and leads him around by his monkey tail. She has succeeded in taking his psychological freedom away and he is under her deadly control. From what I gather, there isn't much left of him mentally.

Every motivation of the malignant narcissist is about killing life and liveliness. There is nothing life giving or life enhancing about them. Even if a MN births a life, she just uses it as a host to parasitize. And although these homicidal monsters are not designated criminals, they are in fact worse because they *elect* to switch off morality in their own home; the place where they know they can get away with their evil deeds. And unlike your average criminal their crimes against humanity are not random; they select those near and dear who place their trust in them to systematically murder.

Families governed by malignant narcissist parents have often been referred to as "god's concentration camps." I believe this to be an accurate description. The normal children of these concentration camps are at the mercy of powerful, life destroying tyrants who operate in a secretive and closed environment where they are free to remove themselves from ordinary restraints of human decency. That's why I believe the last "sacred" institution known as family is so dangerous. The "family" structure becomes like shackles that can be taken to injustice, and that's precisely what happens when malignant narcissists are in charge – they get away with murder. Home sweet homicide.

COMMENTS:

"She is more dangerous than her master" Interesting thing is that each generation is seemingly worse than the previous.

The MN bitch stole my ability to think; my ability to feel happiness, and my very will to live. What other kid would be contemplating suicide to a point of creating a plan at the age of 9 or 10?

When they're not beating you to death physically, they're beating you to death psychologically day in, day out. This is the consistent experience of a child with an MN "Parent" and/or "Sibling." In my experience bruises fade, burns scar over, broken bones mend. It is the psychological homicide that leaves the longest legacy.

My very own mother is a malignant narcissist and wherever she goes, destruction follows.

I don't believe there is such thing as a "benign" narcissist. They all lack empathy and as a result have no capacity to genuinely care for another human being. For that reason, they are all toxic and harmful.

It is so hard to be positive after enduring so much abuse. Never let your guard down, though. One thing I know from first-hand experience trying to figure out their "cruel intentions" is that everything they say, every single sentence has some motive to it - every sentence is a manipulation to fulfill or in the quest to fulfill some need or desire or want they possess. They are very calculating and they are always up to something.

I grew up with a very cold, abusive MN mother, and till date, she has never said "I love you" to me. I am the scapegoat; the one who she projects the worst of herself onto, so she hates me as much as it's possible to hate another person. It wasn't good enough to hate me from a distance; she actively has been trying to destroy me for years! She's alienated me from others, stalked me, filed false reports so that I would be investigated...there's plenty more, but it is my opinion that they only way to even begin healing from the effects of so many years of abuse is to get away from them. Dealing with them any little bit is like pouring salt on our wounds...I have NC (no contact) at all, whatsoever with my MN mother. It's amazing how much more clearly I am able to see, and what I do see I am repulsed by. The day I cut that evil woman out of my life is my new birthday. I feel like this is the first time in my life that I'm actually beginning to live, and my only regret in this is that I didn't initiate NC sooner.

The Malignant Narcissist As Character Assassin

If you have been targeted by a malignant narcissist for serious abuse, be aware that the abuse includes character assassination – the annihilation of who you are as a person. Just as through murder a careful criminal leaves no witnesses, a malignant narcissist is careful to abuse on the sly and destroy the victim's credibility in advance in order to "leave no witnesses." Character assassination is the premeditated murder of the target's image, their good name, their reputation and ultimately their life.

It takes extreme treachery to replace an authentic self with a false image of that person, and who is better skilled to do that than a sneaky malignant narcissist. Take a look at their lives; who they appear to be and who they really are. They don't connect with reality. They live in a fictitious world of smoke and mirrors where *appearances* are all that matter. Narcissists only identify with their false image and they expect you to identify with the false image they invent of you. They NEED you to

285

appear to the world the way they NEED you to be. It's your life according to the narcissist's script.

As Kathy Krajco wrote in her book "What Makes Narcissists Tick":

Narcissists try to make you be what they say you are because, like a psychopath, they view you as an object, not as a human person with perceptions and a mind of your own. They view you as an extension of themselves (like a tool) to control. It is the moral equivalent of control a rapist thinks he has over the body of another, whom he views as but an object, and extension of himself, an executioner of his will. Psychologists call this bizarre behaviour "projective identification," a defence mechanism. The narcissist wants you to identify with the image he projects on you. You are a mirror to reflect his fantasy, so he pressures you to behave as though it is real.

---- Kathy Krajco "What Makes Narcissists Tick" Page 240

Okay… So there's that. We are nothing but objects that the malignant narcissist feels entitled to use abuse and exploit in any way they please. They use control tactics such as lies, slander, projection, triangulation etc. to create a false image of their target which is always about glorifying themselves and degrading the victim. BUT, they also have *motive*. They are very invested in the way the target behaves because they have something at stake: malignant narcissists are continually engaged in post abuse cover-up. The key word here is "behave." Malignant narcissists don't care what the target thinks or how they feel or who they *really* are. ALL people are just objects to the narcissist. The malignant narcissist only care what their targets think and feel insofar as it affects their behaviour. And they will do whatever it takes to *pressure* the target into behaving according to their script.

Like a physical rapist who attacks when there are no witnesses, the malignant narcissist carries-out violent psychological rape covertly. The target, being the victim of the crimes is an expert witness of the narcissist. The narcissist's greatest fear is a credible witness - the target. So, just as a rapist may use intimidation, blackmail, gagging and threats to coerce the victim to silence; the narcissist abuser does the same. But when control tactics fail to silence the victim, the malignant narcissist goes in for the kill.

Character assassination is the narcissist's method of taking a hit out on the target. The idea is to stop the target from reporting the narcissist's crimes to the authorities. Stop the target from being taken seriously by the authorities. Stop the target from taking the stand and testifying. The target is the most credible character witness against the vile malignant narcissist and they know it, so they retaliate like angry vandals smashing-up the target's most precious possession – their character. Character assassination is punishment for unmasking the malignant narcissist and breaking the "no talk" rule. It's about condemning the target to a life in prison for the crimes *the narcissist* commits. Character assassination is about scapegoating the target, so the target ends-up with the reputation and the life the malignant narcissist deserves. Character assassination is about DESTROYING the evidence; the credibility of their most damning witness - their main target(s).

I come from a family with 3 malignant narcissist abusers, so I know how they operate. I've been observing them in action since I slept in a crib. They ALL abuse on the sly. They ALL slander and discredit me behind my back. They ALL paint me as the "problem." And they ALL play the victim. You better believe I'm a "problem" to the malignant narcissist mob. I have escaped solitary confinement of "no talk" prison and my mouth is running loose.

If going no contact is akin to placing yourself in the witness protection program, then what I've experienced is like being framed for a crime I didn't commit, going to prison, breaking out and being hunted with a target on my back. The malignant narcissists will stop at nothing to make their target (me) take the fall. Just as a criminal doesn't want to do hard time, the malignant narcissist doesn't want to face the hardcore reality of who they are. As a result, the fugitive of a MN cult is subjected to the same threat as any defector who escapes with a suitcase full of sensitive inside information that could bring down the regime.

Character assassination, smear campaigns and vandalizing the target's image are tactics used by the malignant narcissist to avoid public shame of the truth. The malignant narcissist is terrified of having their freedom taken away – their *freedom* to abuse and exploit others whenever the hell they want. They are complete frauds and are absolutely terrified of being exposed.

Why are they so scared? Because malignant narcissists rely on using, abusing and scapegoating others to feel superior. And feeling superior is the name of the game. If they were forced to acknowledge their debts and dependencies on others (even if their debts and dependencies are through maltreatment) they would no longer appear superior. The malignant narcissist would be completely humiliated if others knew their limitations – that in order to feel good and appear good, they must make others feel bad and look bad. That's a pretty pathetic existence. Not only that, they would likely be punished for exploiting others opportunistically. So, malignant narcissists cover their tracks, by becoming cunning and devious, concealing their true motives and actions as much as possible. This is where character assassination comes in.

The ability to project an image is relied upon more than ever when the narcissist is close to being outwitted and exposed. At this stage, narcissists become completely deceptive and extremely treacherous in an attempt to sustain whatever dishonesty they are guilty of while not appearing to be dishonest.

If you have been on the receiving end of a malignant narcissist post-abuse cover-up/character assassination then you know this can create terrifyingly bizarre scenes that make you wonder if you are living a nightmare. In fact, things can become so strange and surreal that if you were to try and explain what the narcissist just pulled-off, people would think you are tripping on psychedelic drugs. This is where I have to hand it to those crazy evil fucks; they create scenarios that are so inexplicable their victims are left tongue-tied. Malignant Narcissists will do whatever, and I mean *whatever* it takes to cover their tracks - including, inflicting MORE abuse on to the victim. In fact, the narcissist's post-abuse cover-up is always more destructive than the original crime.

Who would believe a "sister" and "mother" would call the police and accuse their victim of doing to them the exact thing they are in the process of doing to her? Who would believe a sister would lie to police and state her innocent sister is schizophrenic and violent just to avoid the embarrassment of being outed a cyberstalker? Who would believe a sister would lie outrageously to authorities and destroy her innocent sister's reputation just to punish her for breaking the "NO TALK" rule of the MN asylum? Who would believe protesting the malignant narcissist's viciousness, abuse and lies would drive the malignant narcissist cult to even more extreme acts of brutality to dis-empower and silence the victim?

For example, the MN sister is given access by the MN father to clean-out her sister's bank account so she has no money and is forced to endure severe financial stress that's piled onto to the stress of her trying to obtain employment with a massive road block the malignant narcissist *intentionally* laid with her calculated slander; slander that was also spread to the victim's neighbours that resulted in the victim's home environment being unsafe which forced her to have to pack-up and move. That's an example of how malignant narcissists use the weight of mounting pressure to try and break the victim's back. It's called intentional infliction of emotional distress and it's designed to kill, or, at the very least, render the victim neutralized and too mentally and physically weak to fight back.

The severity of the malignant narcissist's crime is of no significance to the MN. Whether they get CAUGHT lying to police or snooping through your sock drawer, the gaslighting and cruelties they inflict to try and silence the witness never match the crimes they are in the process of covering-up. In the malignant narcissist's eyes, the victim is expendable. For example, the malignant narcissist mother doesn't give a damn if she destroys her daughter's life to the point where she ends up destitute and living on the streets, just as long as people never "believe" what the daughter says about her being a bad mother. See what I'm saying? Their maliciousness reaches delusional proportions as they become obsessed with protecting their false image and ruining the victim so they can remain superior... and triumph. It's very important for the malignant narcissist to WIN at all costs.

Character assassination destroys careers, marriages, and relationships, isolating the victim "to the desert" of humankind. Except for the fortunate who have independent means, it's usually a trip down Skid Row, with one ramification after another barring every way out and relentlessly crushing and hammering the victim into ---- guess what? Exactly what their assassin says they are. This is where rag pickers and bag ladies and suicides come from. The victim will ask why he bothered to be a good person when what a person is isn't up to him --- when it's up to whatever others choose to make of him. ---- "What Makes Narcissists Tick" page 246

The malignant narcissist degrades and humiliates others, trashes good names, maligns strong character and ruins reputations because there is a huge pay off for them - protection/cover-up/conspiracy of silence. They will stop at nothing to obstruct the Whistleblower from outing their morally repugnant, debauched, and parasitic existence.

Bottom Line: If you cannot drop off the grid, go into the no contact witness protection program or lay low then the malignant narcissist better fear you, or you better have some kind of power. Because if you decide to fight back, clear your name and expose the narcissist cult you can expect to be under attack from all sides: finances, career/job, home, relationships, reputation, children etc. It's unrelenting and it often ends in marginalization of the victim.

For those of you who aren't convinced of the malignant narcissist's wrath when it comes to loss of control over their false image and their victim, you might want to ask the question "How exactly did Kathy Krajco die?"

Kathy Krajco, ACON blogger and author of "What Makes Narcissists Tick" wrote under her real name, and she wrote extensively about her abusive malignant narcissist father and sister. Kathy's mother died in 1992, and her father died in 2004. So by the time she was blogging about malignant narcissism both her parents had passed away.

According to Kathy's blog, her sister Terese was gainfully employed as a teacher, but lived at home with her parents her entire life. From what I gather, she mooched off her parents while hoarding her own money and even ended up manipulating the MN father into disinheriting Kathy. Kathy was also a teacher and I suspect she was a target of a career smear campaign orchestrated by Terese. Throughout Kathy's blog and book there are numerous accounts of Terese's bullying and abuse. For example, Kathy had a heart condition and one day Terese, who lived across the street, hired a snow plow guy to block Kathy's driveway with snow. This meant that Kathy would have to go out and shovel in order to get her car out of the driveway. It's would appear that Terese wanted to induce a heart attack in Kathy. Only a malignant narcissist could dream-up a scheme like that.

Kathy died unexpectedly in her home on May 9, 2008. She was 56 years old. Her sister Terese was the one who discovered her body. After Kathy died, her blog started being mysteriously dismantled. The only way that could happen is if someone had access to it. I know from experience, that I can leave my blog sitting around dormant for months without it being tampered.

I remember when I read online that Kathy had died, I cried. It was a huge loss to the ACON blogging community. And for years it bothered me that this brave woman who championed for the victims of narcissistic abuse was taken from this world, while an evil malignant narcissist (her sister) lived on.

Anna V of Narcissists Suck blog ordered Kathy's death certificate to find out the cause of death. There didn't appear to be anything suspicious in the report. Apparently Kathy died of natural causes – her heart may have given out.

Despite this information, there has always been a part of me that was left speculating whether or not Kathy's sister played a hand in her death. Perhaps it's because I have a malignant narcissist sister who is capable of anything, and wants to obliterate me for breaking the "no talk" rule. I have witnessed how *out of control* a malignant narcissist can become when they lose even an inch of control over their target and their precious image.

A couple of months ago my curiosity got the better of me and I read Kathy's online obituary and Googled her sister's name. What I discovered is this: Terese Krajco retired from teaching in 2012, and died in her home 5 years to the day that her sister Kathy died. I find it significant that Terese Krajco died on the anniversary of Kathy's death.

Unlike Kathy's obit that stated she died "unexpectedly," Terese Krajco's obit simply said she died alone at home on May 9, 2013 at the age of 59.

Is the date of Terese Krajco's death a coincidence or an indication of a disturbed personality carrying out a ritualistic act? Did Terese assassinate Kathy? Did repressed guilt and shame finally surface to the conscience of a malignant narcissist and prompt her to off herself? Or, was she just fresh out of narc supply and saw no reason to carry on? I don't know, but I know this:

I know if I were to die "unexpectedly" and under "suspicious" circumstances, I would want my sister to be a person of interest and be thoroughly investigated. The bitch is totally capable of murder. Or at least, hiring a thug to do it for her.

I'm living proof (no pun intended) that my malignant narcissist sister is capable of character assassination which is just as violent, if not crueler than a physical assassination.

But then again, according to my brainwashed N dad, whose will has been usurped by the sociopath sister, I am nothing but a paranoid little bitch.

Comments:

If a malignant Narcissist spent as much time BEING virtuous as they spent trying to appear virtuous think about what this world might be like.

Like all of you, the horrors I have lived through can't even be described to a person who does not understand NPD.

You're right about suicide, about ACONS internalizing the degradation to the point of such self- violence.

The satisfaction they get out of feeling superior is so profound. It is asserted in any way possible, from grammatical correctness to parallel parking to being such a great aunt to nieces who appreciate you when your shitty daughters don't! It's so fucking sad --I mean it would be sad if it weren't so destructive, because superiority can only be understood in relation to another's inferiority.

These narcs think they're so wonderful, but their children/family go to great lengths to drop off the grid to escape them. THAT'S how dangerous and destructive they are.

I've never really believed in coincidence and in my experience with narcs, have pretty much ALWAYS tossed aside "coincidences" as being just another one of the tricks in a narc's playbook.

Yes, we can get revenge just by being alive. They really do want us dead, if not physically at least psychologically.

I am SO FRICKEN GLAD I found this. I needed to see this today. You have no idea (actually I think you do) how happy I am that I stumbled upon your blog. I'd love to bend your ear, about EVERYTHING!

I can completely relate to everything that has been written about MNs. My mother is a MN, and I've been no contact with her for 5 years now, and she hasn't seen her grandchildren or anything, but she still stalks me to this very day, crying at how she is the victim. My family is completely oblivious to her true character. She tried to kill me, and she even tried to kill my father. My father kisses her ass though, despite 40 years of cheating on her.

I am the scapegoat of a narcissistic family. But I'd like to tell you what I've begun doing as a way to 'even the score' with my toxic family - because now it's MY TURN! Now when they try to 'set me up' in order to abuse me, I quickly figure out a way to turn it all around to my advantage and make THEM the target!

Your blog has been priceless in understanding my life which up until a few months ago I described as nothing short of a disaster. So many empowering changes have happened. One of the high points happened when describing to a friend the pathology of those freaks and their use of proxy abusers. I said, "we call them flying monkeys". There was never a WE in my vocabulary, there was only me alone questioning my own sanity. I have also just become aware of how big of a threat I am to the Ns delusional world, they have gone in high gear with their isolating tactics. Finally my true calling has been revealed. No longer the family scapegoat, more like the family nightmare. Thanks!

Malignant Narcissists Are Bat Shit Crazy!

Months ago I observed a woman sitting on a bench outside the library having a lively conversation. Her legs were crossed and she was leaning forward with a burning cigarette dangling between her fingers and a cup of coffee in her hand. She spoke with such enthusiasm; widening her eyes, chuckling, sighing, shaking her head in disbelief, and waving her hands to make a point. Sometimes she leaned back, paused to listen, sipped her coffee, took long drags on her cigarette and nodded her head in agreement. When she was done listening she would lean in and carry on her animated chatter. The thing is; she was talking to no one. The conversation existed in her head.

This is what little children do when they play pretend. For example, the little girl who has a tea party and pours imaginary tea and chats with her imaginary friends. It's a sweet thing to see children play make-believe. But when adults do this, it's not sweet, it's insane. Healthy children eventually out-grow playing make believe. Narcissists never do. The malignant narcissist is no saner than the woman I described having an animated conversation with herself. Malignant narcissists are nothing more than masked psychotics.

According to Eric Fromm and Scott Peck, *evil is a severe and specific form of mental illness*. But don't confuse narcissistic personality disorder with mental illness. Mental illness is not the cause of malignant narcissism; it's the result of malignant narcissism. In other words, malignant narcissists are bat shit crazy because they won't stop abusing their minds. They engage in a persistent *pattern* of doing bad things (evil) and then they evade accountability. How do they evade accountability? By avoiding the truth about everything – the world, themselves, their past, their present, you. This denial of reality is what makes them insane. They lie to themselves 24 hours a day and live in a fantasy world so their personal narrative is a complete work of fiction. But it doesn't stop there. They also need to bend your personal narrative to support their delusions – that's where character assassination and smear campaigns come in. Ultimately, the malignant narcissist's outreach of insanity disturbs everything and everyone around them.

Like the crazy woman talking to herself in public, the narcissist's internal world and external world don't match-up. But God help the person who brings this to their attention. What if you told the little girl having the tea party that there was no tea coming out of the pot, she had no friends at the table, and the biscuits she was feeding her guests didn't exist. Well, the little girl might just have a temper tantrum, bawl her eyes out and start stomping her feet in an effort to coerce you into believing, or at the very least, shutting-up so that she can enjoy her fantasy. Other children might get you to play along by using their vivid imagination to convince you that what does not exist does exist and vice versa. This is what narcissists do. They use temper tantrums (narc rage), intimidation tactic and lies to make you play along with their script.

Never underestimate the narcissist's creative union with lies. They play with them, colour them, put their own spin on them, and hide from them. Narcissists ARE lies and they inhabit a parallel universe where they hide from themselves and play peekaboo with the demon at the door – their true selves. Consider their "external" dialogue: *She's mentally ill and I'm concerned for her wellbeing. I care about her and want to see her get the help she needs. She needs medication.*

Now consider their "internal" dialogue: *I psychologically tormented her, harassed her and humiliated her to the point of hospitalization. Yay me! I broke her. Now she's dumbed down and numbed out on meds! Now she IS mentally ill. Maybe I can drive her to suicide!*

Do you think someone who IS a lie is sane? I don't.

Just as through their choices the malignant narcissist's character becomes disordered, as does their mind. The narcissist's brain becomes deformed because they abuse it to avoid reality. The narcissist's brain becomes sick with lies and as a result, the narcissist becomes mentally disturbed.

Malignant narcissists have zero problem embracing their malicious envy, their hatred and rage, their contempt for others, their pathological sense of entitlement and grandiosity. They act on these sadistic impulses every day in every way in an effort to vaunt themselves, but they would never admit this is who they are. No way! Instead they opt to put all their energy into hiding who they are, and in the process they give themselves brain damage and leave a trail of destruction in their wake. Honestly, I would have more respect for malignant narcissists if they manned-up and admitted to their darkness. The only thing worse than a moral deviant, is a moral deviant who believes they are a "good person." Reminds me of the only self-help books my malignant narcissist mother and malignant narcissist sister read. My mother read *Women Who Love Too Much*, and my sister read *When Bad Things Happen to Good People*. That's how delusional they are. Malignant narcissist mother believes she "loves too much." Malignant narcissist sister believes she's a "good person" who bad things happen to. Here are the books they should have read: *Women Who Are Incapable of Love* and *Why I do Bad Things to Good People*.

Oh what tangled webs they weave when first they practice to deceive – themselves. The "tangled web of lies" is of course, their brain. Consider the mess that is their mind. Once they hit the delete key on reality there is no turning back. They can never undo the damage they have done to their brain. The narcissist does not have a psychological injury, they have

297

psychological decay. Every minute of every hour of every day that they lie to themselves they become more and more mentally decompensated. They can never regain their sanity because they can't repair something that no longer exists. Remember those public service announcements with 2 cracked eggs sizzling in a frying pan and the slogan: *This is your brain on Drugs*. Well narcissists, this is your brain on narcissism – fucking fried!

Outwardly malignant narcissists appear normal, but inside they are very different. They are people who have been lying and deceiving themselves and others their entire lives, and they have trained their minds to unknow the truth. They will never stop thinking in lies because by lying to themselves they believe they somehow exalt themselves. For example, thinking the petty torments and suffering they so glibly spread around make them superior. In the end, reality short circuits their brain. This is why all malignant narcissists end up going *outwardly* mad with some form of dementia or psychosis. You cannot keep unwanted knowledge and feelings repressed forever without becoming sick. I have been no contact with my malignant narcissist mother for 26 years, but if I was to have her in my life that would have meant 26 years of swallowing my feelings, repressing my anger, and denying the truth about her unmitigated hatred of me. I can tell you right now, if I had stayed stuck in her web of insanity I might now be crazy too, in a 'folie a deux' shared psychosis kind of way like malignant narcissist sister. That or dead from a stress illness. Relationships are always on the malignant narcissist's terms and that means they control you. It's not just a matter of go along to get along, it's a matter of buying into their lies and special brand of cult-like crazy. It's about believing what isn't instead of what really is. It's about willfully abusing your mind. Sorry, ain't gonna happen. My mind is my most precious possession and I'm not going to hurt it. Never let a narcissist into your head because if you do, you are allowing a violently mentally ill person to control your thoughts and they do not wish you well. If you allow a narcissist to contaminate your mind, your mind will turn on you – I guarantee it. One must employ Robot Mode all the way.

Malignant narcissists expend a ton of mental energy to escape reality – a ton. That is why as the narcissist gets older and mentally weaker, the rare and easily repressed moments of unwanted self-awareness they used to easily deflect, become more frequent and virtually assail them. In other words, they are attacked by reality because their mind is too debauched to protect themselves from it. They've battered their brains so badly that their minds start turning on them and playing tricks on them. The irony here is that when the malignant narcissist's mind plays tricks on them that means reality is sneaking in. Like I said before; masked psychotics. Their minds are mutilated. Hell, I wouldn't expect my arm to function normally if I continually took a baseball bat to it and broke the bones. That's what narcissists do to their brains – self-inflicted mental abuse.

The malignant narcissist is at war with reality 24-7, and at some point their arsenal of mental defence mechanisms becomes so depleted that they must shovel faster to dig themselves out of the black hole of lies they've dug themselves into. What happens is they go deeper and deeper into the hole (madness) to outrun the truth. Consider what they would have to confront in themselves if they let reality in? Hell to the no! Malignant narcissists, as bat shit as they are, are incredibly willful and there is no way in hell they will ever face such a reality about themselves. They would rather die than stop abusing their minds. They would rather die than let the bright light of truth shed light on their dark souls. Going mad is the ultimate break with reality. Madness is a kind of death. Madness is the malignant narcissist's preferred choice over reality. Lunacy is their safe place. They would rather die than admit to themselves who they are. Their deep hole of lies becomes a dark tunnel that takes them farther and farther away from reality and morality and closer to insanity. Sorry, I'm not jumping into the malignant narcissist family rabbit hole where black is white and lies are truth and bad is good.

As a wise person once said to me, "Stay away from your family. They're not lucky for you. They're crazy just not confined."

The malignant narcissist is crazy but not confined. So don't make the mistake of thinking that just because the malignant narcissist is not having animated conversations with herself on a park bench and swatting imaginary flies that she is not insane. Take the malignant narcissist's control away and watch the mask of sanity slip and crash to the ground.

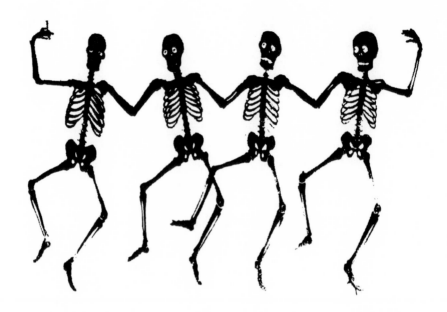

Malignant narcissists exist to control everyone who orbits around them. They see themselves as Kings and Queens lording over a mini Kingdom perched above in their ivory tower. These creatures "blend-in" with society and roam the earth untouched because they are stuffed like pigs with narcissistic supply and their mask is firmly in place. But what would happen if all their little minions and flying monkeys defected, and proclaimed their independence? What would happen if the narcissist's sycophants rose-up and yelled, "Fuck you! You're not the boss of me! I'm outta here!" What would happen if the malignant narcissist lost all control and was abandoned completely? I believe their internal world would become indistinguishable from their external world. In others words, they would no longer be able to mask their psychosis and their mental disturbance would quickly be revealed for all to see.

Losing control of their narrative is agony to a malignant narcissist because malignant narcissism is all about control. If others don't behave the way they need them to, they go out of their minds. It's like chopping off all their limbs. It's like psychological castration. Malignant narcissists are psychologically dependent on others to validate their lies. Feeling in control of the world and everyone and everything in it is imperative to the narcissist's survival. The further along the continuum they are, the more this holds true. Without absolute control over their work of fiction the malignant narcissist's actual mental state is revealed. Here's a little tip: if you want to prove to the world that the malignant narcissist is bat shit crazy, take away some of their control. But be prepared to feel their wrath. When the malignant narcissist loses an inch of control they strike out violently. Sometimes, and I wish this happened more often, they turn the violence on themselves and commit suicide. But the bat shit crazy, evil malignant narcissist isn't offing themselves out of a sense of guilt or shame. They are ending their lives because it's the only thing left that they have any control over. Without a pathological sense of control over others, the malignant narcissist feels completely empty inside and has nothing to distract them from all their repressed thoughts and feelings.

Take for example the story of a malignant narcissist who brutalized, abused and tormented her sister her entire life. She successfully lodged a smear campaign against her innocent sister, assassinated her character all over town and brought her career to ruin. The malignant narcissist did not stop there. Once she had positioned enough road blocks so her innocent sister could not find employment and earn an income, she hatched a plan to make sure she had no future financial security on which to rely. This particular malignant narcissist took absolute control over their aging father and his estate, kept him isolated and blocked the innocent sister (the man's other daughter) from communicating with him. She swindled the old man while he was still alive and had her innocent sister disinherited after his death. The malignant narcissist sister went out of her way to try and drive her innocent sister to suicide. It didn't work. The innocent sister prevailed and went on with her life. This drove the malignant narcissist so crazy that she killed her innocent sister.

It would appear the evil malignant narcissist got it all. She controlled everyone and everything, she got all the money, all the property, she got away with murder and even got her hands on her dead sister's estate. Her ordinary life as a school teacher went on as usual. She should be as happy as a lark, right? Nope. 5 years after she killed her sister, she offed herself on the anniversary of her sister's death. Her pathological greed, and malicious need to have it all meant that she couldn't even allow her sister to have that date as her death – she had to take that away from her too. In the end this malignant narcissist checked-out because there was no one and nothing left to control. She had nothing to live for. There was nothing to fill that empty void within her. There was nothing left to dodge the demon at the door. She would rather die than live a life confronted by the reality of her true self. If that isn't the behaviour of a highly psychotic individual, I don't know what is.

The moral of the story: malignant narcissists go through life clinging to their obsession to control and destroy others, and although their ruthless pursuit often achieves their desires (for example, bringing the object of their malicious envy to ruin or even death), when all is said and done, these desires, these obsessions, ultimately destroy the narcissist.

If the malignant narcissist in unable to maintain their lies then it's game over and they are face-to-face with death = their mental or physical demise. Some bat shit narcissists take the route of psychological death (insanity); others opt for the whole shebang – total annihilation (suicide).

The malignant narcissist's mask of sanity may often *appear* to be held firmly in place, but in reality it is hanging by a thread, a very thin thread. They are completely dependent on narcissistic supply, and without sufficient supply to maintain their life of lies, the cracks in their mask widen. These freaks are highly disturbed and a hair line trigger away from going full on psycho.

Ever wonder why the number one projection levelled against the narcissist's target is that she is mentally ill? It's not just to destroy her credibility so no one will believe her when she exposes the truth about her abusers. That's called lying and slander. Projection is different. Projection is when the narcissist takes the things she detests about herself and calls it you.

Do you think on some level the malignant narcissist knows she's crazy? I do. I don't think it's a coincidence that the most violently mentally ill malignant narcissists that I have come across were all hell bent on painting me around town as mentally ill. In fact, it became an *obsession* for these malignant narcissists to smear me as mentally ill. They went out of their way to do it, and even broke the law in the process. Do you think it's a coincidence that I observed each of them having conversations with themselves, just like the lady on the bench? I don't. Methinks they doth protest too much. Methinks they are bat shit crazy. That is to say, I believe their minds are so warped that they probably hear voices and hallucinate. The most vicious malignant narcissists are always the most paranoid too. In many ways, the mind-set of the malignant narcissist resembles that of a schizophrenic. This makes sense considering their lack of solid contact with reality.

Projection/denial/delusions are all a form of lying, but the person being lied to is the narcissist. The narcissist lies to the narcissist. The narcissist can project whatever the hell she wants onto you, but that doesn't mean you have to believe it. The narcissist can burrow so deep into denial she ends up in Middle-Earth, but that doesn't mean you have to travel there. The narcissist can delude herself into believing she is a superior being, but that doesn't mean you have to share her delusions. The narcissist has a love affair with lies and a generalized disdain for reality because reality does not support her false image of perfection. Don't validate her lies. Choose truth = reality.

And know this: though nothing will ever come between malignant narcissists and their lies, take comfort in the fact that it is their lies that will ultimately be their undoing.

Comments:

When I was a kid and at the height of my mother's criminal activity she would carry on imaginary conversations with imaginary men in the mirror while she put her make up on. She also did this in the rear view mirror while we were stuck in traffic. It was unnerving to hear one half of a conversation and listening to a woman talking to dead air like some guy was there flirting with her. It almost makes me feel sorry for but compassion for her was something that was dangerous to show her.

303

Such an excellent post! You have so accurately described narcissistic sister and the made up slander that has prevailed. The business of what is made up in her head that now becomes HER reality, when it is based on her jealousy and competitiveness. I am grateful for this writing of yours. It is dead on. Thank you.

The narcissists always focused on calling me crazy. There's no such thing as recovery in the narcissist universe. I have to remind myself, that mine showed a lot of insanity on a daily basis, even the screaming and wailing over one thing.

I think narcissists go insane from hiding from their true selves. They know right from wrong, but this doesn't speak of a conscience, it just means they know how the game of life works. When their mental gymnastics, lies, manipulations and deceit are no longer effective or backfire on them, they are forced to face their true selves. They don't want to confront the demon at the door. "They can't handle the truth." So, in order to maintain the lie, they push themselves further and further from reality. Living a lie, in and of itself, is a form of insanity. Playing make believe your entire life is insanity.

The most dangerous people on earth and the quintessence of evil. I am the scapegoat for a family of malignant narcissists and psychopaths. These three score full marks on the Hare PCL.

Beware the psychopath and remember this fact. Not all narcissists are psychopaths but all psychopaths are narcissists. Your life may depend on knowing this. And don't think that you can see through them. Too many people think that they can see through lies and that makes them that much easier to fool.

I am curious does their control falter as they age? I am so used to seeing mine in absolute control, even the idea of her ever becoming weak is foreign to me. I know the ravages of time even will bring a person to fragility but I am so used to this one holding all the cards and power that it is hard to picture it

I think they're all insane, whether or not they end up on a park bench babbling away depends on their circumstances. I don't think their control necessarily falters with age. Their control hinges on those who orbit around them.

I just want to say thank you for this blog. My mother is a covert N and sometimes it's hard for me to put her bizarre, erratic behavior into words, but you really seem to "get it."

They are so bat-shit crazy. I see that now in hindsight as I no longer am in contact with any of the narcs. Seriously, why did I put up with that crap for so long?

Thank you so much for these posts and insight into the reality and mindscape of the narcissist. I came upon these about a month ago after the behaviour of my NSIL (?) left me flabbergasted and I went looking for insight.

I'm a long-time reader of your blog, first time commenter. Your posts are like deep tissue massages, really getting in there and relieving the bad shit. I hope this isn't too familiar or awkward of me to say, but I'm SUPER sorry these people were your close relatives. You're an inspiration to write about your experience(s) with such a powerful voice.

From what I have seen this blog gives the most accurate representation of what MN's/ psychopaths are like behind closed doors. Your blog is very validating.

How To Bring Down A Malignant Narcissist

Addicts do really stupid and reckless things to get a fix of their drug. Picture if you will the high out of his mind meth head who thinks he can get away with hitching a portable ATM to the back of his truck and dragging it down a busy street in broad daylight. Did he ever stop to consider how he will get the money out of the machine? Narcissists are no different. They do really stupid and reckless things without any consideration of the consequences just to get a hit of narcissistic supply. Think of the husband who cheats on his wife with not one but six other women. Oy vey! The lies, the plotting, the planning, the manipulations, the acting, the sheer logistics is mind boggling, but this asshole believes he can pull it off. Wrong. Like the ridiculous meth head, the ridiculous narc head will get busted, and if he's famous, a public shaming will ensue. Just like the meth head's stupid criminal stunt will go viral with a catchy Auto Tune like – "We eat ribs with this dude, and we didn't have a clue that the girl was in that house….. DEAD GIVEAWAY"

You can use the narcissist's addiction and their grandiose delusions of invincibility (aka STUPIDITY) to control them, manipulate them, and steer them down a path of legal problems, criminal charges, financial troubles, social shunning, paranoia, reclusion, mental illness, or all of the above. You can use the narcissist's addiction, in all its various manifestations, to expose them and bring them down. You can turn the tables on the narcissist. Are you game?

Perhaps you think this sounds too far-fetched? Or way too much effort? Or, maybe even a little psychopathic? Maybe. But I think I will take a stab at it anyway. And as for it sounding psychopathic, well, if you're feeling even a smidgen of empathy for a malignant narcissist, they've already got you beat.

I watched the first episode of the British crime drama *Luther* because the plot revolved around a character named Alice Morgan who is a malignant narcissist/sociopath. Having a sister who is a malignant narcissist/sociopath, I was curious to see how the disorder was depicted on screen.

30 something Alice Morgan was a child prodigy who enrolled in Oxford University at age 13. She received her Ph.D. in Astrophysics at age 18, for her study of dark matter distribution in disc galaxies. Alice is a genius, as well as a sociopath and malignant narcissist. She states that she felt as though she was a freak growing up, and hated her parents. Sound familiar? For those of you who have seen *Gone Girl* one can certainly draw parallels between *Luther's* Alice Morgan and *Gone Girl's* Amazing Amy. Both of these malignant narcissist/sociopaths are portrayed as child prodigies and dazzling dark souls with over-the-top Machiavellian brilliance. They are also both homicidal maniacs that get away with elaborate murder schemes.

Geesh, how I wish a malignant narcissist would be depicted in a realistic way. You know, make her a low-functioning hoarder who never leaves her cluttered lair because she's paranoid and delusional. We could see her operating her "control room" of evil surrounded by boxes, junk, various busted-up electronics and numerous TV screens that display video surveillance covering every corner of her condo inside and out. She's perched in front of two long tables where she has set-up multiple computers, phones and fax machines. On one screen she cyber stalks her sister, on another screen she checks her elderly father's financial investments, while on another computer she transfers money from his bank accounts to her own, and then angrily taps away at a keyboard composing a "poor me… I'm such a good person" email, and on yet another computer she browses the Apple Store and greedily selects item after item to purchase using her weak and vulnerable father's VISA card. She does all this while spewing nasty gossip and complaining about her ill father over the telephone to her equally malignant mother. In between her slime and malign fest with her mother, the multi-tasking malignant narcissist barks orders over a cell phone speaker, commanding her Flying Monkey to swoop in and take whatever he can from her ailing father's home. On another cell phone she texts outrageous lies to her brother about assorted family members, while sending an I LOVE YOU!! Fax to her lonely and isolated father, followed by a demand list of all the possessions she wants from him. After she hangs-up the phone with her evil mother, she looks over at the computer screen where she is cyber stalking her sister and becomes red-faced and infuriated. She huffs and screams and smacks the computer monitor sending it crashing to the ground. Still fuming, the malignant narcissist dials 911 and calmly asks for the police to do a "wellness check" on her sister because she is "concerned" about her. The malignant narcissist states her sister is mentally ill and just threatened her. She does this while gazing at her distorted reflection in all the various monitors and mouthing the words, "You're brilliant."

But I digress. Back to Alice Morgan. She hates her parents so she kills them… and their dog too. One bullet in mom's head, one bullet in dad's head, and 4 bullets to blow-away the dog so she can hide the murder weapon in its gaping carcass. Alice thinks she's so damn clever. She even fake cries. But Detective John Luther is no fool. He's on to the crazy bitch the moment he begins her interrogation. Alice is as cool as a cucumber but claims to be SO tired from the incident - her parents being shot dead in cold blood and all. Luther consoles her a bit, saying it's natural that she's fatigued because she's just been through a very traumatic experience. Then he lets out a big over-the-top yawn, and Alice just sits there calmly with perfect posture and her hands crossed on the table. Luther knows right there and then that she is what he suspected – A MALIGNANT NARCISSIST. The way Luther sees it, yawns are contagious and because she didn't yawn back that means she has no empathy. Yeah, that and she's a liar. That bitch is not tired. She's pumped-up on an intoxicating power high.

Typical of crime shows with a tormented brilliant detective and an empty brilliant psycho, a game of cat and mouse ensues. Alice knows that Luther knows that she killed her parents. And Luther knows that Alice knows he knows. But Alice also knows that Luther can't prove it. And this makes Alice damn proud of herself because getting away with murder is a sign of prestige and self-affirmation that she is so clever, so cunning, so superior, and SO untouchable.

Well, we'll see about that. Alice and Luther have one psychological show-down after the other and at one point Luther says to the gloating Alice:

Your compulsions make you weak in ways you can't see or understand.

Your compulsions will bring you down.

Boom! Dude nailed it! And THAT my gentle readers (I mean fighting machines) is what I want to discuss in this blog post. But before I do, I want to mention something else. As I was watching *Luther* and observing the character of Alice, it struck me how often I forget that malignant narcissists are not like us. They look like us, they mimic us, but inside they are *very* different. They never have and never will experience love and all the good stuff that comes with it. This lack makes them empty to the core. They are ice-people and they do not bond with, or feel any sense of attachment to the human race – not their children, spouse, best friend or neighbour. Yes, they can fake it. They have to in order to blend-in. Yes, they can be dependent. But dependence is not love. The narcissist doesn't give a damn about love. How can you desire something you've never had?

Malignant narcissists view humanity with contempt because they see themselves as superior beings liberated from the burden of love and all the "perceived" weaknesses that spring from it. They truly believe their deficit gives them the upper hand in life, and in many ways it does. When most of us feel good about helping others and shame at betraying them, there's a lot of room for successful predation. But the deficit also makes for a life plagued with crushing boredom and an inner emptiness that needs to be filled.

My point is narcissists and especially malignant narcissists are driven by entirely different motives than the rest of us. You cannot figure them out, predict their moves, or bring them down by projecting your normal human behavior and emotions onto them. They lack the very things that define the "human" experience – they have very bleak inner lives. As a result, they are hungry and restless and constantly on the prowl to fill their inner emptiness and alleviate boredom. It's time to pull back the curtain of their control rooms and figure-out what makes them tick and ultimately implode.

How does the malignant narcissist satiate their hunger, the big black hole, the endless void? They can't fill themselves up emotionally the way we normal people do, so they try to fill the dark chasm through their compulsions to control, dominate, exploit and win at all costs. And remember what Luther said: The malignant narcissist's compulsions make them weak. Weak in ways they cannot see or understand.

How do you fight back when a malignant narcissist is hell-bent on destroying you? Notice I didn't ask how to "stop" a narcissist. That's because I don't know how to stop them, short of having them locked-up in jail or a psychiatric institution; I know they will NEVER stop. If you have ever tried asking a malignant narcissist to stop, you will have learned the hard way that this makes them do it all the more. From my experience, malignant narcissists get worse when you try to confront them, hold them accountable, defend yourself and fight back. That's not to say, you shouldn't fight back – you should! In fact, you should always use any means necessary to protect and defend yourself against abuse. Just keep in mind that malignant narcissists are crazy drug-fueled addicts.

The way they see it, life is a war of control over a precious commodity known as narcissistic supply. All channels of this drug must flow to them. The evil drug lords think they own the market so they make all the rules.

Not giving in to their exploits and corruption, in their twisted minds, is a crime against them! In this drug war the narcissist is *entitled* to launch any attack necessary to get a stash of the good stuff. You get none. In fact, they expect you to submit, run for cover, duck and hide, live in fear, end up maimed, seriously injured, neutralized or dead.

Look at it from their perspective: if the malignant narcissist did stop trampling anyone who got in their way, they would be terrified of retaliation from those they have wronged. They violate others so maliciously that they desperately hold on to their power at all costs. They cling to this power because they are playing for high stakes – possessive control of people, families, fortunes, property, businesses or entire nations. Malignant narcissists literally play for life and death. They go all the way to the end over the big things and the small. And once the malignant narcissist has begun to defy the law, morality, and common decency, there is almost no way they can stop. They don't want to stop. They are in it too deeply, and hooked on the glorious power rush they get from exploiting and destroying, or as they see it - WINNING. Unlike your typical addict, malignant narcissists have NO rock bottom.

So, malignant narcissists are unstoppable. That's pretty scary, right? I know in my case, the malignant narcissist sister and mother will never stop trying to destroy me. I have not seen the MN mother in over 26 years and she found a way to get to me, to hurt me – she got her evil MN daughter to have so much power over her ex-husband (my dad) that she now possesses him. The evil bitch and her evil daughter are trying to destroy me through a man who no longer belongs to himself and is simply carrying-out the will of the malignant narcissist mother/daughter team. Predators never stop preying. And the war rages on.

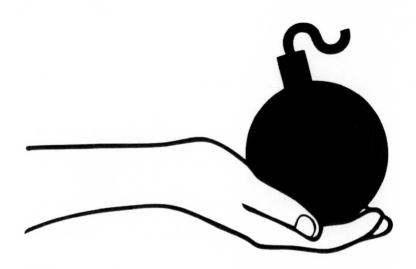

HOWEVER, not being able to stop IS the malignant narcissist's weakness. Remember what Luther said? Their compulsions make them weak and their compulsions bring them down. Malignant narcissist's are out of touch with reality, especially the reality of their power. The irony is, the more delusional they are about their invincibility, the more over extended and reckless they become. But the narcissist can't see this because they are knee deep in it. Look at it this way: the only thing stopping a runaway freight train is for it to fly off the rails and crash and burn. Would you expect a runaway freight train to stop just because there is a person on the tracks? Don't expect a malignant narcissist to "stop" just because people are getting hurt. Ha! Destruction fuels their compulsions. They are always chasing the rush of their biggest high.

What is a "compulsion"? It's an uncontrollable urge – an addiction. Having no control over their predatory urges means that malignant narcissists are a slave to their addiction. If you are a slave to anything, *anything* – it means you are controlled by it. The malignant narcissist will never see this or understand this because they view themselves as superior beings who are not only in control of themselves, but the entire world and everything in it. Their irrational belief in their invincibility and their blindness about the compulsions that control them make them stupid and weak and this is how you can bring them down.

Yes, malignant narcissists are free from the constraints of love, empathy, decency, honesty, shame, remorse, a conscience etc., and these deficits *appear* to give them a lot of self-control and self-control usually translates to power. But it's not real self-control or true power. It's merely a dead emotional state supplemented by the application of lies and manipulation to score a fix. Any addict will become dead inside and a practiced liar and manipulator over time. And like any addict, malignant narcissists do really stupid and reckless things to get their supply. Their compulsions make them weak, and we can exploit those weaknesses to our advantage. But first, in order not to end up prey, you need to understand the mindset of this predator and how they view us.

What do you do with your life when you are agonizingly empty inside and excruciatingly bored with a ravenous hunger that needs to be fed? To fill the void, satiate the appetite and alleviate the boredom you turn life into a game and people into chess pieces. So what's the game? Exploitation is the name of the game and you're it! Predators need prey. Parasites need hosts. Chess boards need pieces.

Exploitation is the most powerful signifier of malignant narcissism. If you want to know how dangerous someone is then beware their response or *pattern* of responses to your vulnerabilities. How someone responds to vulnerability indicates empathy, or exploitation. Malignant narcissists respond to vulnerability the way a junkie responds to a shot of smack – they have ZERO control over their urges. They gotta do it. They gotta get that high. It's no surprise that when I have been at my most vulnerable in life the malignant narcissist sister couldn't resist taking advantage of my predicament and inflicting more harm. It's no coincidence that the malignant narcissist sister is exploiting our sick and helpless father. Again, it is how someone responds to vulnerability that tells you who they are.

Malignant narcissists are by definition exploiters. Their compulsion for narcissistic supply = exploitation = fraud. Like I said before, malignant narcissists do not have true power or true self control. They get their drug fix through lies and manipulation – fraud. You know that line in *It's a Wonderful Life* – "every time a bell rings an angel gets its wings"? Well, "every time a person is exploited a narc gets its supply." All that matters to the malignant narcissist is their perceived gain and greedy satisfaction. There is absolute indifference to the loss, damage and suffering to others resulting from the malignant narcissist's shockingly callous exploits.

Malignant narcissists do not like us. Malignant narcissists do not respect us. The only thing they *feel* toward us is contempt. They truly believe that they are superior beings and we are mere "items", "things", "its" to be used for their selfish gratification. This condescending attitude is conveyed either covertly or overtly in *every* interaction with a narcissist.

The malignant narcissist lives in a world where others are the ultimate objects to jerk around, toy with, menace, steal from, control, dominate and generally entertain themselves. Hurting people is fun. It makes them feel drunk with power. In this game of life, this world they live in, the malignant narcissist believes they can do pretty much anything they want to anyone, while enjoying, if not relishing immunity from accountability. By relentlessly exercising their power over others, narcissists convince themselves that human limitations do not apply to them. Given that no one has stopped them before, they find it impossible to believe that they are not invincible. And because no one has stopped them before, there is no reason to believe they will be stopped now. It must be one of the headiest drug highs to be so convinced of your invincibility that you can brazenly pull off shit that other people would simply find too risky and too shameful to consider. It's a mindset steeped in a profoundly, grandiose sense of omnipotence; a mindset that leaves the malignant narcissist feeling empowered and at liberty to crush others to get their way and do so without worry and constraint.

Because malignant narcissists have no control over their addiction to narc supply and no capacity for self-restraint, they begin to play god/Wizard of Oz in more outrageous ways for even just a momentary fix. This temporary fix = confirmation of their absolute power. Since continuous power is the only thing that matters to them they will sacrifice anyone or anything to hold on to it – that means you. Their compulsion to sacrifice anyone and everything to hold on to their power makes for staggering audacity and their behavior becomes more absurd and obscene. Ironically, refusing to back down when backing down is the smartest move to make, and stubbornly clinging to whatever power they believe they have by carrying-out even more outrageously cruel and malicious acts is precisely what makes the malignant narcissist vulnerable. It's at this point that the malignant narcissist's mask of sanity begins to unravel and they are nakedly insane for the entire world to see. I have learned there is no reasoning with the insane, but you can give the insane enough rope to hang themselves. Believe me, even these delusional fuckers know on some level that they can't hold-out forever against the force amassed against them by truth and reality, but there's nothing stopping them from attempting to destroy everything they can before they crash and burn.

Daring to run interference on a malignant narcissist's unchecked power, control, greed, abuse, exploitation, lies, etc. etc. will definitely make them worse. They are vindictive mother fuckers and they react to anyone challenging their delusions of superiority by becoming even more crazed and ruthless. BUT, and this is a big but (no pun intended), defending yourself and fighting back makes them worse mentally. And it's the malignant narcissist's deteriorating mental health that makes them vulnerable.

The very act of psychological defence: refusing to have your sense of reality eroded by the narcissist's relentless gaslighting and devious deceptions; refusing to be disarmed and disoriented even slightly by the narcissist's shocking assertions of entitlement and jaw-dropping callousness; refusing to have your attention arrested and your emotions toyed with through the narcissist's sneaky pity-ploys and diversion and intimidation tactics; and refusing to be threatened by the malignant narcissist's state of murderous rage - your refusal to be "gamed" by the narcissist will torment and frustrate them and advance their mental deterioration. Even the thought of not getting their way or losing an ounce of control can make a malignant narcissist go berserk. As for new predators; they will learn you are not easy prey and go find someone else to mess with. Good riddance!

Absolute power corrupts absolutely - this includes the mind.

Instead of trying to stop the crash of the runaway freight train, we should ask ourselves how can we speed up the crash and mitigate injury at the same time. How can WE exploit the narcissist's weaknesses – audacity, recklessness, delusions, grandiosity, a pathological need for control and a predatory compulsion to exploit and dominate? How can an aggressive impulse to use and abuse others make the malignant narcissist weak in the first place? Because when they don't get their way they tend to feel anxious, threatened and paranoid. So they defend themselves against this anxiety by acting out and impulsively striking first in an attempt to destroy before they are destroyed. See what I'm getting at? There is no other ending for the malignant narcissist. They will *always* go too far and either get busted, burnt-out or go insane. So how are you going to make this human freight train derail? Yes, you can starve them and slow them down, but that's a long drawn-out kill. This post is about accelerating the malignant narcissist's inevitable demise.

Before you answer, you need to ask yourself this: How do you expose a ruthlessly sadistic exploiter without becoming one yourself? Do you have to become ruthless to fight ruthlessness? Unjust to fight injustice? How far should you go to protect yourself from a predatory malignant narcissist/sociopath who destroys without remorse? Does doing things a narcissist would do, make you like them? I say NO!

Why are you following the narcissist's rules in the first place? To drive home this point further: You cannot continue to do everything "right" by people who only do "wrong" by you in return. You either have to get away, as with no contact, or if there is something you must claim as your own, and dealing with them is a precursor to it, then you go in and do whatever you have to (within the boundaries of the law) and fight fire with fire! Unless you are simpleton, you do not respond to constant face-slapping with a smile.

So how do you fight fire with fire? I don't have all the answers. You have to figure-out this stuff on your own. I'm just laying the groundwork and suggesting you change the state of play. Besides, I'm way more interested in hearing your ideas. So, before I bring this post to a close, here's another question to ponder:

Is the ability to destroy a reflection of real power? Who is more powerful, the person who destroys a city or the person who builds one?

Comments:

I bet every ACON has thought of ways of "fighting back" and getting "revenge".

I think you are correct in your theory that if someone challenges them and fights back, they will raise the ante and go from covert and overt and many will break the law and cross all sorts of societal lines.

I would love to have a way to fight back. I can make a MN spin their head and spit pea soup.

Your blog is amazing. I feel some semblance of mental relief just reading it tonight for the first time...after 39 years struggling under the smoke of my mother's narcissistic rages, in a family crawling with narcissists and enablers. Thank you.

Thank you! Thank you! Thank you!! And I mean all of you!! :) I didn't know there was a name for my horrid sister's lifetime abusive and absolutely horrific conduct. What a monster she is!!

My sister is a MN. She is far more covert than other descriptions on this blog but cruel and destructive nonetheless.

This is a fantastic piece. "Self-control usually translates to power." It's spot on. I also loved "you can't continue to do right by people that only do you wrong." That's a lesson I learned years ago that helped me greatly. Your writing explains these monsters better than anything else I've read.

I'd like to avoid them all but that is not possible. The world is a breeding ground for them. I have my guard up all of the time now and I don't trust anyone until I know who they really are. If they are narcs, the real person will eventually come out. It could take a week or many months. Some that have come across my path have shown their true colors within a day or two. Unfortunately even brief encounters with these vampires are unavoidable.

So validating to discover there are others who have lived through this...I am cutting my narcissist sister off completely! I FEEL SO FREE to be away from the monster and oppressor!!!

Lisette, I want to thank you for sharing your experience dealing with narcissistic family members. I connect and can relate to most everything you have to say and it's been a godsend. I think your writing on the subject is probably the best I've been blessed enough to stumble upon. When my mother starts her shit and the 'flying monkeys' come out I sit and read your writing and it gives me strength, calms me down and instead of being self-destructive I can close my heart and mind off to her.

To the people who CHOOSE to be in relationships with Narcs: Boo hoo ... So you got your feelings hurt bad by your narcissistic relationship and that has never happened to you before. Well welcome to our fucked up world. Because, (and I learned this all from you Lisette) we have been dealing with these relationships our entire lives! Like you have taught me, our narc radar was smashed, stomped on, and torn to shreds from day one. We have been like flypaper to these narcs ... Friends, co-workers, boyfriends, husbands ... You name it, we have been there. But the big difference and I mean Big difference, is we have no safety net, no soft landing ground, no family to run home to. In fact what do have? Soul suckers who are only there to stick their claws in deeper. Need some comfort? Some kind words? A hug? Ha! Ha! Ha!

Fight Back Against The Malignant Narcissists!

If you are reading this book because you have had the misfortune of being targeted by a malignant narcissist then you are well aware that these thugs feel *entitled* to do whatever they want to whomever they want. In getting away with a lifetime of abuse, and never being held accountable for their crimes, malignant narcissists develop delusional ideas about themselves and the extent of their power. They truly believe there is nothing wrong with them. They think all of their problems and conflict in the world lie outside themselves in the environment. So they attempt to dominate and control the environment and everyone and everything in it – that means you!

The most glaring example I can offer are the slime infested words that oozed from the mouth and dripped off the serpent tongue of the malignant narcissist sister: *"Why do you expect ME to act a certain way?! Why can't YOU just be complaisant?!"* Get it? The malignant narcissist feels entitled

319

to abuse the living shit out of you and *expects* you to bend-over to the abuse without any resistance or a word of protest. With this warped mind-set driving their behavior, malignant narcissists have zero ability to set limits on their actions. This means they are capable of anything. They can seriously harm others. They have no rock bottom.

What is missing in the malignant narcissist is the ability to identify with other human beings. Their gargantuan egos choke-off any capacity for empathy. They don't give a damn if they are right or wrong as long as they get their way. They feel that their own needs and desires are the only ones that count – that they alone are the only ones with rights. They play Master/Mistress of the Universe, relating to the environment and everyone and everything in it as superior beings who are more powerful than anyone or anything else. This might makes right philosophy creates a personality that is completely ruthless, cruel, and tyrannical. Malignant narcissists oppress people; take away their rights, their freedom, their dignity and sometimes their lives.

What is especially dangerous is the malignant narcissist's willingness, even eagerness, to use psychological and/or physical violence with very little provocation. They are always ready to raise hostility levels and the smallest hint of aggression from others will bring an avalanche of retaliation. Some people resort to violence when there are no alternatives for defending themselves. And when they do, they usually feel guilty and fear retribution. Not so the malignant narcissist.

Malignant narcissists think nothing of using violence and they do so without guilt. They are entirely *capable* of feeling guilty for their actions, but they defy guilty feelings so that they will not have to modify their behavior. They intentionally set-out to make themselves blameless. This is why malignant narcissists react with vengeful acts of cruelty and control when held accountable. Defying guilt and other emotions such as empathy and fear of retribution allows the malignant narcissist to escalate their abuse of power and act even more ruthless. Intimidation is the name of the game.

So....

320

When is it time to show the malignant narcissist YOUR fangs and claws?

When should you fight back?

These are stupid questions!

You ALWAYS have the right to use any means necessary to protect and defend yourself against abuse.

You must NEVER accept abuse or deny yourself the right to put up a fight.

The victim NEEDs to do EVERYTHING they can to resist the abuser(s).

"Narcissists don't merely abuse, they FORCE SUBMISSION TO ABUSE. This makes them God, whose punishing wounds we are to shamefully accept as our fault. We are not to resist: we are to simply hang our heads as deserving of them.

--- Kathy Krajco "What Makes Narcissists Tick" page 105

Let me rephrase the question. If a malignant narcissist/sociopath is hell-bent on destroying you ARE you going to fight back?

Most of us who have experienced the total darkness of a malignant narcissist, and are wading through the trail of destruction left in their wake, would agree that they are evil. Your attitude about evil reflects your stand on evil. We need to think about evil and the fight against it in simple terms. The most tragic mistake you can make is to sort of believe in evil, sort of believe in its existence and sort of believe in the malignant narcissist's designs on your life. When you approach the threat of the malignant narcissist in this way you are sending them a clear message. You are saying to your enemy that you understand *intellectually* that they are evil fuckers plotting and scheming to destroy you, but then you act as though they have nothing to do with *all* the tragedy that befalls you. You do nothing. You don't strike back. You run and hide, or you lay down and die because you don't want to "feed" the narcissist or "appear vengeful." Who the hell dreamed-up THAT excuse to stop victims of narcissists from exercising their right to self-preservation?! Guess what? The malignant narcissist is already engaged in a blood and gore feeding frenzy of YOU, and they are not going to unclench their talons unless you pry them off or scare them away.

You need to recognize the extreme treachery of the malignant narcissist and understand how all of your misfortune can be traced back to them. If you don't understand the far reaching effects of their malice and take a stand to fight back and protect yourself then....

YOU IN DANGER, GIRL!

For example, the malignant narcissist has been tormenting and brutalizing you for months, even years – this makes you extremely vulnerable. You fall down a flight of stairs and damn near break your neck. The malignant narcissist didn't push you down the stairs. They aren't even in the same city as you, so it can't be the fault of the evil narc. Right? WRONG. The malignant narcissist is responsible for making you vulnerable and that vulnerability – be it mental, emotional, physical, financial, social etc. are the eggs they plant that hatch into bad shit happening. It's the domino effect. The first domino has to fall for the rest to come tumbling down and the malignant narcissist is the one that tips it. The "bad luck" that the victims of malignant narcissists experience is no coincidence. It's just all part of the domino effect of evil.

I experienced a violent physical assault soon after I unwittingly "trumped" a narcissist. I was simply exercising my rights. But looking back, I see how a disturbed personality like the malignant narcissist sister could view my success at exercising my rights as her being outsmarted and LOSING. Having a modicum of power and control of my own life – after the malignant narcissist has worked like hell to STEAL it ALL from me – enraged the evil bitch. Even though I had not seen her in 25 years, I have to question whether or not it was merely a coincidence that I was attacked 3 months after the malignant narcissist sister got a taste – *for the first time in her life* – of her own medicine and not getting her way? Her "way" being able to steal from me and abuse me with impunity. My attack was planned and I was targeted. So did the malignant narcissists take a hit out on me? Or, was my fragile state of constantly trying to recover from ongoing

322

attacks and trauma inflicted by the malignant narcissist sister and her gang of brainwashed goons a huge blinking neon sign on my forehead flashing "VULNERABLE." Was I simply spotted as easy prey by a predator? Either answer leads back to the malignant narcissist being responsible for the attack. See what I'm saying? These evil fuckers are *always* either directly or indirectly involved in our demise. We may not see them strike the match, but we know they set the fire.

Malignant narcissist predators thrive on their prey being unaware of their presence and the hand they play in indirect and covert attacks. Spiders spin translucent webs. Sharks have sensors that can detect objects in their environment before the object senses them. Jungle animals use stealth, stillness and camouflage to get near enough to attack their unsuspecting prey. In all these cases, the victim doesn't see their end coming. Our bodies and minds are engineered with warning systems. It's damn time we start to listen to them. A HUGE part of the malignant narcissist's programming is about turning their victim into prey. They train us to ignore our warning systems. That's why it's critical to show the malignant narcissist our claws and fangs. Cockroaches scurry and hide in order to avoid the static of an electric field when the lights come on, and malignant narcissists run and hide when they are faced with the bright light of truth. Of course, not before they rage, threaten, bully and intimidate you into silence. It's time to strike back.

You have experienced the worst atrocities a human being can inflict on another. Character assassination is a form of murder. Gaslighting is mental cruelty. Shunning is social torture. Mobbing is a violent gang assault. Financial abuse is theft. Control is imprisonment. Domination is enslavement. Narcissistic abuse is intentional infliction of malice. Silence = death.

Evil intentionally attacks with symmetrical force to bar any way out for the victim. Remaining emotionally distant and ambivalent toward the malice embodied by the malignant narcissist will leave you wide open to more abuse. It's also important to understand that as your understanding of evil grows so does your power and that means the attacks the MN launches will change too. For example, an evil person is not going to attack the naïve the same way they attack the knowing. The malignant narcissist's tactics change based on your resolve. That's why I believe I experienced a *physical assault* after every attack the malignant narcissist launched at me failed to crush me. She had run out of options. Naturally her abuse would escalate from psychological violence to physical violence. Physical murder is only step away from psychological murder.

What the malignant narcissist is now learning is that I have linked her to my assault. Psychological violence is difficult to prove, but physical violence is not. I know she is entirely capable of masterminding the crime and to me that means there is a possibility she is behind it.

Unfortunately for the malignant narcissists, I am aggressively aware of their nature. I've studied their moves and I know they will continue to harm me as long as they can get away with it.

If you have been targeted by a malignant narcissist are you going to fight back? Are you going to flee? Are you just going to stand there like a deer in the headlights? When you are not awake and aware then you are asleep and vulnerable. It's only when you recognize the reality of evil that you can be effective in your fight against evil. Reality demands that you do something. You know the old saying: Evil thrives when good people do nothing.

I am a strong believer in no contact because it IS self-defence and sometimes it is the wisest and safest choice to make. Not communicating with a malignant narcissist or any clan member makes good sense. However, I'm also of the mind that no one should be bullied out of their life. Malignant narcissists/sociopaths/anti-socials are bullies. And bullies love to intimidate others into submission: silence, running and hiding. This works great for the bully, but it does nothing for the victim except to provide temporary relief. Cut the fuckers off, yes, but claim your turf and don't back down.

My malignant narcissist mother and sister did not want me living in the same city as them (my home city), they made that abundantly clear and I think that's why I spent the better part of my young adulthood living at the opposite end of the country. I didn't move with a plan, I fled while in

324

flight mode and just sort of hid-out. I truly believe that on a deep sub-conscious level I was obeying their order. One time during a telephone call I mentioned to the malignant narcissist mother that I was thinking of moving back home and she became filled with rage and screamed, "Why do you want to move back here?! What the hell are you coming back here for?!" I told a couple of friends about this and one reaction was: "Why are they so threatened by you?" The other response was: "Move back there and when you're all settled-in call-up the bitch and tell her you're baaaack and you're not going anywhere!" During a previous conversation with the MN mother, she was trying to convince me to marry a man she never met. He was American and wanted to move me to Boston. I told a friend of about this and she said, "What the hell?! Does she *need* you to move even *farther* away?"

From my experience, uprooting one's self to avoid the manufactured terror of the little man behind the curtain is a temporary solution, a band aid. Sometimes I think it's better to face these fuckers head on – show them your fangs and claws and dig in to the interior rot of their soft flesh and tear it to shreds. After all, malignant narcissists are all slimy little cowards. They usually only intimidate people they are sure they can beat. Before they act, they find some weakness in their opponent and strike at the most vulnerable point. Only if their back is to the wall does the malignant narcissist confront someone whose strength is equal to or greater than their own.

For example, the malignant narcissist sister has always used others to attack me – mommy, daddy, her monkey, third parties etc. etc. She's a depraved monster that is currently hiding behind our sick father and using him and *his* money as a weapon to hurt me while simultaneously exploiting and abusing him. Yup, that's right. The craven and cowardly bitch is getting a dying old man to fight her battles. What's her battle? Me daring to object to a lifetime of her abuse. Poor baby. Not only does she *always* need to get her way – her way being abusing and exploiting others with impunity. She retaliates without mercy if anyone dares to run interference on her getting her way.

My dad was going to send me a small amount of money that would enable me to get hip replacement surgery that will help me walk again. She aggressively put a stop to him and would only allow him to give me the money if I was bound by degrading and humiliating contractual terms and conditions - terms and conditions of *her* making. Guess what psychological control tactics she came up? Terms whereby I had to agree to a "diagnosis" for an "alleged" mental illness and seek "treatment" for it. Remember, I haven't seen her in over 26 years. Yet she has stalked me on my blog since its inception. She's blatantly trying to silence me. In an effort to get through to my dad, who appears to have zero free will left, I launched a pre-emptive strike and sent him a *private* information package about undue influence. Of course she stole it (as I predicted) and it infuriated her. So she dropped the "mental illness" card and her mouth piece/puppet (my dad) informed me that the terms and conditions require that I "leave the malignant narcissist sister alone." Yup, it's DARVO and Triangulation all rolled into one. Not to mention projection.

I have asked my dad to send me a copy of the so-called terms and conditions and he has done nothing. They are bluffing. That is not to say that all malignant narcissists are all bluster and no substance. Far from it. They are insane and their insanity makes them dangerous. But someone like the malignant narcissist sister would rather get her way by bluffing than by risking defeat. She doesn't want me to get the money, period. She doesn't want me to have an operation that will relieve me of pain and help me walk again. Incidentally, I suffer from a genetic disease, and both the MN mother and MN sister have received hip replacements. But, if I receive the money, the sister would see that as losing. And losing is catastrophic to the malignant narcissist. Not only would she lose what's at stake – control over me – but she would also lose her sense of self, and her pride, and she would be totally crushed. That's why it might be revealed that she is behind my physical attack that occurred shortly after I experienced a minor victory over her. I even allude to the possibility of her physically harming me in *Malignant Narcissist As Character Assassin*.

Evil people are not that clever. They are rats that have learned a few tricks, and most of their tricks rely on you doing their dirty work for them while in devastated emotional states. Believe me when I say, if I wasn't educated on how these fuckers operate, their bag of tricks may have worked on me. The seeds they planted may have erupted into a tangled mess of vines that eventually strangled me, my identity and my sanity. Knowledge truly is power when you are under attack. I know from experience that evil is out there and it will feed on you without mercy unless you fight back. So are you going to fight back?

Consider the school yard bully who terrorizes his target every day and steals the kid's lunch money. The targeted child gives-in to the intimidation tactics and every day automatically hands over their lunch money. The bully need not exert more effort than a "look" to scare the target into compliance. So what happens next? Do you think the bully is going to back off? Hell to the "NO." The bully is going to see that kid as easy prey, get bored and ramp-up the abuse. The abused kid will soon end up with not only anxiety, dread, depression and no lunch, but a black eye too. That's why I believe when you come across a malignant narcissist bully the first time they try to steal your lunch money you need to steal it back AND kick-em' in the shins to let them know you mean business. Mirroring back their behavior teaches them a lesson.

Malignant narcissists are always trying to intimidate us into compliance with their, don't poke the grizzly routine. We should do the same. If they continually poke at us we should immediately respond by roaring in their faces. *They* feel *entitled* to rage at us like a wild animal, so we should rage back. Or, give them a metaphorical whack on the snout to make them back off. Running and hiding, maintaining your silence and keeping the peace is exactly what they want. These predators rely on the fact that we don't have or won't show our capacity for violence. They control the narrative, and re-write the script to suit their agenda knowing full well we will not stand-up to them or stoop to their level. I say we do both.

All of the Blogs, Vlogs, Websites and books related to the subject of malignant narcissism can no longer be ignored – these are a few ways we ACONs can show our fangs and claws. It takes a serious amount of courage for someone who has experienced extreme psychological violence at the hands of their malignant narcissist family to put their face in front of a camera and speak-out about the abuse. You'll never see a narcissist take centre stage to *defend* their outrageously cruel behavior. They know damn well they haven't got a leg to stand on morally or legally or factually. They gang-up, bully and threaten on the sly. Their defence is merely offense with the intent to chill and terrorize the victim into believing silence is safer. Of course silence is safer. Of course going along to get along is safer. But you don't remove the threat by submitting to the narcissist's abuse and complying with their rules – you only keep the threat at bay. And eventually the predatory malignant narcissist will get hungry and go on the prowl again.

So how do you *remove* the threat?

How do you fight back when a malignant narcissist is hell-bent on destroying you?

More importantly, what are WE as a civilized society going to do about these malignant narcissists?

Do we fight or do we flee?

Do we remain in a worldwide denial of everyday evil?

Seems to me the time is now to expose them and give them a good ass kicking in the process!

Keep on spreading the information!

Comments:

In my FOO, it was generally agreed upon that you get what you deserve.

Expose them and their abuse. They are threatening you about your blog and using your financial vulnerability and need for surgery to make you sign a contract that never materializes for money that doesn't exist. That's psychological control and mental cruelty. Your MN sister and the rest of the evil crew are clearly doing what you mentioned in your blog post - they are forcing your submission. It's times like this when we ACONs get to see how hateful and cruel our "families" really are. Sounds like they are all feeding-off you.

I had thoughts about running and going into hiding but mine have the connections to "find" me. I just want them to stay away from me for the rest of my life and the favour will be returned.

I know full well these MNs plot revenge against those they "previously" could control but no longer can. They are greedy pigs who get away with a lifetime of dominating others and manipulating situations and circumstances to advance their agenda. As a result, not only do they feel entitled to everything including all material possessions, money and attention, they even feel entitled to control the will of others. Asserting our rights enrages them. But I suppose if home appliances, electronics and vehicles started asserting their rights, the human race would be pissed-off and put a stop to the uprising. That's how the MN sees us - as objects.

Woe to the Adult Child who has the absolute gall, the incredible (insight) audacity to WALK AWAY-FOREVER! The MN Perp demands the AC's head on a platter! "NOW!" she commands her minions/monkeys who willfully collude in the on-going War of Domestic Terrorism against that "selfish, ungrateful, willful, overly-sensitive, brat" etc. An adult child who simply chooses to live their life in peace.

They keep it covert on purpose. They do what they can to get someone to react or act out, and then they use it to their advantage. One has to be careful to stay NC or stay with legal channels alone if forced to deal with any narcissists.

Your sister must be so jealous of you to go to all this trouble to sabotage you to this extent, because why else would anybody do this to another human being? She is a true sociopath! She needs to know that you have your own personal army here to protect you but let's not call us your flying monkeys because we are not here to attack her ... She is attacking you ... We will only be exposing her! So let's call us your guardian angels ... ;) and yes I am writing this in hopes that she reads this and stops this bullshit ... This woman is truly sick.

Your sister is a ruthless bully trying to marginalize you into oblivion. She is scary because she is crazy, but she is in no way more formidable than you, and I sincerely hope you give her a run for her (your) money, and take your power back. Even if you need to break your NC to do it!

I'll send her a signed copy of my book.

Sometimes, There Just Aren't Enough Bricks

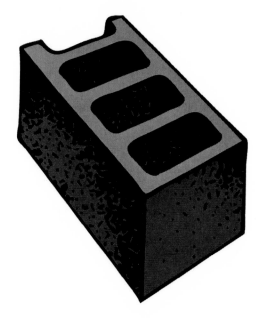

I gave a draft of my book *Breaking Free: A Way Out for Adult Children of Narcissists* to a writer for feedback. This individual does not know me very well, nor has he had any experience with narcissistic abuse. From what he tells me, he thinks he has known a narcissist or two, but he has never been targeted by one for destruction. So, for all accounts and purposes, this guy doesn't know much about malignant narcissism. But what he does know about is story. He has written many screenplays that have been produced in film and television. So he really knows how to grab an audiences' attention and keep them hooked through escalating story arcs that "raise the stakes" of the protagonist's dilemma.

Here's what he had to say about my book...

"The ending reminds me of the final scene in *The Sopranos*. It's abrupt. There's no resolution. No closure. Or is this a cliff hanger? What are you trying to say with your ending?"

I was a huge fan of the HBO Television series *The Sopranos* so I knew the exact scene he was talking about. The Sopranos arrange to meet at a Diner. Tony arrives first and watches customers come and go. Each time someone enters and exits the Diner, a bell rings. The bell rings and Tony looks up and Carmela arrives. The bell rings and Tony looks up and AJ arrives. Meadow arrives late and parks her car outside. Just as the bell rings and Tony looks up there is an abrupt cut to black screen followed by silence. That's the end of the series - going dark.

Naturally I found it interesting that this writer paralleled the ending of my book to the ending of a television drama series about a mob family. Being raised in a family of narcissists is like bearing witness to an underground crime ring. There is corruption and collusion and a very rigid pecking order. In these so-called "families" the higher up the ladder of hierarchy, the more your apparent personal worth. The narcissist at the top is of greatest worth and is the most powerful. As a result, the merest whim of the "Boss" narc is infinitely more important than the direst need of the member below. In these sick and twisted "family" political systems, all energies and resources are first diverted to the Boss and Underboss narcs with the perks trickling downward to their soldiers and associates (Monkeys). The members at the bottom get scraps – if that.

You must always respect the *delusion* of "family" and there is grave punishment for anyone attempting to escape the oppression or who rebels against the unjust system and their role of servitude.

There is also a code of silence in the narcissist mob family. Break the code and you bring dishonour to the family. Bring dishonour to the family and receive the kiss of death. Actually, I'm making a joke. There is no "honour" in narcissist families. They are shady political systems based on bloated egos, greed, dirty little secrets and lies. What I meant to say is; expose the lies, exploitations and abuses and the malignant narcissists will take a hit out on you. Normally the "hit" travels through various channels of psychological violence such as mobbing and bullying and shunning.

The bullet then makes contact through financial abuse and character assassination which lead to social isolation of the target. Without a support system to navigate the assault, the target becomes extremely vulnerable and possibly desperate enough to surrender – still alive but not a threat. Character assassination is the method the gangsters in the narc mob family employ to "rub-out" and silence the Whistleblower.

"Um…no… the end of my book is not a cliff hanger," I told the writer. "It's just the way it is. There is no closure when it comes to narcissistic abuse within a family because the narcissists never stop abusing. But that doesn't mean you can't have peace of mind… or find freedom… or seek justice."

This book does not have a sunshine and lollipop summary that ties everything up in a neat little bow at the end. I have no intention or ability to guide you through a field of daisies and force you to hop on a talking Unicorn and marvel at the double rainbows all the way.

I am a realist and it is totally unrealistic to believe that an ACON can reach "closure" with an abusive narcissist family. But there is a light at the end of the tunnel, a way out of the prison and a route to lasting freedom. This does not mean the narcissists will stop the brutality. They never stop. If you've been targeted for character assassination you know it's a crime in progress that follows you for the rest of your life. It's a psychologically violent form of annihilation that ruins lives and sometimes even takes lives. Just because the victims of character assassination do not all end up in the hospital emergency room does not mean the narcissists have failed to seriously injure in their attempt to kill. Freedom comes at a price.

In my experience, an achievable outcome for ACONs is to erase all the lies the narcissists planted in our head, begin to self-reference and stake a claim to our life. We must also have a profound understanding of the enemy – the narcissists. And because it is so easy to slip back into self-blame, we must love and trust ourselves and be gentle with our selves. When you treat yourself with love, kindness and respect you will not accept abuse. We are only human, we are bound to make mistakes and so are others, but the intentional infliction of malice is no mistake. Malignant narcissists aim to destroy those closest to them.

One of the reasons we cannot be gentle with ourselves is because of the shame we carry - shame the narcissists burdened us with by demolishing our boundaries and using us as a depository for their all their faults, failings and bad acts. Shame is not a feeling; it's a state of being.

I lived in a state of shame for most of my life because I prostituted my "self" to abuse. I degraded myself by allowing others to treat me like dirt without putting up any resistance. In the aftermath of the abuse I would quietly walk away, turn the other cheek, take the high road, stay silent and NOT fight back. In other words, I would submit – the narcissists taught me that. They taught me that I am nothing more than property that others are entitled to exploit. Even after I escaped the narcissist family mob, I continued to deny myself the right to respectful treatment. I was brainwashed into accepting abuse as normal. The build-up of shame became a paralyzing burden and I ended-up stuck and immobilized - imprisoned. But an ember ignited by outrage burned inside me. I just didn't know what I was so angry about. When I learned about NPD I found my answers and allowed myself to embrace my righteous anger.

It is bad enough that these malignant narcissists get away with willfully abusing their own children and family members for a lifetime, but they become so sadistic that they break the victim to the point where the victim is programmed to just take it. The same people who trained me from birth to bend-over to abuse are the very people who should have loved and protected me the most. It's a travesty of justice that these bullies continue to deny me a defence by terrorizing me into submission - even after over 25 years of no contact! Can you imagine the extreme perversity in someone who desires that level of control over another human being? The malignant narcissist's end goal is to usurp the will of others. THAT is the very definition of evil. They are not fit for human interaction.

I will not sit back and just take it. I have learned that docile victimhood is not a virtue. It destroys minds. It ruins lives. And every time you allow a person to degrade you, you allow them to steal a piece of your soul. What happens is that you end up with a deficit of self. You no longer belong to yourself. You become possessed by the abuse. In effect, the narcissist puppet master continues to control you on a deep subconscious level.

The shame and anger we feel at tolerating the narcissist's bullshit projections and unprovoked abuse is infallible proof that it is wrong. No one needs a book to teach them that. We KNOW it's wrong because it goes against the laws of human nature and our instinct for survival. Accepting abuse is the worst betrayal you can deliver upon yourself. You commit the act of treason against yourself when you surrender yourself to abuse. There is nothing right about this.

When you have the power to put up some resistance (even just mental resistance) and don't, you will be haunted by this breach of faith against your worth as a human being. Your lack of loyalty to yourself will torment you. It will follow you around like a dark cloud. Shame is an unbearable state of being. Joan of Arc preferred the stake.

Malignant narcissists get an exhilarating power high vilifying those they are in the process of destroying. They want their victims to suffer the agony of shame – so much shame that they submit to the abuse and feel unworthy of their most basic human right – SELF PRESERVATION.

I refuse to appease the narcissists or be intimidated into a docile state of victimhood. Character assassination is not nothing. It is character ASSASSINATION. I have every right to vindicate myself and blame my abusers by hurling the accusations right back and shattering the projections and lies. In fact, it's my only defence.

"Okay. So there's no closure with these abusive narcissists. But what are you trying to say with the last line?" asked the writer.

"This book is my brick," I said. "This book is every ACONs' brick."

….. And our ending is not darkness followed by silence.

SMASH CUT TO:

335

Breaking Through

Living Free!

House-of-mirrors.blogspot.com

Validating ACONs since 2011

Lisette SQ

Lisette SQ graduated from the University of Toronto. She studied Cinema and went on to work in the film and television industry where she earned producing credits and received development grants for her screenplays and documentary ideas.

When Lisette discovered narcissistic personality disorder a lot of the pieces of her family puzzle fell into place. She delved into the subject matter and launched her blog House of Mirrors in 2011. The author writes about malignant narcissism and narcissistic abuse and draws not only from personal experiences, but from observation of the world around her.

Lisette's first book **Breaking Free: A Way Out for Adult Children of Narcissist** is also available in a two volume set of eBooks **Breaking Through the House of Mirrors: Clarity for Adult Children of Narcissists** and *Exit the House of Mirrors: Freedom from Narcissistic Abuse.* A third book is in the works that the writer describes as creative non-fiction.

Lisette SQ is Canadian and lives in Vancouver, British Columbia. She considers herself a Cinephile and an Anglophile. She loathes bullies and tyrants and noise. She loves privacy, peace and quiet, the mountains, the ocean, the great outdoors, BBQ, dogs (not barbequed dogs, hot dogs – yes, dogs that bark – no, she does not barbeque them).

Made in United States
North Haven, CT
22 July 2022

21726741R00209